Microsoft® Internet Explorer and the World Wide Web

Microsoft® Internet Explorer and the World Wide Web

FRITZ J. ERICKSON
Michigan Technological University

JOHN A. VONK
University of Northern Colorado

Web management by Karl L. Erickson

Boston • Burr Ridge, IL • Dubuque, IA • Madison, WI • New York
San Francisco • St. Louis • Bangkok • Bogotá • Caracas • Lisbon
London • Madrid • Mexico City • Milan • New Delhi • Seoul
Singapore • Sydney • Taipei • Toronto

Irwin/McGraw-Hill 
A Division of The **McGraw-Hill** *Companies*

MICROSOFT® INTERNET EXPLORER AND THE WORLD WIDE WEB

This book is printed on acid-free paper.

1 2 3 4 5 6 7 8 9 0 VNH/VNH 9 3 2 1 0 9 8

ISBN 0-07-365739-5

Vice president and editorial director: *Michael W. Junior*
Senior sponsoring editor: *Garrett Glanz*
Developmental editor: *Kyle Thomes*
Marketing manager: *Jodi Fazio*
Project manager: *Carrie Sestak*
Production supervisor: *Lori Koetters*
Designer: *Jennifer McQueen Hollingsworth*
Compositor: *GTS Graphics, Inc.*
Typeface: *10.5/12 Caslon 224 Book*
Printer: *Von Hoffmann Press, Inc.*

Library of Congress Cataloging-in-Publication Data

Erickson, Fritz J.
Internet Explorer and the World Wide Web / Fritz J. Erickson, John A. Vonk : Web management by Karl L. Erickson. —4th ed.
p. cm.
Includes index.
ISBN 0-07-365739-5
1. Microsoft Internet explorer. 2. World Wide Web (Information retrieval system) I. Vonk, John A. II. Erickson, Karl L. III. Title
TK5105.883.M53E75 1999 98-34638
005.7′13769—dc21

http://www.mhhe.com

Preface

We wrote *Microsoft® Internet Explorer and the World Wide Web* because we wanted a Web-based textbook to help us teach. At the time, most Internet texts were written like cookbooks. Do this, do that, follow these steps. There was little or no explanation about why you should carry out specific tasks. Most books simply described a series of elaborate keystrokes or mouse clicks. While these types of textbooks work fine as a personal reference, they did not help us to teach or our students to learn. These types of texts certainly did not help our students master working with Microsoft Internet Explorer and the World Wide Web with a high degree of understanding.

One of the primary reasons so many books of this type fail as instructional tools is that most are not written by people like us, people who teach in the classroom. Unlike our *Microsoft Internet Explorer and the World Wide Web*, most texts are written by professional writers—people who have not been in the classroom in recent years or who have never taught. Their books are not guided by teaching experience, experience working with students on a day-to-day basis, or an ongoing educational pedagogy. Our goal was to take our ongoing classroom experience and use it to guide us in the development of a computer text that would serve as a true instructional and learning tool. The outcome of this effort is a pedagogical model we call Success-Based Learning.

Success-Based Learning

Success breeds success. You may have heard this simple statement before. As simple or as trite as this statement may sound, it is at the basis of our thoughtfully planned instructional pedagogy. We base our Success-Based Learning pedagogy on one primary assumption: The most successful teachers are those who have a strong desire for all students to learn. This desire serves as a threshold in the sense that teachers who want their students to learn, and who hold high expectations for student learning, have students who are successful in the classroom.

Putting high expectations into practice is the foundation for the five principles in our Success-Based Learning model. By combining five separate elements, students learn the material quicker, have a better understanding of how the Internet operates, and retain and recall the material more easily. It also makes it easier to teach. Most of our principles are based on social psychological theories that have been around for a long time. They are not new, nor are they exclusively ours. What is different here is that we have taken principles we use to teach in the classroom and have used them to guide us in writing this series of books.

Learning is most likely to occur when students make a decision that they want to learn. If a student makes a conscious decision to learn something, and the teacher also wants that student to learn, the teaching–learning process becomes very easy. Unfortunately, in many instances this is not the case. One of the benefits of Success-Based Learning is that it provides a motivation, and a stimulus, to help students develop a desire to learn. The elements of Success-Based Learning are

- **Identifiable outcomes.** Students learn with confidence when they can anticipate the results of their work. In other words, students must know when they have learned something correctly. The important component here is not that students must know when they have learned something, but that they have learned it correctly. The example we like to use here involves the activity of making an omelet. Before you start to make an omelet you should know what an omelet looks like. This way, you will know if you have been successful in your attempt. Otherwise, when you try to make an omelet you might end up with some concoction of eggs and other ingredients that looks vaguely like scrambled eggs and not realize that you have made a mistake.

  Each of our lessons begins with a set of objectives, followed by an extensive overview of what students can expect as they proceed through the lesson. We include several screen shots to show students exactly what to expect from their actions. Further, each major section within the lesson begins with a conceptual discussion of the reasons why an activity is important, what outcome should be gained from the activity, and how this is related to the overall goal of the lesson. From this students know what to expect throughout the lesson and what they should understand at the end of the lesson. They know when they have been successful. Knowing when you have been successful is key in learning any behavior.

- **Structured success.** Generally, when attempting any new behavior, if people experience immediate success they become more willing to try additional behaviors in that activity. On the other hand, if they experience failure, they become reluctant to attempt any further activity. Students need the opportunity to experience their own victories in order to reinforce what they learn and instill confidence in their abilities. So we provide highly structured activities and tightly correlated exercises early in every lesson. These activities and exercises are designed to provide opportunities for immediate success. When students experience this early success, they are more likely to make a decision that they want to learn more.

- **Guided exploration.** Most of us agree that the best way to learn how to use the Internet is to solve a problem on the World Wide Web. But this "hands-on" approach should not be left to trial-and-error learning. It is important to provide a step-by-step road map through each new topic. This is the explanatory aspect of lecturing or working through class activities. It may also be referred to as the "how to" component of instruction. The goal here is to explain how to use this new idea, or new information, in their own experience.

  We include exercises in each lesson that are directly tied to an activity that is carried out throughout the lesson. Not only are these exercises tied to an activity, we provide several applications at the end of each lesson that are linked directly to lesson objectives. In this manner, students are provided with a map. That is, they are guided very closely toward achieving the objectives of each lesson.

  Exercises embedded throughout each lesson and application projects at the end of each lesson provide personally meaningful experiences throughout the learning process. We also provide a comprehensive problem at the end of the lesson that is designed to link concepts in previous lessons to the current lesson. This helps students understand the connection between concepts and processes throughout the entire learning experience.

- **Deductive reasoning.** We think it is best to provide students with broad general principles and then to reduce these global conceptions to more specific, existential ideas or components. Most scientific reasoning is deductive rather than inductive, so it makes sense to follow this model when teaching scientific subjects. The second lesson introduces students to the broad, general, or global aspect of the Internet. By moving from a global procedure to more specific activities in subsequent lessons, retention and recall are facilitated. Tips, Tricks, and Ideas boxes are used to suggest alternative strategies for a task or to provide very brief instruction on a limited topic. The combination of Tips, Tricks, and Ideas and the organization of the book helps facilitate retention and recall.

- **Critical mass.** This is an aspect of teaching that comes with experience and ongoing contact with students. Those of us who teach must carefully determine how much material we can safely introduce in one lesson. Too much and the student is overwhelmed. Too little and the student is not challenged.

Identifying the critical mass for a classroom lecture, chapter topic, or even an entire course becomes a crucial variable for successful instruction. With an introductory course on Microsoft Internet Explorer and the World Wide Web, not everyone needs to know every command, procedure, or nuance. What is important, however, is that students learn enough to feel comfortable with what they have learned, and feel comfortable enough to experiment. In several of the projects at the end of each lesson, we provide activities designed to encourage students to experiment.

Would you prefer a textbook written by professional writers who have not stepped into a classroom in years, or who may have never been in the classroom? Or would you rather use a textbook written by people who teach, who care about their students, and who want their students to learn? We know this pedagogy works.

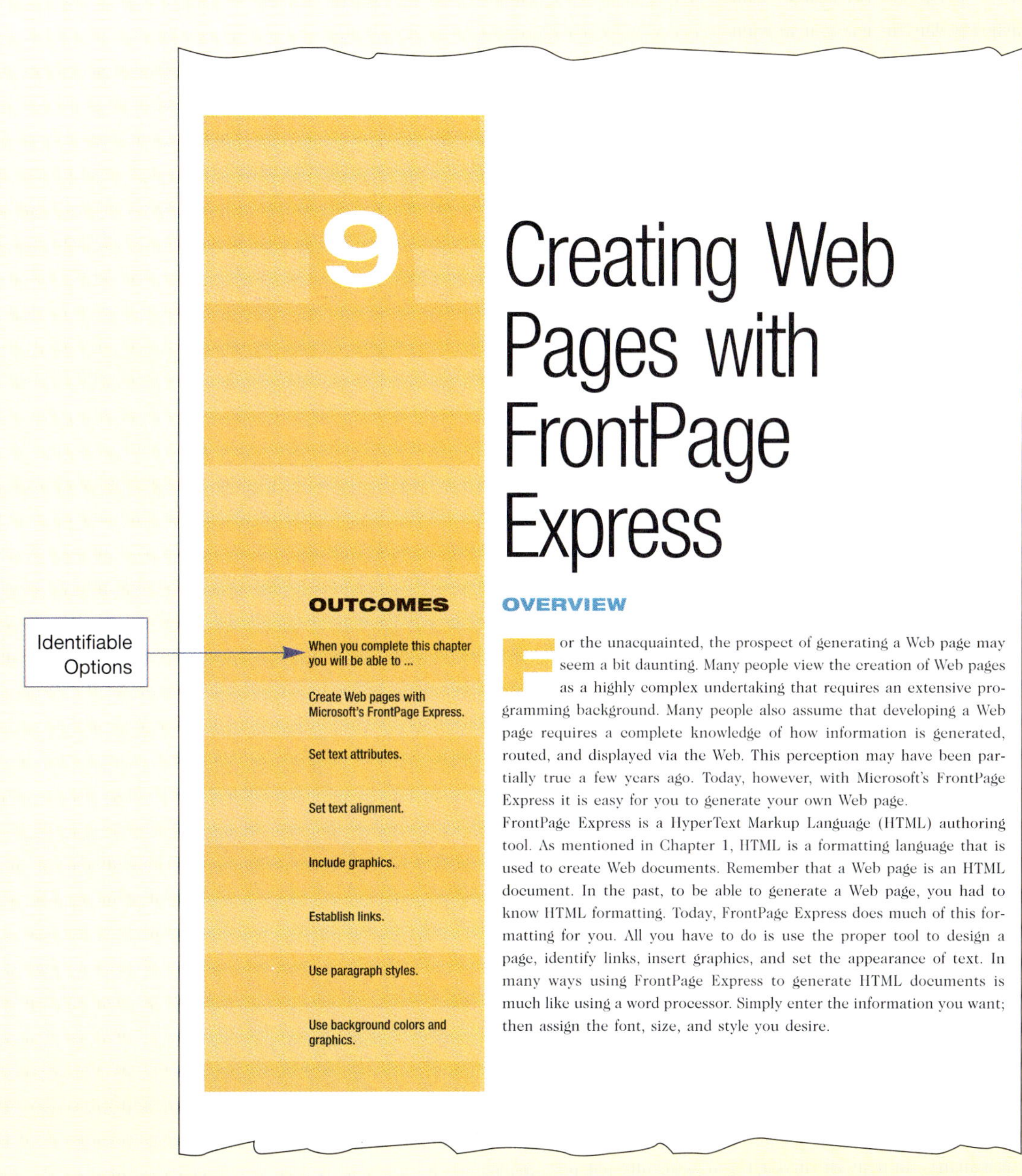

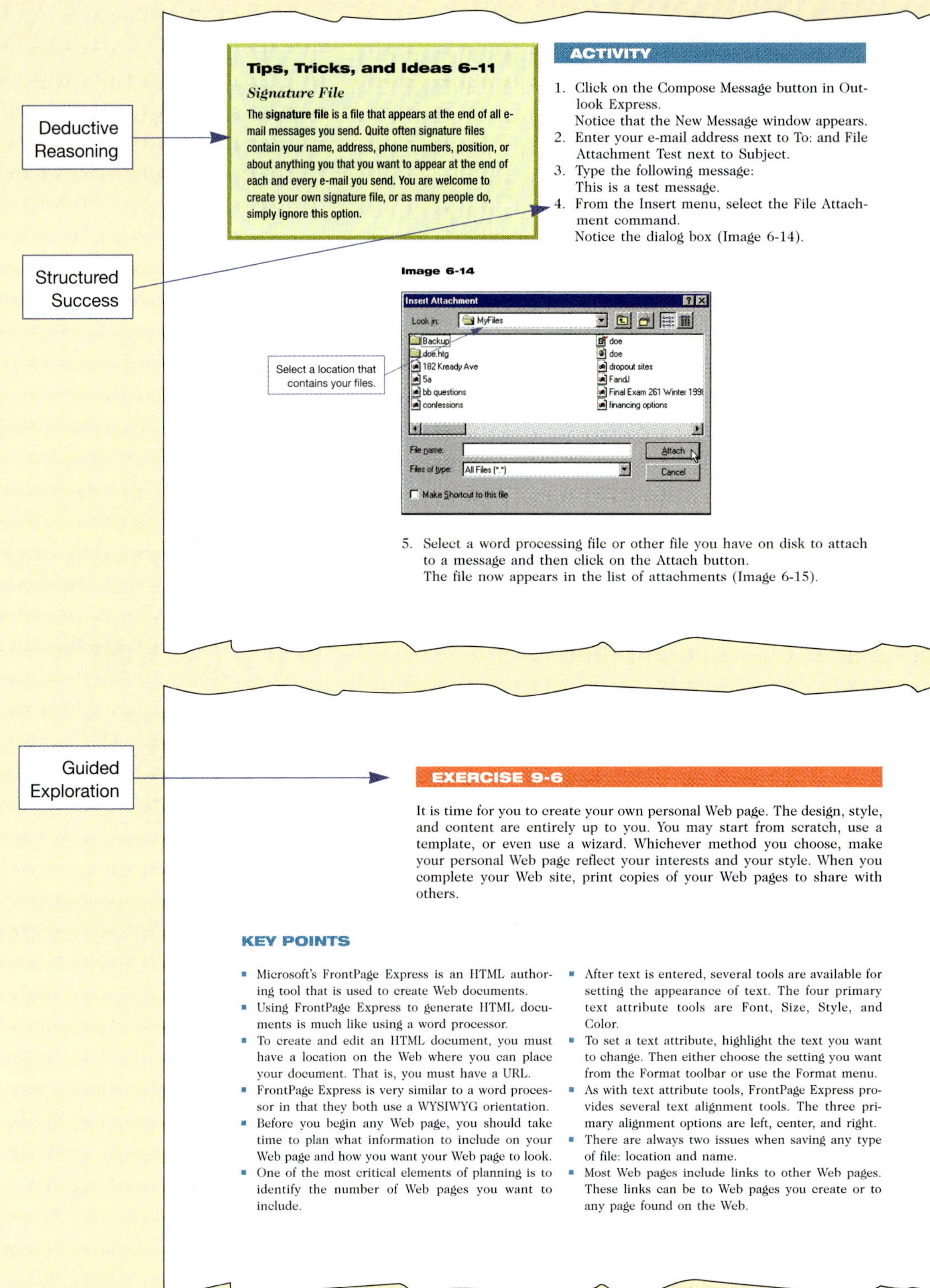

Tips, Tricks, and Ideas 6-11

Signature File

The **signature file** is a file that appears at the end of all e-mail messages you send. Quite often signature files contain your name, address, phone numbers, position, or about anything you that you want to appear at the end of each and every e-mail you send. You are welcome to create your own signature file, or as many people do, simply ignore this option.

ACTIVITY

1. Click on the Compose Message button in Outlook Express.
   Notice that the New Message window appears.
2. Enter your e-mail address next to To: and File Attachment Test next to Subject.
3. Type the following message:
   This is a test message.
4. From the Insert menu, select the File Attachment command.
   Notice the dialog box (Image 6-14).

Image 6-14

5. Select a word processing file or other file you have on disk to attach to a message and then click on the Attach button.
   The file now appears in the list of attachments (Image 6-15).

EXERCISE 9-6

It is time for you to create your own personal Web page. The design, style, and content are entirely up to you. You may start from scratch, use a template, or even use a wizard. Whichever method you choose, make your personal Web page reflect your interests and your style. When you complete your Web site, print copies of your Web pages to share with others.

KEY POINTS

- Microsoft's FrontPage Express is an HTML authoring tool that is used to create Web documents.
- Using FrontPage Express to generate HTML documents is much like using a word processor.
- To create and edit an HTML document, you must have a location on the Web where you can place your document. That is, you must have a URL.
- FrontPage Express is very similar to a word processor in that they both use a WYSIWYG orientation.
- Before you begin any Web page, you should take time to plan what information to include on your Web page and how you want your Web page to look.
- One of the most critical elements of planning is to identify the number of Web pages you want to include.
- After text is entered, several tools are available for setting the appearance of text. The four primary text attribute tools are Font, Size, Style, and Color.
- To set a text attribute, highlight the text you want to change. Then either choose the setting you want from the Format toolbar or use the Format menu.
- As with text attribute tools, FrontPage Express provides several text alignment tools. The three primary alignment options are left, center, and right.
- There are always two issues when saving any type of file: location and name.
- Most Web pages include links to other Web pages. These links can be to Web pages you create or to any page found on the Web.

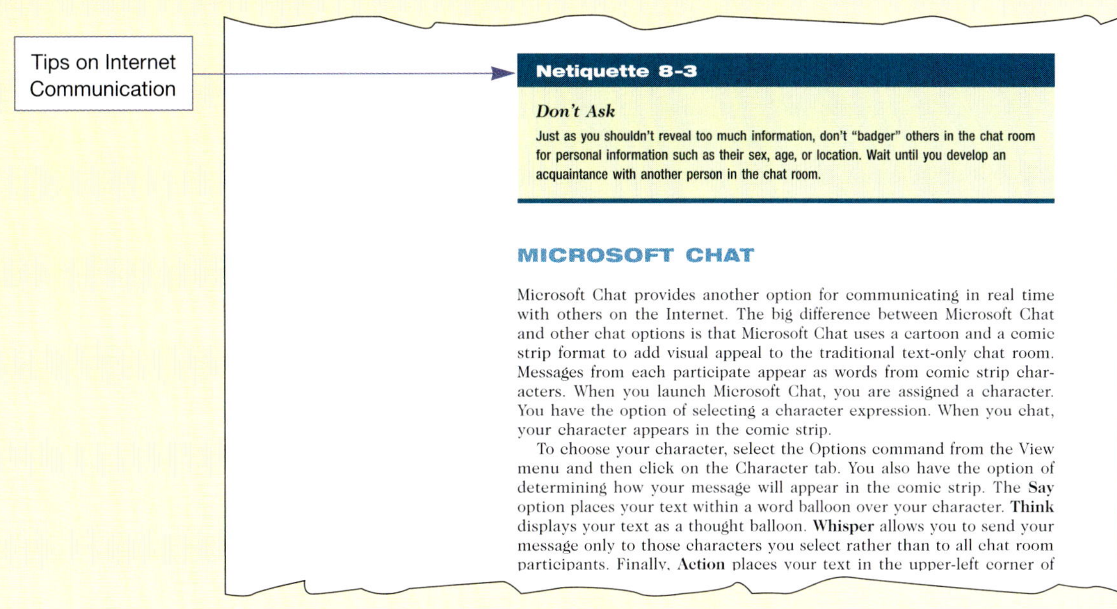

Key Points, Key Terms, and Commands

At the end of each chapter we conclude the lesson with a summary of the key points and key terms. The key points are important topics covered in each lesson while the list of key terms calls attention to a series of important concepts, commands, and procedures highlighted throughout the text.

Study Questions, Practice Tests, and Fill-ins

In addition to the key points and key terms, we have included numerous questions that help the reader review important concepts in the lesson. The study questions tend to be open-ended, discussion-type questions. The practice tests are multiple-choice questions. These multiple-choice questions are followed by a series of fill-in-the-blank questions. As students review and try to answer these numerous questions, they are reinforcing important topics covered throughout the lesson.

Projects

Anyone teaching the Internet knows there is no substitute for hands-on activities. Each lesson concludes with a group of projects. Throughout these projects the students carry out a number of activities learned in the lesson, and they are encouraged to experiment on their own.

Learning Online Web Site

One frustration of teaching the Internet is compiling Web site addresses and keeping them up to date. So, we have done this for you. Students will learn to maneuver and use Microsoft Internet Explorer and the World Wide Web through the *Learning Online* site. This site (http://www.mhhe.com/cit/net/learning) contains several links to interesting and useful sites dealing with such topics as FTP, Gophers, and Cool Games along with a variety of other topics. This site's address will not change, but it will be kept current so teaching and learning will occur more seamlessly. We do the work of finding educational and interesting sites for you.

Accuracy

Class time is important. You shouldn't have to use your class time trying to deal with an inaccurate activity. All of the books in this series are developed as carefully as possible to ensure their quality and accuracy.

Acknowledgments

To write a book like this takes a great deal of help and support. We have been extremely fortunate to have the very capable assistance of a number of dedicated people at Irwin/McGraw-Hill publishing. We are very grateful for the assistance of Garrett Glanz, Kyle Thomes, Carrie Sestak, Lori Koetters, Jennifer Hollingsworth, and Tony Noel.

Thanks to Timothy Gottleber at North Lake College for providing a thorough technical review.

We would also like to thank our families. Thanks Jan, Jenna, John, Edsel, Ruth, Petie, Jennifer, Cody, Julie, Jacqui, Joey, and Helen. All of you made a labor of love less labor and more love.

Fritz J. Erickson
John A. Vonk

Contents

Microsoft® Internet Explorer and the World Wide Web

1 Welcome to the Internet

OUTCOMES

When you complete this chapter you will be able to . . .

Define the Internet.

Describe some of the uses of the Internet.

Identify various information resources.

Use the Domain Name System (DNS).

Identify various ways to connect to the Internet.

List various resources available such as e-mail and the World Wide Web, and others.

Start an Internet session and access the World Wide Web through Internet Explorer.

THE ELECTRONIC FRONTIER

For many people, the electronic revolution began with the advent of the personal computer. At that time people rushed to praise the promise of computers as providing access to a world of information that would be accessible to all and become interwoven into the fabric of our daily lives. It has taken a bit longer than the early futurists proclaimed but the promise of instant and universal access to the world of information has arrived. Its name is the Internet.

Although the Internet has been around for a number of years, it has only recently captured the imagination of the business community, schools, governmental organizations, and almost every industry. It is almost impossible to turn on the television and not see commercials listing locations on the Internet for obtaining information. The rapid acceptance of the Internet as the means of accessing electronic information has made learning to use the Internet as fundamental a skill for the future as using the telephone or operating an automatic teller is today.

Image 1-1

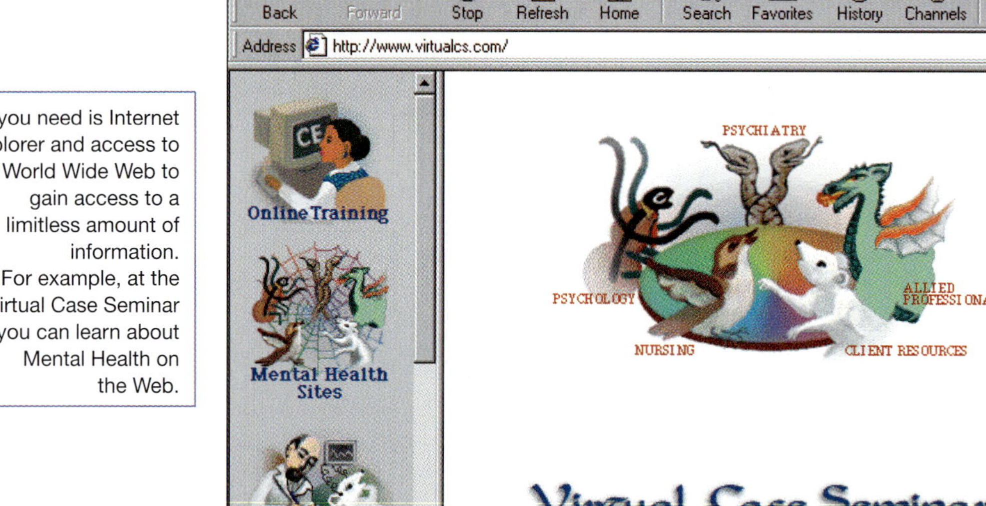

All you need is Internet Explorer and access to the World Wide Web to gain access to a limitless amount of information. For example, at the Virtual Case Seminar you can learn about Mental Health on the Web.

Yet the Internet is still in its infancy. It changes daily. Information is added. Information is removed. Changes occur on the Internet at such a rapid rate that no one can keep up with all of the information that is available. How we access information on the Internet is also changing. Methods of incorporating text, audio, video, and animation have made the Internet a vibrant tool. The Internet is truly an electronic frontier, but not without its problems and not without its promise.

If you look in the computer section in almost any bookstore, you will see a large number of expensive books on how to use the Internet. Many of these books are filled with technical jargon and loaded with acronyms such as TCP/IP, SLPP, POP, HTTP, DNS, VT100, and X.400. The size of the books and the large number of acronyms suggest that learning to access the world of electronic information through the Internet is a complicated process. Not so. Learning to access information resources on the Internet is not very difficult. All you need is a little guidance. That is the purpose of this book. When you complete this book, you will not be an Internet expert, but you will be a capable and competent user of our new electronic frontier.

WHAT IS THE INTERNET?

For much of the last two decades, teachers, scholars, the media, and many others have used the term *information age.* With the wide acceptance of personal computers, beginning in the early 1980s, many spoke of a societal change from industry to information. Ten years ago some people predicted that information would be the commodity of the future. However, 10 years ago few could have predicted the amazing growth and near universal acceptance of an electronic system for sharing and exchanging information. The Internet initiated a communications revolution: Millions of people now send messages, listen to music, check live video cameras, participate in global discussion groups, read magazines and newspapers from across the world, and watch video news segments as routinely as they turn on a television or talk on the telephone. The Internet bridges time, distance, and culture; it is where you can learn about virtually any subject and communicate with just about anyone almost instantly.

The term *Internet* is one of those terms that you know when you see it, but it is hard to define. For some, the Internet is a system of telephone wires, fiber optics, satellite links, and other links that allow computers to connect to each other. Others define the Internet as a means for sending electronic mail or as a system for accessing information from sources all over the world. Still others view the Internet as an agreed-upon software standard for sending and receiving computer data. All of these definitions are partially correct. However, the Internet is much more than a giant computer network. It is a cultural phenomenon that has made our desire for instant information and communication a reality.

Tips, Tricks, and Ideas 1-1

Learn Your Operating System

The operating system you use to access the Internet makes little difference to the outcome. An *operating system* is the set of controlling commands for your computer system. For users of **Internet Explorer,** the operating system of choice is Microsoft Windows. Before you proceed you should have at least a rudimentary understanding of your operating system.

The Physical Internet

A *network* is a collection of computers linked together to achieve some common goal. In most cases networks allow users to share information. In business, networks enable one computer to send messages or get information from another computer. For example, a business may have a network that allows the sales department to access inventory files, new product announcements, and demonstrations of services. In schools, networks allow teachers to access student records, library catalog listings, and class registrations. Conceptually, the only difference between the Internet and any other network is that the Internet is bigger.

The Internet is a network of networks. The networks use very precise rules that allow any user to connect to and use any available network or computer connected to the Internet. When you use any single computer to connect to the Internet, you have access to many other computers connected to the Internet. In other words, connecting to the Internet means connecting to tens of thousands of other networks, millions of individual computers, and tens of millions of other computer users.

Tips, Tricks, and Ideas 1-2

Just the Beginning

If you really want to become an effective Internet user, you need to learn more about the communications processes that make the Internet operate. Although these topics are beyond the scope of this book, you should try to learn more about the history and the technical issues associated with Internet communications. On our Web site, we have included access to several documents to provide you with more detail on the technical nature of the Internet. Try us at http://www.mhhe.com/cit/net/learning.

The Soft Internet

The Internet is also a communication system that uses physical connections (usually telephone lines, direct wires, fiber optics, satellite transmissions, etc.) to link one computer network to another. The Internet uses a standard of communication, called a **protocol,** that enables one computer network to "speak" to another. During the 1970s a new communication language, or protocol, emerged; it is called **Transmission Control Protocol/Internet Protocol (TCP/IP),** and it created a communication standard. In short, any computer network could communicate with any other computer network as long as they both used the TCP/IP standard protocol.

After TCP/IP was established, it became relatively easy for one network to communicate with other networks. The National Science Foundation (NSF) established one of the initial networks of networks, primarily for governmental agencies and universities to communicate and share research information. This initial link of university networks to five supercomputers, called **NSFnet**, became the backbone of the Internet.

Image 1-2

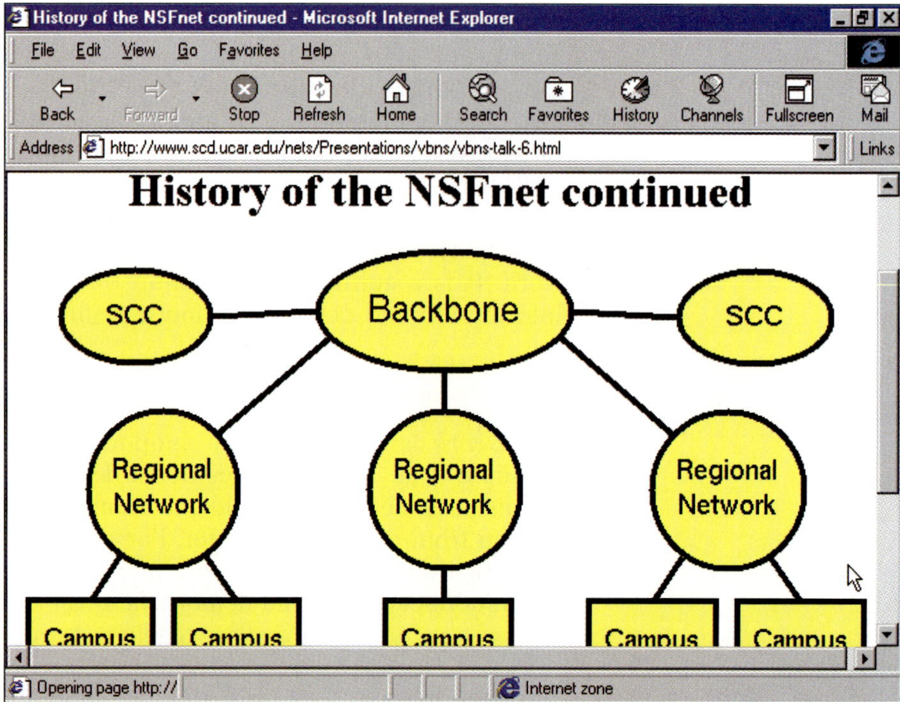

The real strength of NSFnet and TCP/IP was that the design of the network made it very easy for other networks to join. Originally, NSFnet did not allow other networks to join (especially commercial or for-profit networks). However, new rules were adopted, and soon it became very easy for commercial entities to join and participate on the Internet. This move opened the communication capabilities of the Internet to the people, organizations, and governments around the world.

The rules that govern the Internet rest with the **Internet Society.** It is a voluntary organization and is not run by the government or by any individual. Rather, the Internet Society is a board that meets to set standards and determine resources. For example, the **Internet Architecture Board (IAB)** determines addresses for users, as well as the rules for accessing and using these addresses.

Netiquette 1-1

Internet Etiquette

There are no formalized rules about how to behave when using the Internet, but a code of conduct, sometimes referred to as *network ethics* or *network etiquette,* has evolved. This standard for network etiquette is called *netiquette.*

DOMAIN NAME SYSTEM

Another important factor that makes the Internet possible is an agreed-upon standard for addresses. Addresses on the Internet are, in many ways, similar to home addresses. Every network and every computer user must have a unique address. Without this address, information cannot be routed to its destination. The structure of Internet addresses is, therefore, very important.

The addressing system for the Internet is actually quite simple because of a process called the **Domain Name System (DNS).** Internet addresses are numerical and are called **IP addresses** (for example, 128.116.24.3). However, most users never see or use IP addresses directly because DNS provides a more meaningful and easier-to-remember name. The host computer converts a DNS to an IP address in the background, so you don't need to know the numbers.

Image 1-3

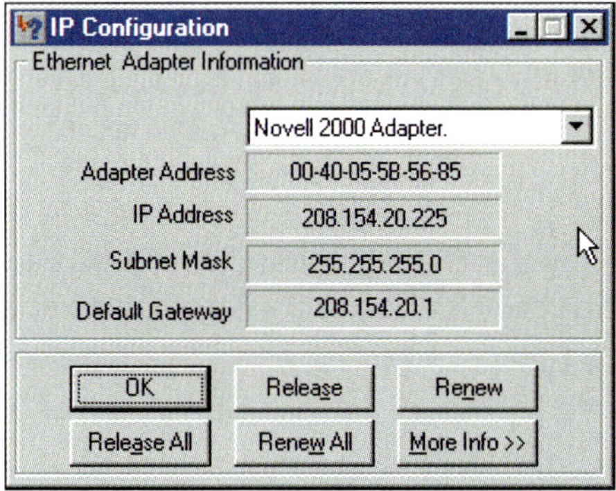

A DNS name is made up of a domain and one or more subdomains. For example, www.ed.mtu.edu uses the domain edu (educational institution) and has three subdomains, mtu, ed, and www. Each subdomain identifies a particular computer or network. If you read this address backwards, it is the educational institution Michigan Technological University (mtu), using the education (ed) computer, which is available on the **World Wide Web (WWW).** The key point is that the DNS is specific to a computer.

Popular Domains

.com	commercial
.edu	educational
.gov	governmental
.mil	military
.org	organization
.net	network

Tips, Tricks, and Ideas 1-3

Interpreting a DNS

Learning how to read a DNS is important because it can help you locate people and resources on the Internet. As you come across various locations on the Web, take a few moments to look at the DNS and translate it to English. For example, bentley.unco.edu is the Bentley computer at the University of Northern Colorado, which is an educational institution. www.mcgraw-hill.com is the McGraw-Hill Companies computer, which is a commercial site.

Because the Internet is worldwide, some addresses indicate the country in addition to the network type. For example, a DNS ending with .ca is Canada; similarly, .uk is the United Kingdom.

In addition to identifying and locating a specific computer system through the Internet, it is also important to identify specific individuals who have accounts on a specific computer. This is the reason for the @ (at) symbol. For example, fericksо@mtu.edu indicates a specific individual at (@) Michigan Tech (mtu), which is an educational institution (edu). Of the millions of people using the Internet, no two people have the exact same address.

INTERNET RESOURCES

There is no single way to access and use all the information and resources available on the Internet. In fact, diversity is one of the Internet's real strengths. Different information processes are available, and different types of software are used to access these various information resources. Connecting to the Internet is only the beginning. What you do once you are connected depends on your individual needs and the type of software you have at your disposal.

The Internet is made up of several different components, and each component requires a unique piece of software to access that component. For example, to use electronic mail (**e-mail**), you must have e-mail software. To access electronic bulletin boards called newsgroups, you need a **newsreader.** Internet Explorer contains most of the important pieces of software you need to access the various components of the Internet. Although these various components may be a bit confusing at first, you should remember that different Internet resources require different software and Internet Explorer provides that necessary collection of software.

Image 1-4

The World Wide Web can be fun. With Internet Explorer you can access and download a wide variety of games.

> **Tips, Tricks, and Ideas 1-4**
>
> ***Don't Be Intimidated***
>
> The Internet was developed by computer scientists. As in most specialized fields, a unique language exists to describe the various functions and procedures. Don't let the new terminology intimidate you. As you progress through this book, many of these terms will become second nature.

The following sections provide a very brief overview of some of these Internet components. Each component is described in much more detail later.

World Wide Web (WWW)

The World Wide Web is what most Internet users use most of the time. The Web has made the Internet popular by enabling people to access text, graphics, audio, video, animation, virtual reality, and a host of other types of information. The Web is a universal system for sharing information on the Internet. With the Web, you can establish your own Internet location. This is called a **Web page.** Every Web page has a specific address, called a **Uniform Resource Locator (URL)**, which looks something like http://www.mhhe.com/cit/net/learning, where http:// is the protocol, www.mhhe.com is the domain, and /cit/net/learning is the path. The protocol and path make up the DNS.

Image 1-5

The Uniform Resource Locator (URL) identifies a unique Web page. It contains the DNS name plus the type of document (http://).

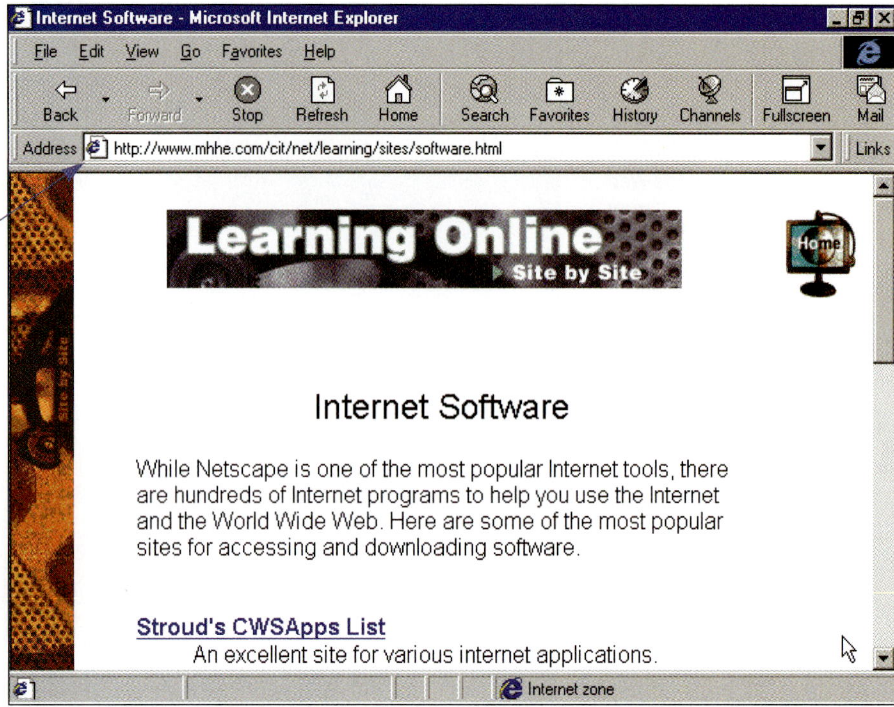

To access the World Wide Web, you must have specific software—known as **browsers**—designed to interpret and decode Web pages. Internet Explorer is an extremely popular Web browser. This book focuses on how to use Internet Explorer to successfully access and use the World Wide Web. However, other important information resources that can be accessed by using Internet Explorer are covered in this book as well.

E-Mail

Many people believe that e-mail is the fundamental service of the Internet. It is what Internet users employ to communicate with other Internet users. As described earlier, e-mail can work because users have unique addresses based on their user names. Most Internet e-mail systems allow you to create mailing lists from which you can send mail to hundreds of thousands of users (depending on the capability of the software you are using).

Within Internet Explorer you can use the program **Outlook Express** to create, read, and manage e-mail messages. If you prefer, you can use Microsoft Exchange or almost any other e-mail program.

Image 1-6

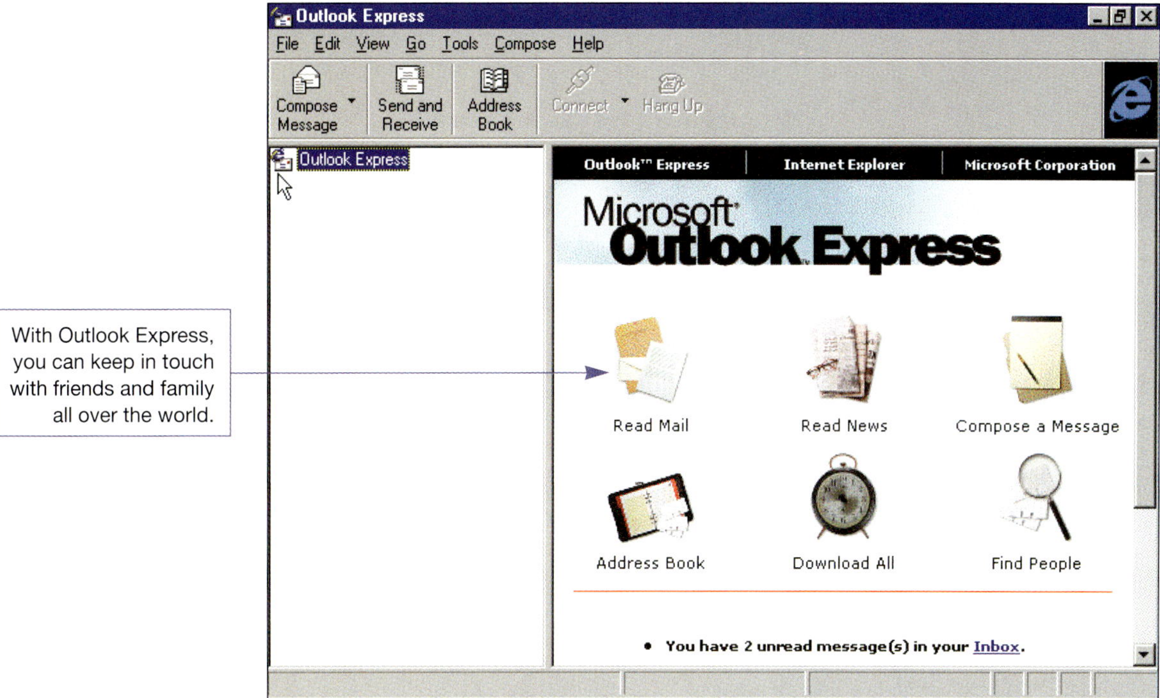

With Outlook Express, you can keep in touch with friends and family all over the world.

Telnet

Telnet allows you to use any host computer on the Internet as if you were directly connected. For example, if you want to connect to the University of Michigan's computer, you need the DNS or IP address for that computer and permission to use the system. When you telnet (the term *telnet* can be used as a verb) to another computer, your computer operates as if you were sitting in a computer lab for that computer. Usually, you need a password to access and use the computer at the remote location.

One of the big advantages of using telnet is that you can be anywhere in the world, and as long as you can connect to the Internet, you can use your home computer system. For example, if your e-mail is held on a university computer in Maui, you can be in New York or Fargo or Sarasota and access your e-mail account.

Tips, Tricks, and Ideas 1-5

Get an E-Mail Account

You will not be able to take full advantage of the Internet without an e-mail account. Check with your university or provider and request an e-mail address. Do it now so that you will have the address when you get to Chapter 6.

Netiquette 1-2

Privacy

Keep in mind that when you are using e-mail, or writing a Web document, your communication may not remain private. It is a good idea to assume that anyone on the Net may be able to read your words.

Image 1-7

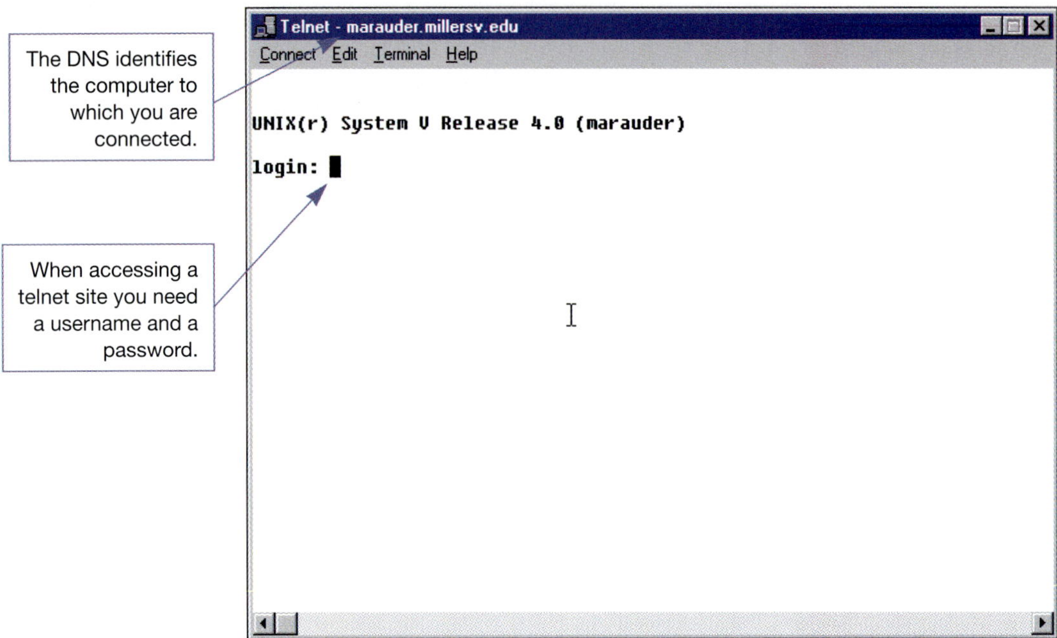

Gopher

Gopher is a navigational tool that uses a system of standardized menus to navigate among various computers on the Internet. By linking several Gophers together on a menu, you can move through the Internet and locate all types of information. Gopher is very easy to use; once you enter the Internet through a Gopher, you simply follow a set of menus or directories to browse for information.

The World Wide Web and Gopher are both tools for locating information on the Internet. The Web is the more flexible of these tools. Gophers force you to move through the Internet with a series of menus, but the Web enables you to go directly to any home page you desire. In fact, you can use the Web to access a Gopher, or any menu within a Gopher, by using the URL address.

Image 1-8

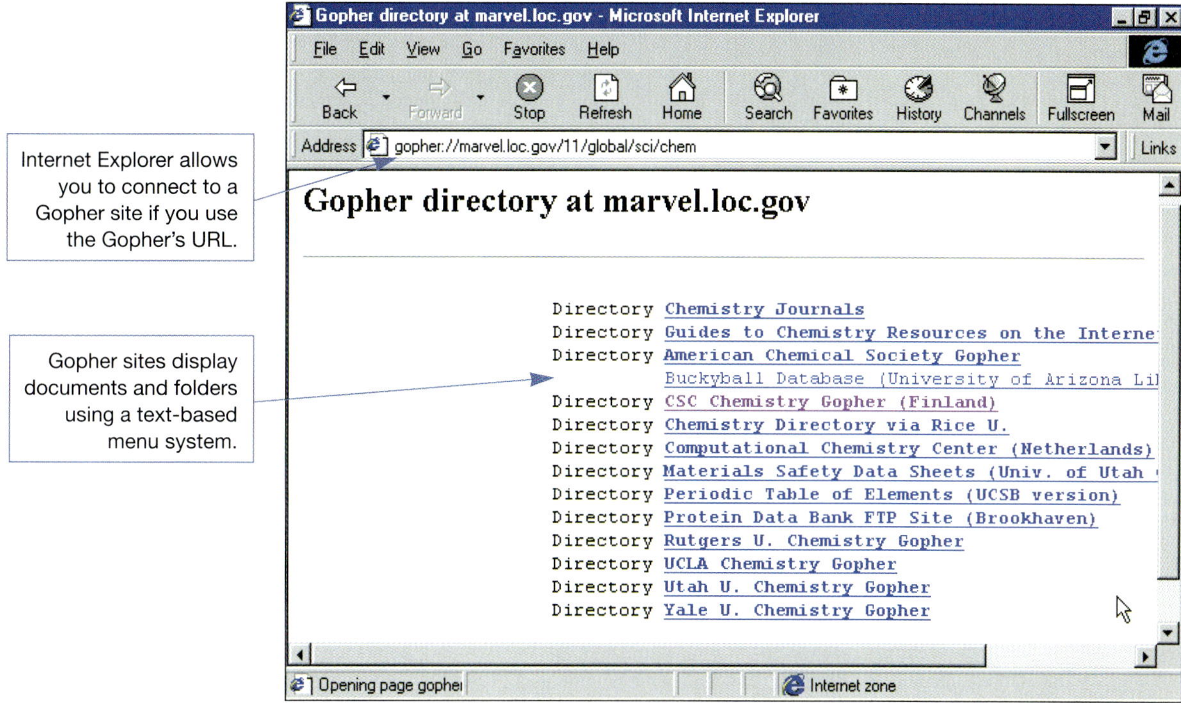

File Transfer Protocol

File Transfer Protocol (FTP) enables you to send and receive files stored on other computers on the Internet. These files include data files and program files, called binary files. With FTP you have access to millions of files, both public and private. Of course, with private files you will need access privileges. However, there are many public files commonly known as an anonymous FTP. You can use FTP to obtain copies of software, documents, or games. With FTP you can obtain almost anything on the Internet that is available for public use.

Usenet

Usenet has been called the world's largest bulletin board; it is a public place where users can read and post messages. Each location for reading and posting messages is referred to as a *newsgroup*. The Internet is home to thousands of newsgroups on a variety of topics, and Internet Explorer provides Outlook Express for accessing and using newsgroups. (As well as being an e-mail client, Outlook Express can also function as a newsreader.) Newsreaders enable you to read and post messages as well as to select and control the groups to which you belong or subscribe.

Image 1-9

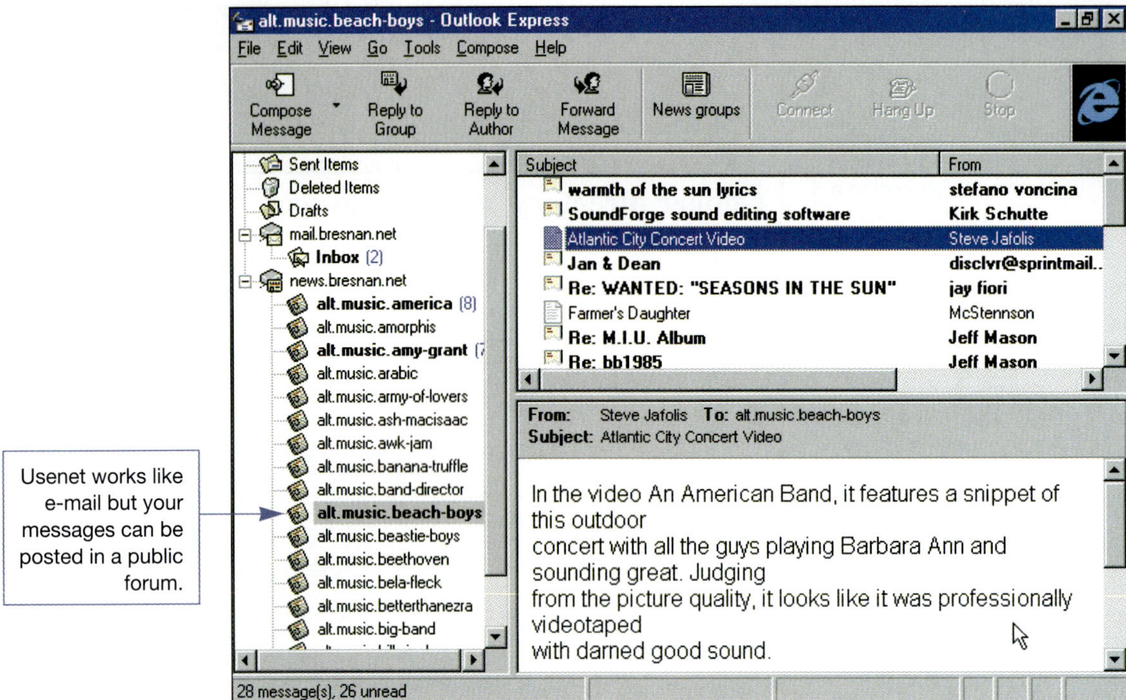

Usenet works like e-mail but your messages can be posted in a public forum.

Listserv

Listservs are automated mailing lists. When you join a Listserv, any mail sent to the Listserv will also be sent to you. Also, any mail you send to the Listserv will be sent to all members. Although Listservs are very popular and cover thousands of topics, they do pose a bit of a danger. If you join a Listserv with thousands of active members, you could receive hundreds of e-mail messages a day.

Image 1-10

There are thousands of lists you can join.

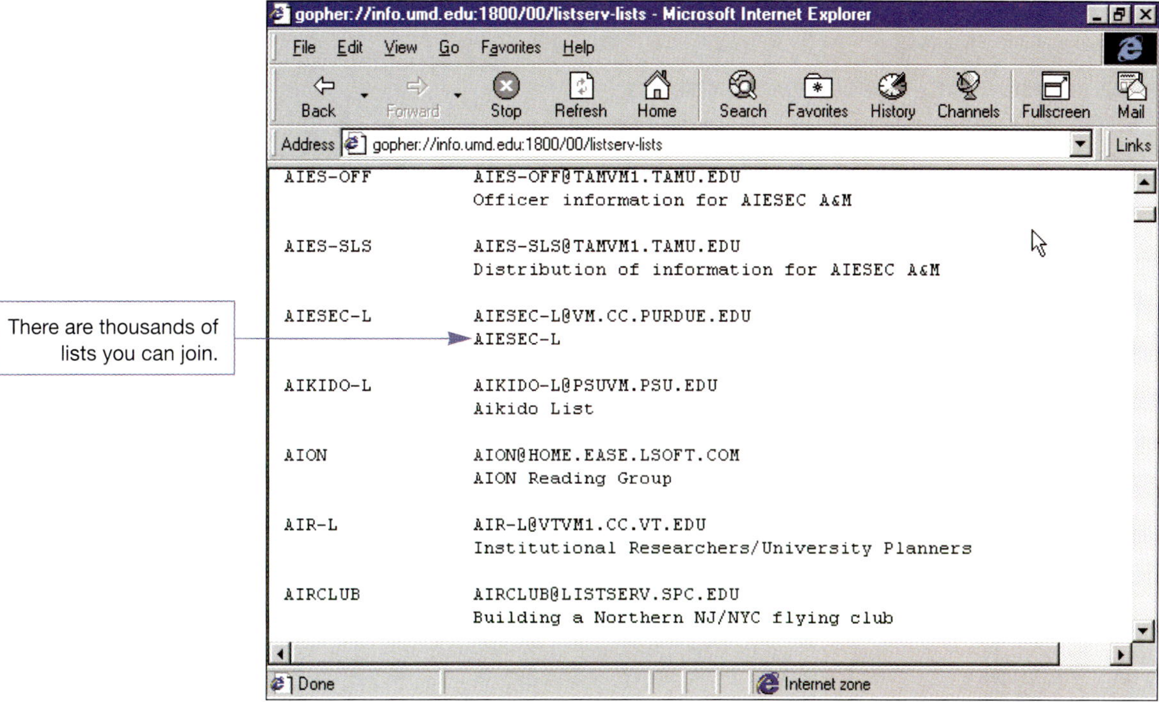

GETTING CONNECTED

Connecting to and using the Internet requires two processes. First, you must make a physical connection to the Internet. There are a variety of ways to physically connect to the Internet, including a direct or hard-wired connection or a dial-up facility where you can connect to the Internet through telephone lines.

After you make the physical connection, the second concern becomes one of selecting and using Internet Explorer software resources. Computer labs normally provide Internet access. So all you need to do is launch Internet Explorer. For dial-up facilities, you normally have many more software options. However, this software must be installed on your computer.

The Physical Connection

The way your computer physically connects to the Internet determines what you can do and how you can do it. The first factor to consider is whether the computer you are using is directly connected to a computer linked to the Internet or whether you are going to use a dial-up facility. A dial-up facility enables you to access a computer through telephone facilities from virtually any location. In other words, as long as a phone jack is available and you have a **modem**, you should be able to connect to the Internet.

> **Tips, Tricks, and Ideas 1-5**
>
> *Cellular Phones*
>
> Some modems work with cellular or mobile telephones. Telephone jacks and telephone lines are not required for access to the Internet when you use this type of telephone and computer hardware. You can have access to the World Wide Web from the beach, your car, or your isolated mountain cabin.

Direct connections through computer laboratories are popular at many colleges and universities. With these connections you get the advantages of simplicity and speed. It normally takes less time to access the Internet directly than to use a dial-up facility through the college or university computer or through an independent provider. If you are connecting through a computer lab, you access the Internet by turning on the computer to make the physical connection. Then all you need to do is launch whatever software is available for accessing and using the various services (e-mail, World Wide Web, FTP, etc.) on the Internet. The same holds true for other forms of direct connections including through the local cable company at home.

Image 1-11

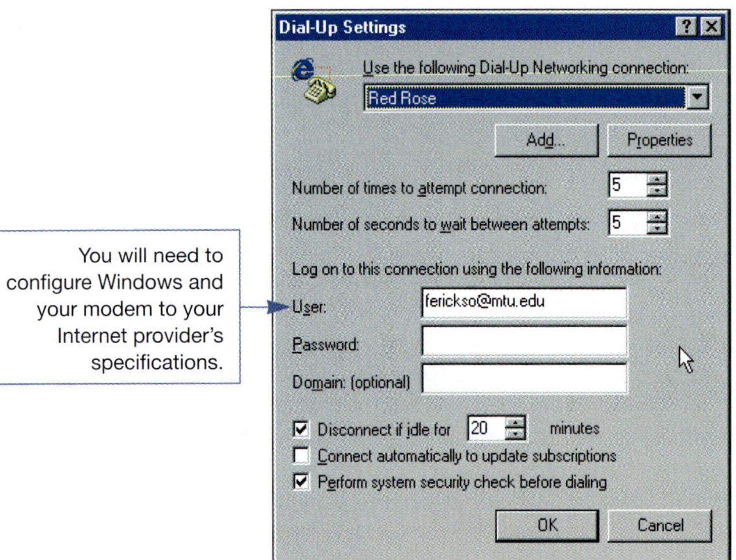

If you are using a direct connect (for example, a terminal of a computer), you will need to learn to operate your terminal. The same holds true if you are using a dial-up facility. However, with a dial-up facility you will also need to become familiar with your communication software. The communication software controls your computer and links it through a modem and through telephone lines to another modem into your Internet provider's computer. Hundreds of communication programs are available. Each software program connects your computer through a telephone line to a host computer; however, the exact process depends on the software. There are several key considerations when using a modem.

> **Tips, Tricks, and Ideas 1-6**
>
> *Communication Software and Modems*
>
> How you install and use communication software depends on a number of factors. One of the most critical is the operating system. Each one offers a different process for installing communication software and connecting a modem. Be sure to check the user manual for the necessary procedures.

The first consideration for using a dial-up facility is the modem, and the most important consideration with a modem is speed. The faster the modem operates, the faster you will be able to send and receive information from a host computer (the computer you are calling). Modems come in a variety of speeds including 14,400 bps (or 14.4), 28,800 bps (or 28.8), 33,600 bps (or 33.6), 56,600 bps (or 56.6), and higher. There are also electronic modems, called ISDN, for electronic phone systems and cable modems for connecting to community cable television lines. Both electronic and cable modems operate at higher transmission rates than phone modems do. No matter what type of modem you are using, the actual transmission speed of the modem is limited by the lower speed modem in the link. If you have a 28.8 modem, but the host has 14.4, then you will send and receive at 14.4.

In addition to having a modem, you also need communication software. The communication settings in this software must match the settings of the host computer. These settings include the character length, stop bit, and parity. Once these match, you must set your computer to "behave" like a terminal of the host computer. This process is called *terminal emulation.* The emulation you use is determined by the computer to which you are connecting for Internet service.

The Software Connection

How and where you connect determine how you use the Internet. The interface (how the Internet appears to you) can differ. Some interfaces are graphical, whereas others are character based. In addition, various Internet service providers use different software for accessing and using the Internet. This diversity poses a bit of a problem. What you can do is fairly standard, but how you do it is not. Although less and less popular, some providers (usually colleges and universities) provide a text-only system. The reason is that colleges and universities provided the early backbone of the Internet—before graphical software was popular.

With graphical software interfaces, you can use software that is written for Microsoft Windows® (or Macintosh®) to access the Internet. Consequently, you can use the point-and-click features of a mouse with pull-down menus and all of the advantages of Windows (or Mac). The big advantage of graphical software is that you can view graphics (pictures) directly on the Internet. You can also access sounds, video clips, and other multimedia information directly. Many colleges and universities offer both types of interfaces (graphical and character based). Character-based systems provide the same access as graphical systems, but do not allow you to view graphics directly. With character-based systems, you must use command-driven software. Typically, you cannot use a mouse with this type of software. You must type commands or make selections from menus.

Within the basic framework of character-based and graphical software, there are many different program choices. For example, you can access the Internet with a wide range of general

Tips, Tricks, and Ideas 1-7

Point and Click or Click and Drag

There are two ways to use the mouse to select menu items. You may point the mouse at a menu item, click the left mouse button, point the mouse at the desired selection, and click again. This technique is known as *point and click.* To *click and drag,* place the mouse pointer on a menu item, press and hold the left mouse button, drag the mouse until the desired item is highlighted, and then release the mouse button. Both techniques work equally well. Try each technique, and use the one you like best.

Tips, Tricks, and Ideas 1-8

Internet Explorer Desktop

Internet Explorer can be used as a desktop in Microsoft Windows. In other words, with Internet Explorer you can change the desktop in Windows to operate like a Web browser. Although many people use this option, it can be confusing when you are learning to use Internet Explorer. Therefore, this book does not deal with this popular feature.

graphical software (e.g., Netscape Navigator, Mosaic, Internet Explorer) including specialized software from specific providers (America Online®, Microsoft Network®, etc.). Many character-based systems are also available. The way all these systems operate depends on the provider.

INTERNET EXPLORER AND THE WORLD WIDE WEB

The resources and the ease of use of the World Wide Web have made accessing and using the Internet popular with millions of computer users. In fact, most people use the World Wide Web for accessing and using the Internet, and many people use Internet Explorer for accessing the World Wide Web.

The World Wide Web is made up of documents created with a special language called the **HyperText Markup Language (HTML).** HTML supports the full use of hypermedia including text, images, graphics, sounds, and other types of multimedia. Because HTML is a special language, it requires special software to access the Web. This type of access program is known as a browser. Lynx is a character-based browser that allows you to view only the text portions of home pages and other resources created with HTML. Internet Explorer is one of several full-featured graphical browsers that allow you to use color graphics, a mouse, and all of the features common to Microsoft Windows. Other browsers are specific to providers or services such as America Online.

Although many browsers are available for accessing and using the Web, one of the most popular is Internet Explorer. This Web browser will be used for all the Web examples in this book. However, most browsers operate in the same way. Therefore, even if you are not using Internet Explorer, you will be able to transfer the examples in this book to your browser with only slight modifications.

Tips, Tricks, and Ideas 1-9

Internet Explorer and Other Browsers

Most browsers are remarkably similar. If you are not using Internet Explorer, don't worry. Most of the processes described will work with any browser. With a little common sense you will be able to perform all of these tasks no matter which browser you use.

Tips, Tricks, and Ideas 1-10

Launching from Windows

As with so many other features of Windows, there are multiple methods for starting Internet Explorer. In many cases Internet Explorer appears as an icon on the desktop. If this is the case, simply double-click on the icon to launch Internet Explorer. Another easy method is to click on the Start button and then choose Programs from the Start menu. When the folder appears, select it; then point and click on Internet Explorer.

ACTIVITY

1. Connect to the Internet.
   The exact procedure for making your connection depends on whether you are working in a computer lab or using a dial-up facility. Ask your instructor for the basic connection procedures or consult with your Internet provider for details.
2. Launch Internet Explorer. Again, this process depends on how Internet Explorer is installed on your computer system. Check "Tips, Tricks, and Ideas 1-8" for details on Windows 3.1 and Windows 95. The opening screen for Internet Explorer should look something like Image 1-12. Most users automatically connect to a specific location on the Web.

Image 1-12

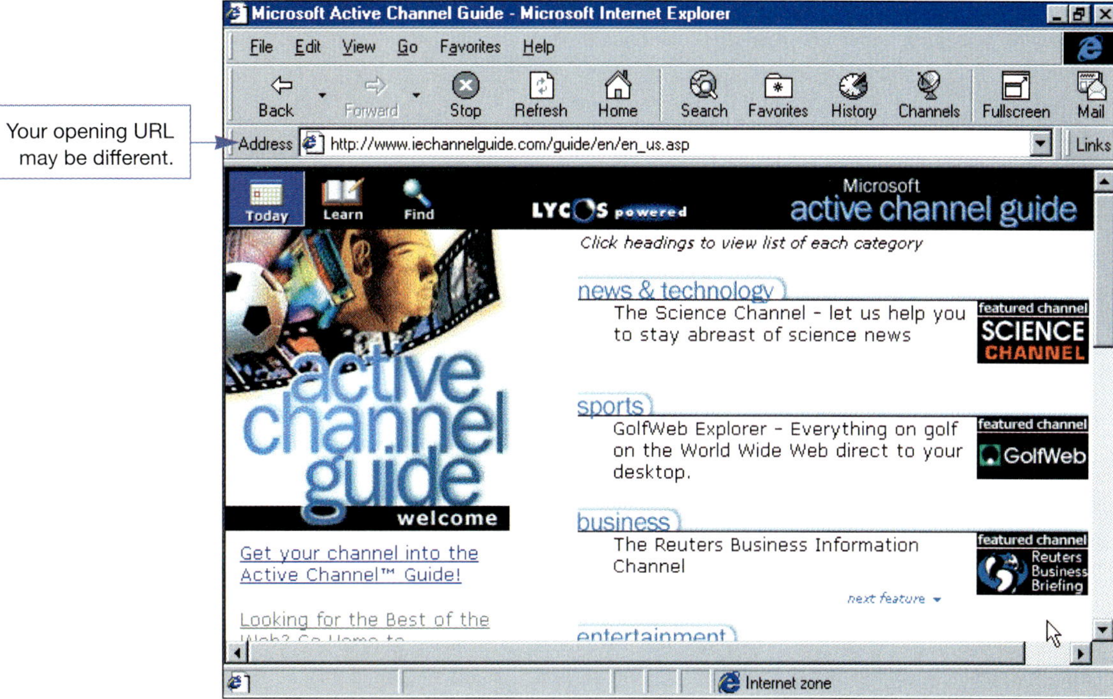

3. Place the mouse pointer to the right of the URL identified next to Address: and click to place the insertion point. Use the Backspace key to delete the existing URL.
4. Next to Address: type http://www.mhhe.com/cit/net/learning. Then press Enter.
   Pressing Enter causes Internet Explorer to search the Web and return the identified Web site. In this case the site is the Learning Online Web site for this book (Image 1-13).

Image 1-13

The URL for *Learning Online.*

Use the scroll bars to scroll down the page.

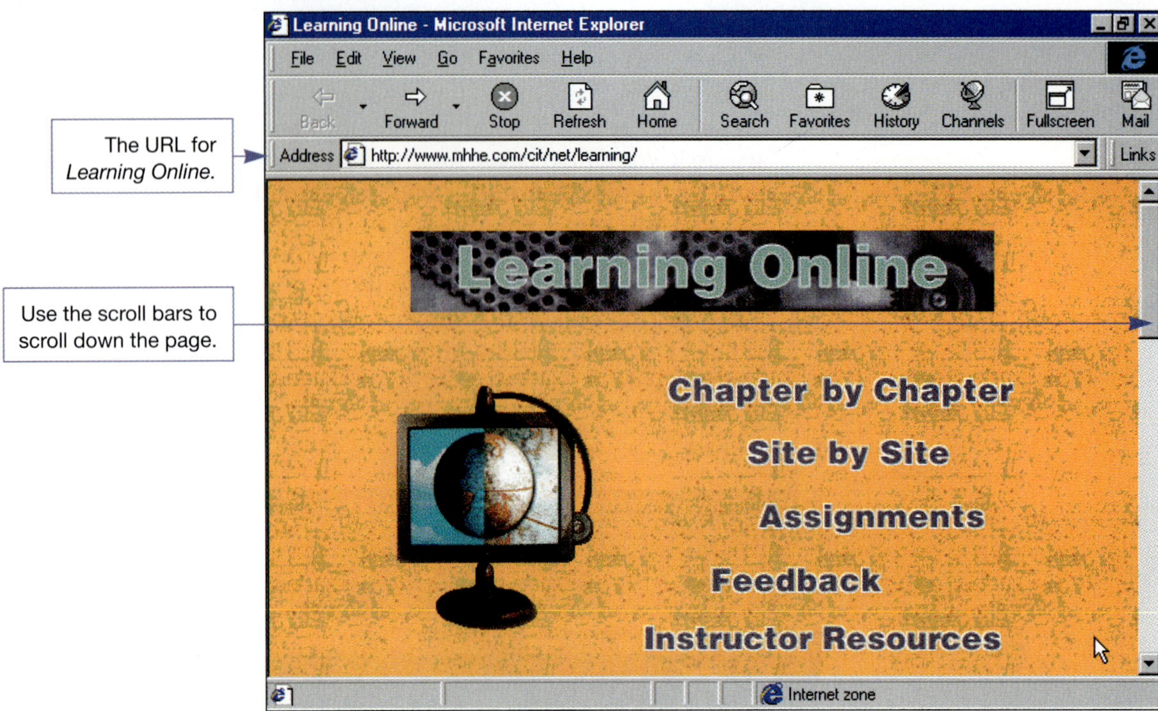

5. Select the Site by Site link.
6. Use the scroll arrows to the right of the screen and scroll through the Learning Online Web site.
   Several links appear in color and are underlined. Links allow you to go to various other locations on the Web (Image 1-14).

Image 1-14

Use the scroll arrows to scroll down the page.

Links normally appear as underlined text.

Point at a link and the pointing finger will appear. Click once to move to a new URL.

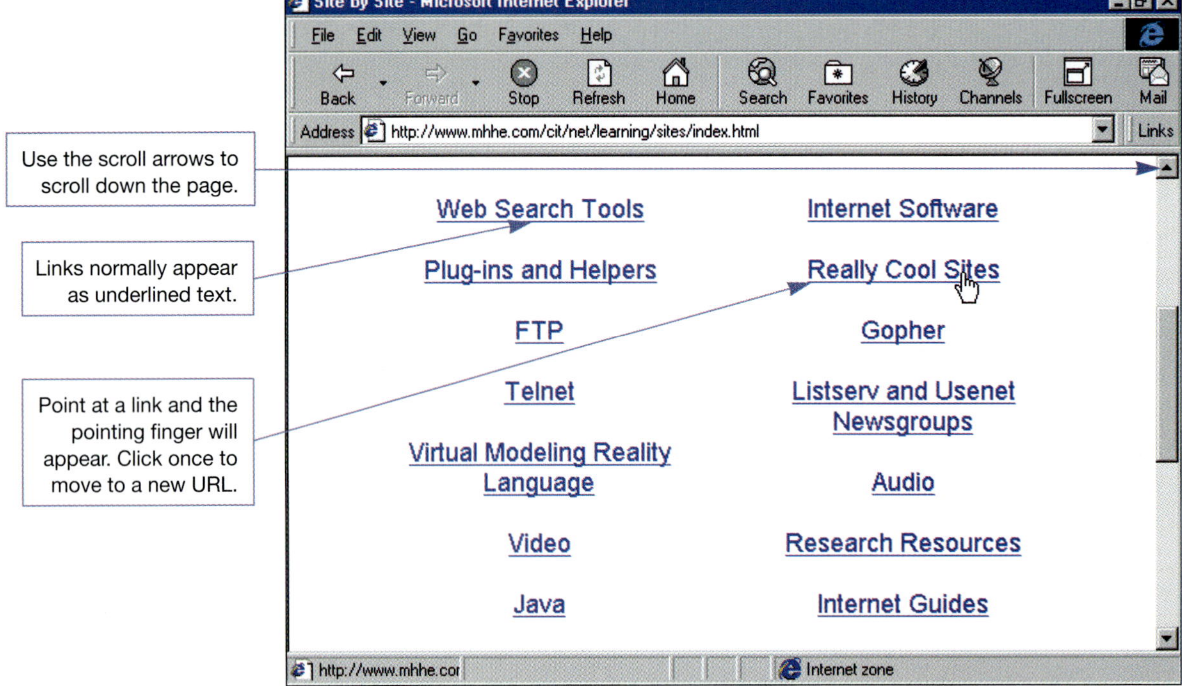

7. Point at the Really Cool Sites link and then click the mouse button. Notice how the URL changes and a new Web site appears (Image 1-15).

Image 1-15

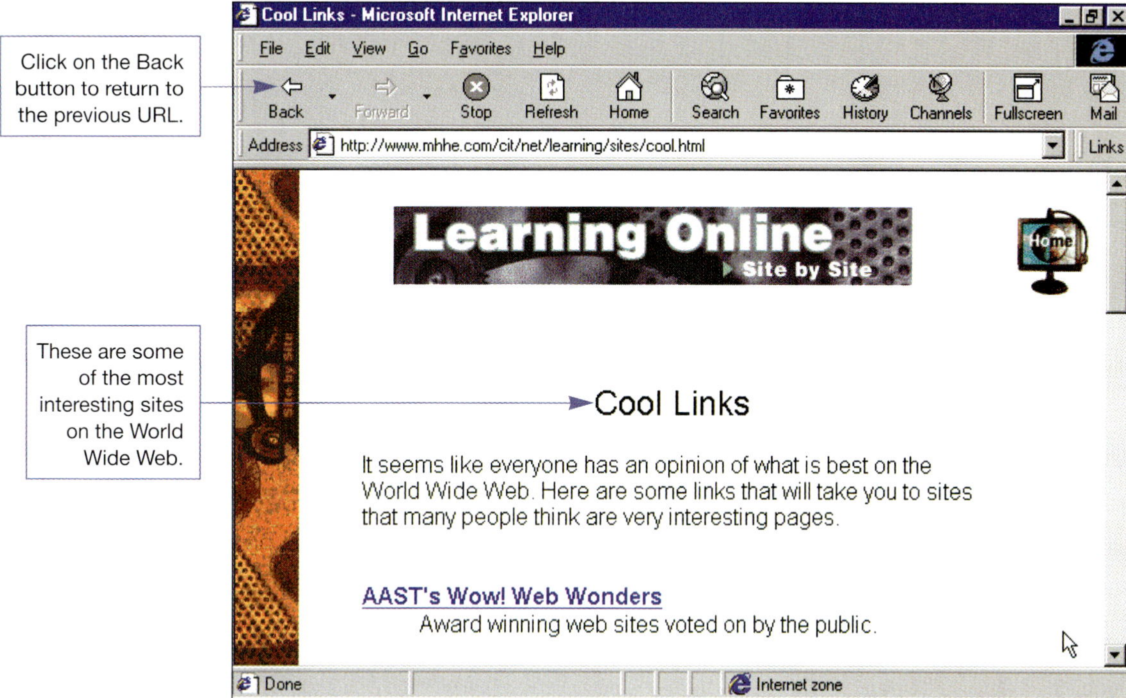

8. Click on the Back button below the File menu to return to the previous Web site.
9. Take a few minutes to explore this Web site and some of the available links. These will be discussed in later chapters.
10. Click once on File to display a list of commands (Image 1-16).

Image 1-16

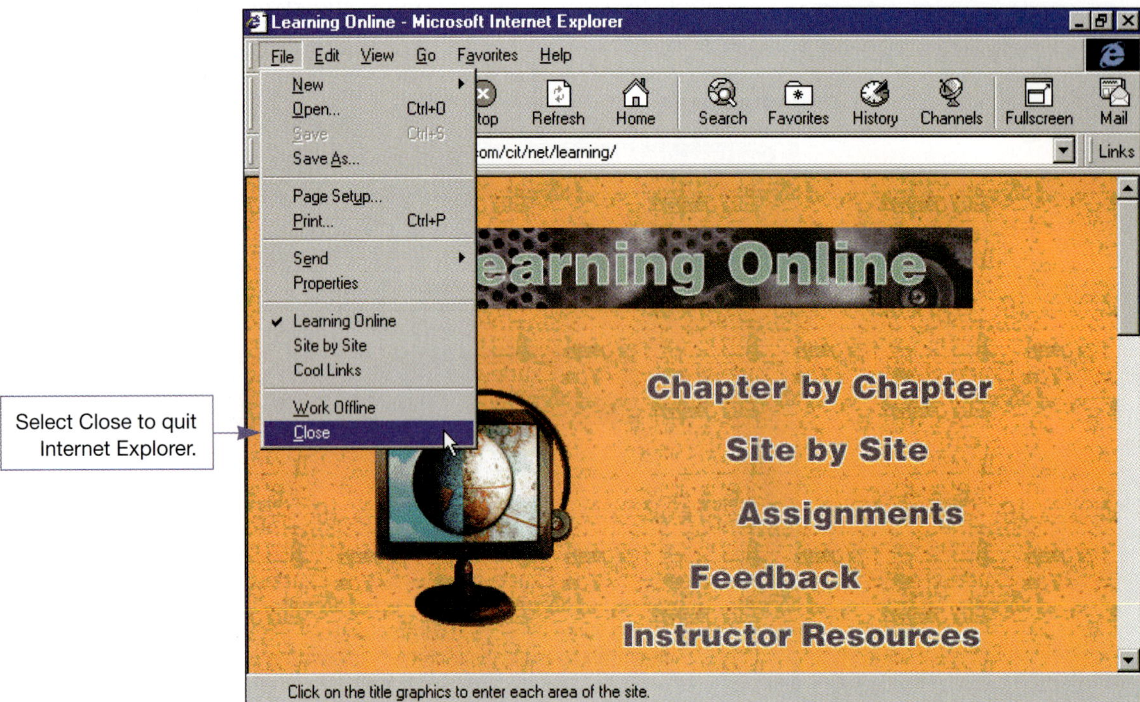

11. Click on Close.
    This step terminates Internet Explorer and ends your session.

EXERCISE 1-1

Don't be afraid to dive right in and start browsing. We provide the *Learning Online* Web site at http://www.mhhe.com/cit/net/learning to get you started, but you can also look for other ways to start browsing the Web. Your school may have a Web site for locating information on the Web, or you may find other locations on your own. The more you begin to explore, the more you will learn about the Internet.

KEY POINTS

- Internet Explorer contains a collection of software resources for accessing various components of the Internet.
- The Internet initiated a communications revolution; millions of users send messages, listen to music, check live video cameras, participate in global discussion groups, read magazines and newspapers from across the world, and watch video news segments as routinely as they turn on a television or talk on the telephone.
- The Internet bridges time, distance, and culture. It is where you can learn about almost any subject and communicate with almost anyone.
- The Internet is much more than a giant computer network. It is a cultural phenomenon that has made our desire for instant information and communication a reality.
- A network is a collection of computers linked together to achieve some common goal.
- The Internet is a network of networks. It is a series of networks linked using very precise rules that allow any user to connect to and use any available network or computer connected to the Internet.
- The Internet uses a standard of communication, called a protocol, that enables one computer network to "speak" to another.

- During the 1970s a new communication language, or protocol, emerged. Transmission Control Protocol/Internet Protocol (TCP/IP) allowed one network to communicate with other networks with relative ease.
- An initial link of university networks of five supercomputers, called NSFnet, became the backbone of the Internet.
- The real strength of NSFnet and TCP/IP was that the design of the network made it very easy for other networks to join.
- The rules that govern the Internet rest with the Internet Society. The Internet Architecture Board (IAB) of the Internet Society determines addresses for users, as well as the rules for accessing and using these addresses.
- Actual Internet addresses are numerical and are called IP addresses.
- The addressing system for the Internet is quite simple because of a process called the Domain Name System. A DNS name is made up of a domain and one or more subdomains.
- E-mail is a fundamental service of the Internet.
- Telnet allows you to use any host computer on the Internet as if you were directly connected.
- Gopher is a navigational tool that uses a system of standardized menus for navigating through various computers on the Internet.
- File Transfer Protocol (FTP) allows you to send and receive files stored on other computers on the Internet. These files include data files and program files, called binary files.
- Usenet has been called the world's largest bulletin board because it is a public place where users can read and post messages.
- Listservs are automated mailing lists. When you join a Listserv, any mail sent to the Listserv will also be sent to you.
- With the World Wide Web, you can establish your own Internet location, called a home page.
- Every home page has a specific address, called a URL (Uniform Resource Locator).
- The World Wide Web and Gopher are both tools for locating information on the Internet.
- How and where you connect determines how you use the Internet. The interface (how the Internet appears to you) can differ. Interfaces can be graphical or character based.
- The World Wide Web comprises documents created with a special language called the HyperText Markup Language (HTML).
- HTML supports the full use of hypermedia, including text, images, graphics, sounds, and other types of multimedia.
- Because HTML is a special language, it requires special software to access the Web. This type of access program is known as a browser.
- Internet Explorer is one of several full-featured graphical browsers that enable you to use color graphics, a mouse, and all the features common to Microsoft Windows.

KEY TERMS AND COMMANDS

browser
Domain Name System (DNS)
e-mail
File Transfer Protocol (FTP)
Gopher
HyperText Transfer Protocol (HTTP)
Internet Architecture Board (IAB)
Internet Explorer
Internet Society
IP address
Listserv
modem
newsreader
NSFnet
Outlook Express
protocol
telnet
Transmission Control Protocol/ Internet Protocol (TCP/IP)
Uniform Resource Locator (URL)
Usenet
Web page
World Wide Web (WWW)

STUDY QUESTIONS

1. What is the Internet?
2. How would you describe the physical Internet?
3. How would you describe the soft Internet?
4. What single development was most significant in the emergence of the Internet?
5. What is TCP/IP and how did it get started?
6. What is the function of the Internet Society?
7. Describe how addresses are defined on the Internet.
8. What is the difference between e-mail and telnet?
9. Why is a browser, such as Internet Explorer, necessary for the Internet?
10. What are two of the most popular tools for locating information on the Internet?

PRACTICE TEST

1. Actual Internet addresses are numerical and are called
   a. Domain Name Systems
   b. DNS
   c. IP addresses
   d. Domain addresses
2. Using any host computer on the Internet as if you were directly connected is called
   a. FTPing
   b. e-mailing
   c. telneting
   d. PPPing
3. The most important development in the emergence of the Internet was the development of
   a. IP addresses
   b. TCP/IP
   c. Domain Name Systems
   d. e-mail
4. Which of the following do you use to send and receive files stored on other computers on the Internet?
   a. FTP
   b. FAQ
   c. telnet
   d. SLIP
5. Automated mailing lists are also known as
   a. Usenet
   b. FACS
   c. Listservs
   d. Amls
6. The World Wide Web is made up of documents created with a special language called
   a. HTML
   b. HTTP
   c. URL
   d. HTML
7. Which component of Internet Explorer enables you to participate in newsgroups?
   a. News Service
   b. Outlook Express
   c. IAB
   d. Mail/News Server
8. Which group is responsible for directing the Internet?
   a. Internet Society
   b. Microsoft
   c. America Online
   d. World Wide Web
9. Internet Explorer provides a software resource for creating and reading electronic mail messages. This resource is known as
   a. Receiver
   b. Outlook Express
   c. Emailer
   d. Outmessager
10. HTTP refers to
    a. HyperText Transfer Protocol
    b. HyperText Transfer Procedure
    c. Home Text Translating Process
    d. Hyper Type Telephone Practice

FILL-INS

1. A ________________ is a collection of computers linked together to achieve some common goal.
2. The Internet uses standard communication, called ________________, that enables one computer network to "speak" to another.
3. On the Internet, any computer network can communicate with any other computer network as long as they both use the ________________ standard protocol.
4. An initial link of university networks to five supercomputers, called ________________, became the backbone of the Internet.
5. The real strength of NSFnet and TCP/IP was that the design of the network made it very easy for other networks ________________.
6. Responsibility for the rules that govern the Internet rest with the ________________.
7. The addressing system for the Internet is actually quite simple because of a process called ________________.
8. ________________ has long been considered to be the fundamental service of the Internet.
9. ________________ allows you to use any host computer on the Internet as if you were directly connected.
10. ________________ is a navigational tool that uses a system of standardized menus for navigating through various computers on the Internet.
11. ________________ is newsreader software that allows you to read and post messages.
12. ________________ allows you to send and receive files stored on other computers on the Internet.
13. ________________ provides a software resource for creating and reading e-mail messages, as well as a tool for managing the e-mail you receive.
14. ________________ has been called the world's largest bulletin board because it is a public place where users can read and post messages.
15. When you are using a dial-up facility to connect to the Internet, the communication settings of your software must match those of the host computer. These settings include the character length, ____________, and ____________.

PROJECTS

1. Before you can proceed with any activities on the Internet, you must have access. As discussed previously, there are several methods for obtaining access. If you are working in a college or university computer lab, see your instructor for the procedure for obtaining a user account. Write your account information in the margin of your text. Don't list your password. Keep that private.
2. Develop your own black book. As soon as you get on the Internet, you might want to send a message to friends, family members, professors, former teachers, or anyone else you know, to let them know that you are now on the Internet. Although most systems allow you to store Internet user addresses, it is a good idea to keep a list of Internet addresses for the people you might want to contact. If you have a personal phone book, you should include Internet addresses whenever possible.

INTERNET AT WORK

Throughout this book you will be working on a problem that places you at the Agee Candy Company. This fictitious company employs many people who operate computers every day. Many of the computer-related activities use the various functions and procedures of the Internet. To be a useful employee, you must master the Internet. You must also be able to use Internet software and resources in an efficient and effective fashion.

The Agee Candy Company is a family-owned and family-run business founded by Edith G. and George D. Agee. Edith's recipes for candy and keen business sense made this business a success. George's experience in manufacturing made the business run. On your first day at work, Mrs. Agee walks into your cubicle with an article from *The Wall Street Journal.* The stock value of Microsoft has rocketed. She knows that Internet Explorer is one of the most popular tools for using the Internet, but has never seen the Internet or Internet Explorer in action. She wants you to write a two-page summary describing the Internet in your own words. Mrs. Agee is a stickler for detail and expects a complete, yet brief, summary of the Internet.

2

Exploring the World Wide Web with Internet Explorer

OUTCOMES

When you complete this chapter you will be able to . . .

Describe the World Wide Web.

Define HTML, HTTP, and URL.

Use Internet Explorer to examine Web pages.

Identify links.

Locate Web pages.

Use navigational aides on the Web.

UNDERSTANDING THE WORLD WIDE WEB

As discussed in the previous chapter, the World Wide Web (WWW), or as it is commonly called, the Web, has quickly become the most popular way to access and use the Internet. The reason is simple. The Web allows full, high-quality color graphics and sound that makes it an attractive multimedia tool. But what exactly is the World Wide Web? Just as it is somewhat difficult to define the Internet, it is also difficult to define the World Wide Web. You know you are on the Web when you are connected. The Web is very distinctive, but if you ask most users what the Web is, they have a difficult time responding.

The World Wide Web is not the Internet, although many people make this mistake. The Web is not software, although you need a browser such as Internet Explorer to gain access. The Web is not hardware, although you need a connection to the Internet to get there. In its simplest form the World Wide Web is a huge collection of documents that are located on computers around the world. These documents, called **Web pages**, or **Web sites**, are all interconnected. Because these documents are interconnected, it is easy to access information from around the world in only a few seconds. However, users must follow a standardized set of requirements to access that information. Therefore, using the Web involves a specific communication standard and a specific set of requirements for developing information for distribution over the Internet.

The World Wide Web was conceived by the European Laboratory for Particle Physics as a means of linking objects (text, graphics, sound, etc.). By using HyperText Markup Language (HTML), anyone can create documents consisting of several objects for inclusion on the Web. The documents that most people create with HTML are called Web pages or Web sites. However, documents can also be sound, pictures, graphics, animation, and video.

HTML, HTTP, AND URL

Every discipline has its own language and acronyms. The Internet seems to have more than its share. For using the Internet, and the World Wide Web, there are three key terms—HTML, HTTP, and URL.

The foundation of the World Wide Web is the millions of Web pages created with a special language called the **HyperText Markup Language (HTML).** HTML is similar to a programming language. However, it is usually referred to as a formatting language. HTML provides a computer with instructions in much the same manner as BASIC, Pascal, C, or many other programming languages do. However, HTML is much more limited than most computer programming languages. HTML was specifically designed to provide a standard format for creating, sending, and displaying information in the form of pages on the Internet—hence the term *formatting language.* HTML programs are referred to as documents. Anyone accessing and using the Web is accessing and displaying HTML documents.

To access and display HTML documents, you must use a communication standard. **HyperText Transfer Protocol (HTTP)** is the standard communication protocol for sending and receiving HTML documents over the Web. There are other communication protocols you can use in addition to HTTP, such as Gopher and FTP. However, when you access any information on the Internet, you must identify what you want to access and how you are going to access that information. HTTP tells the Internet that you are accessing an HTML document. By including the method of transporting data, you are telling the computer what type of information you want to access and display.

Image 2-1

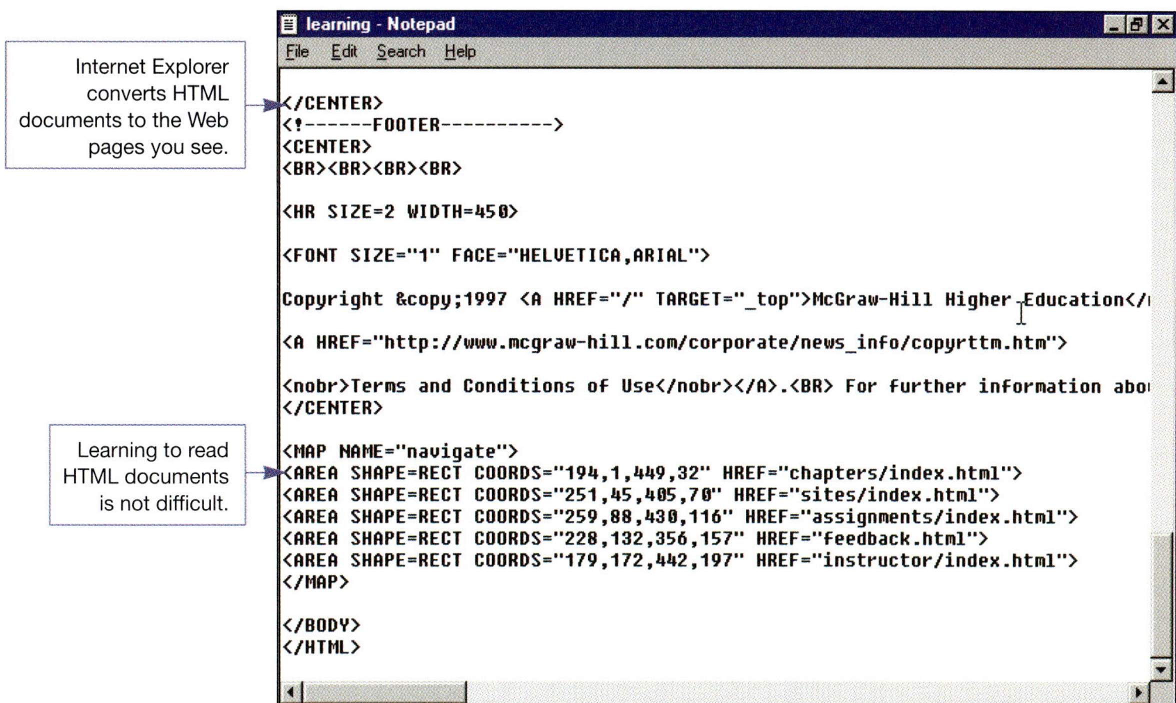


```
</CENTER>
<!------FOOTER---------->
<CENTER>
<BR><BR><BR><BR>

<HR SIZE=2 WIDTH=450>

<FONT SIZE="1" FACE="HELVETICA,ARIAL">

Copyright &copy;1997 <A HREF="/" TARGET="_top">McGraw-Hill Higher Education</

<A HREF="http://www.mcgraw-hill.com/corporate/news_info/copyrttm.htm">

<nobr>Terms and Conditions of Use</nobr></A>.<BR> For further information abo
</CENTER>

<MAP NAME="navigate">
<AREA SHAPE=RECT COORDS="194,1,449,32" HREF="chapters/index.html">
<AREA SHAPE=RECT COORDS="251,45,405,70" HREF="sites/index.html">
<AREA SHAPE=RECT COORDS="259,88,430,116" HREF="assignments/index.html">
<AREA SHAPE=RECT COORDS="228,132,356,157" HREF="feedback.html">
<AREA SHAPE=RECT COORDS="179,172,442,197" HREF="instructor/index.html">
</MAP>

</BODY>
</HTML>
```

A **Uniform Resource Locator (URL)** identifies both HTML and HTTP when accessing Web pages. The Uniform Resource Locator is a standard that allows you to enter the name and location of information, as well as the method for transporting that information over the Internet. In its simplest form, a URL is an address (actually, it is much more) that identifies specific information, where that information is located, and the transfer protocol employed. If you want to access an HTML document or any other type of information on the Web, you must identify its URL. For example, if you want to access the *Learning Online* Web site for this book, the software you are using to access the World Wide Web (Internet Explorer) requires the URL. In this case the URL is

http://www.mhhe.com/cit/net/learning

Each HTML document has its own URL made up of a specific **Domain Name System (DNS).** For example, the URL http://www.mhhe.com/cit/net/learning instructs the Web to locate the default document in the /learning directory, which is a subdirectory of both the /net and the /cit directories located at the McGraw-Hill computer, and to use HTTP protocol.

URLs are not limited to using HTTP. You can also use URLs to access any resource on the Internet, including resources such as Gophers, FTP, telnet, and others. For example, if you want to locate the Gopher at the University of Minnesota, you would use the URL Gopher://umn.edu. In short, if you know a URL, you can go directly to it on the Internet.

Tips, Tricks, and Ideas 2-1

Precision

There is no room for error when identifying a Web page by its URL. If you try to access a Web page, but are unsuccessful, check to be certain the URL is correct. Any deviation, no matter how minor, will prevent you from accessing the Web page.

NETIQUETTE 2-1

Questionable Material on the Web

There is a substantial amount of material on the Web that has questionable value or is offensive to many people. Generally, you have to look for this type of material; it does not just suddenly pop up on your screen. One bit of advice is that if you don't want to view material that might be offensive to you, don't look for it—and be precise when typing in a URL.

NETIQUETTE 2-2

Caveat Emptor—Let the Buyer Beware

Keep in mind that the Internet bridges the world. As you visit different Web sites, you may be visiting cultures that are quite different from your own. Some material that is very offensive in your culture may be acceptable elsewhere.

USING INTERNET EXPLORER

Internet Explorer is a full-featured and powerful Web browser. Internet Explorer displays images as buttons, icons, or the actual image. With Internet Explorer you can use a mouse to access these objects, display graphics directly, and take full advantage of all HTML features. In addition, Internet Explorer provides a unique procedure that allows you to access and use the Web with ease. One feature allows you to store your favorite locations within the Web. For example, with Internet Explorer you can create **bookmarks** with the Favorites menu. Bookmarks are URLs that you save so you can revisit these sites in the future very quickly and directly. You simply select your bookmark by clicking the mouse button on the name of the site in the Favorites menu.

One of the great features of Internet Explorer is that it is very intuitive. Once you understand the basics, you can quickly locate any URL you desire. In most cases the first step in using Internet Explorer (after you have made the connection to the Internet and launched Internet Explorer) is to activate an HTML document identified through its URL.

Many colleges and universities, service providers, or on-line services automatically display a Web page as a helpful starting point. In fact, most providers, including colleges and universities, have Internet Explorer automatically retrieve an HTML document when you start the software. If a Web page is displayed when you launch Internet Explorer, you should see the location of the page listed next to Address. This information indicates the URL for the current document.

NETIQUETTE 2-3

Check Your System First

If you have problems getting on the Internet, begin your problem-solving activity with your own system. Don't assume the problem is the fault of your provider. Determine whether your software settings are accurate and whether your network configuration is correct.

Tips, Tricks, and Ideas 2-2

Page Source

Internet Explorer interprets HTML documents. If you want to see what an HTML document looks like in its native form, first activate a Web page and then select the **Source** command from the View menu. As you look at the HTML document, see whether you can determine the function of each command. HTML is not a difficult language to understand.

The Address text box in Internet Explorer is critical because it identifies the location of a Web page or other document. With this text box you can enter any valid address (URL) you desire. Pressing enter after typing in a valid location causes the document, or Web page, to appear. The real secret to using Internet Explorer is not just knowing the software, but knowing the locations of information that you wish to access.

All HTML documents on the Web appear in Internet Explorer's document view window. When you access an HTML document, Internet Explorer interprets the document and then displays the results of the document including any graphics, sounds, animations, video, and, of course, text. Text appears in the format (font, size, and style) set forth in the HTML document. This interpretation of a document is the reason that a browser is required to use the Web.

Image 2-2

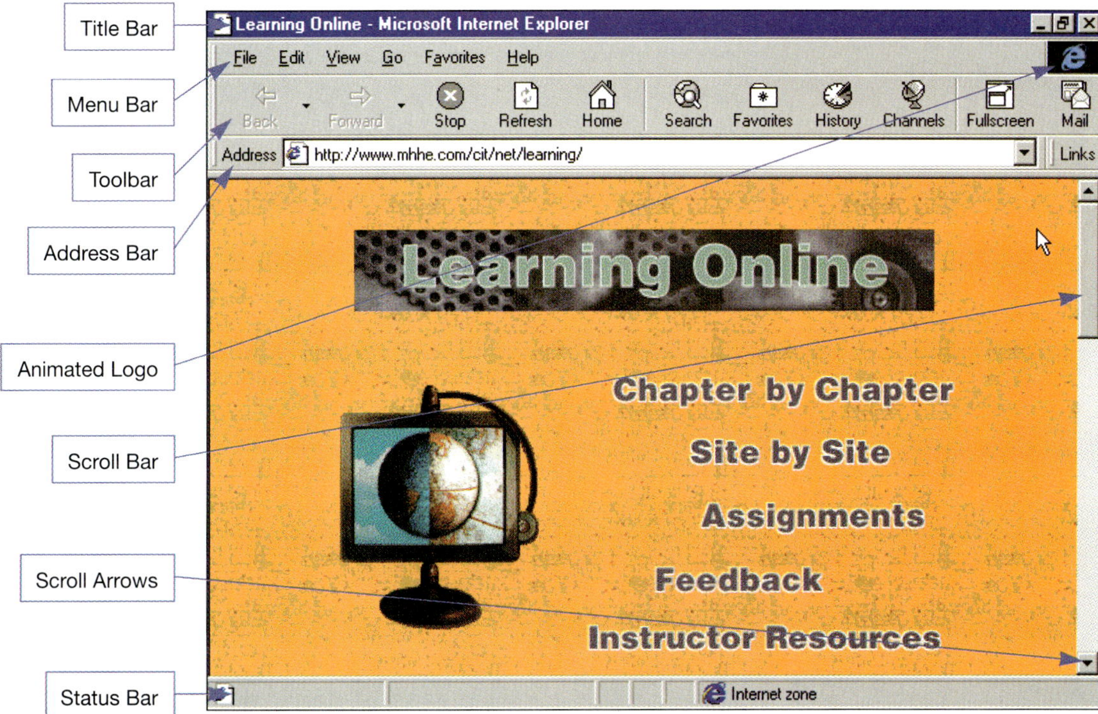

Internet Explorer displays a logo with a ring around an *e* in the right corner for the toolbar. When you make a connection to an HTML document, the ring around the *e* moves and the earth appears, indicating that Internet Explorer has sent out a request to locate, load, and interpret a document. You can stop the locate, load, and interpret process at any time by clicking on the **Stop button.**

The **status bar** at the bottom of the Internet Explorer screen displays any link to a URL address. For example, if you point at an icon in the document view window, the link of that object is another URL. The status bar also displays the process of downloading and interpreting. When you are downloading an *inline image* (Internet Explorer's name for graphics that appear on an HTML document), Internet Explorer tells you how many objects are yet to load. If you do not want to wait for a large image to download, click on the Stop button.

ACTIVITY

1. The way in which you connect to the Internet depends on whether you are directly connecting through a computer lab or using a dial-up facility. Before you start this activity, make sure you have an Internet connection.
2. Launch Internet Explorer.
   Your screen may differ from Image 2-3 because each user can set a default Web page to appear upon launching Internet Explorer (Image 2-3). The way in which you launch Internet Explorer depends on the way your computer system is set up. Normally, you can select Internet Explorer through the Start menu in Windows 95 or through the Internet Explorer icon.

Image 2-3

3. Click the mouse button at the end of the URL listed next to Address and then use the Backspace key to delete any existing URL.
4. Enter http://www.mhhe.com/cit/net/learning next to Address (Image 2-4).

Image 2-4

Enter and edit the URL here. Press the Enter key to go to a new Web site.

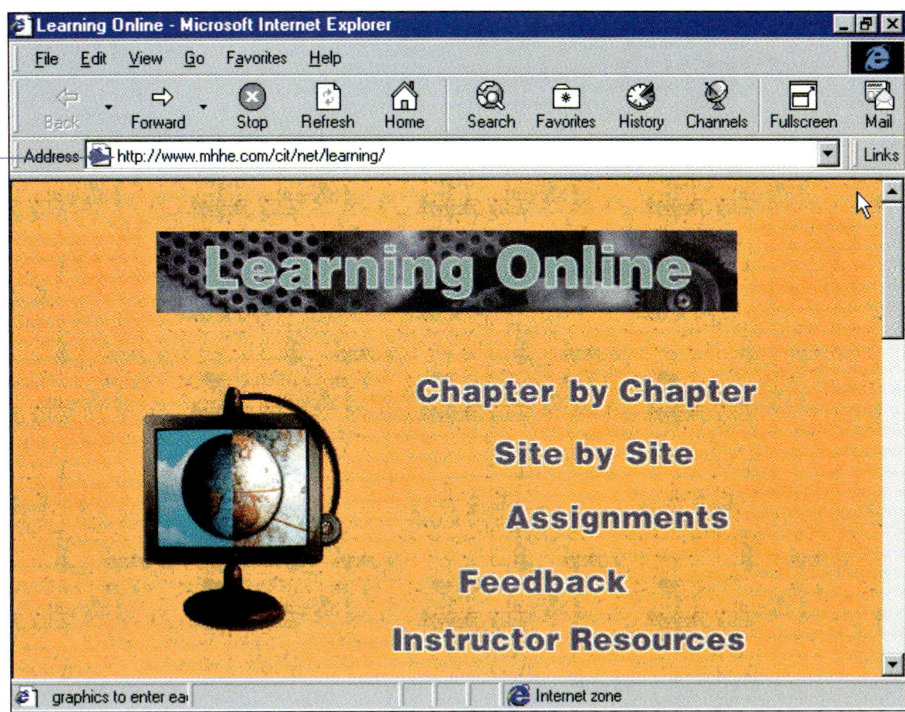

5. Press Enter.

   The Internet Explorer icon comes to life, indicating that the browser is locating and loading the specified HTML document. Notice the status bar. In a few moments the *Learning Online* Web site appears (Image 2-5).

Image 2-5

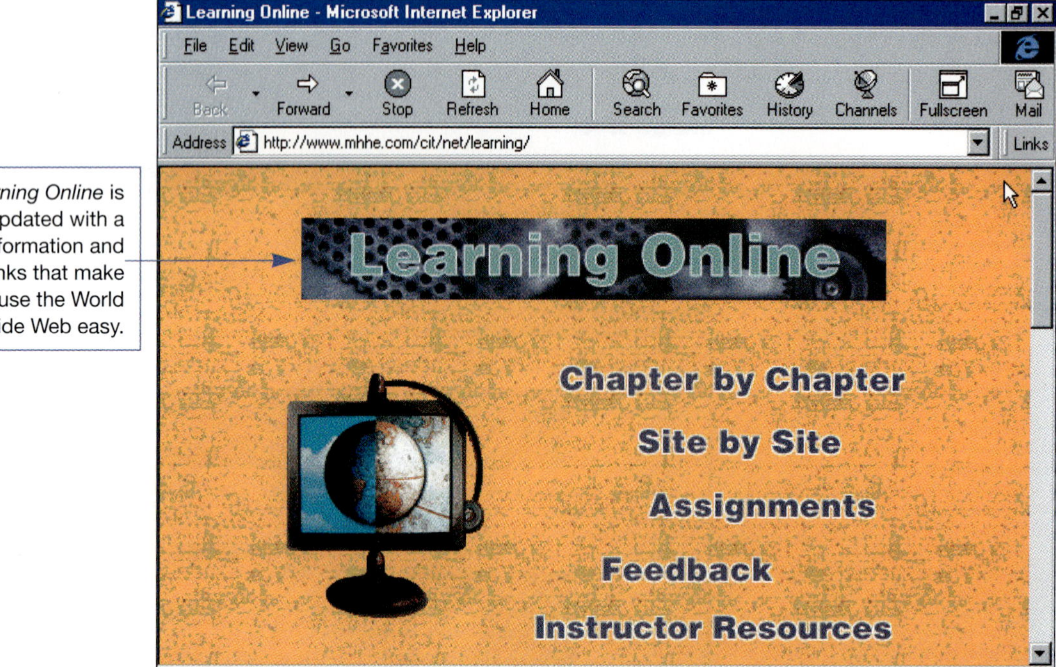

Learning Online is constantly updated with a wealth of information and current links that make learning to use the World Wide Web easy.

Links and Other Navigational Aids

Navigating through the World Wide Web is very easy with Internet Explorer or with any other browser. As you scroll through a Web page, you will probably see some text that is underlined or in a different color. This special text represents a link. A **link** may be an internal link to the HTML document or an external link to another URL. There is no visual difference between the two types of links. Each link takes you to a new location.

Clicking on an external link causes Internet Explorer to access the specified URL. The two documents are linked, but they are separate documents. For example, if you are at the *Learning Online* Web site and click on Audio, Internet Explorer jumps to a new HTML document at the URL http://www.mhhe.com/cit/net/learning/loaudio.htm. This Web site lists several links to various audio capabilities on the Web. You can choose to go to any of these sites by clicking on any available link.

As you start moving from one link to another, you may find yourself wanting to return to a previously accessed Web site. Internet Explorer offers navigation buttons to assist you in locating various URLs. Click the **Back button** to return to the previous page. For example, if you access http://www.mhhe.com/cit/net/learning and then link to http://www.mhhe.com/cit/net/learning/loaudio.htm, you can return to the previous site

Tips, Tricks, and Ideas 2-3

Your First Link

In most cases when you start Internet Explorer, a URL will be identified and an HTML document will be displayed. If you are working in a college or university computer lab, it is likely that your college or university Web site will be automatically accessed. If you are accessing the Internet through a provider, then your provider's Web site, or even Microsoft's own Web site, will appear.

Tips, Tricks, and Ideas 2-4

History

In Internet Explorer you can also use the **History button** to return to previously accessed Web pages. Click on the History button to open a list of all the Web pages you have visited during the current session. To select any of these, click on the desired URL and then click on the Go To button.

by clicking on the Back button one time. The **Forward button** works in reverse. It sends you forward through previously selected pages up to the most recent page you accessed.

The **Home button** returns you directly to the initial URL identified when you launched Internet Explorer. This button is very useful when you get deep into the Web and want to start browsing all over again.

To go to a specific URL, you can type the URL address in the Open Location dialog box that appears when you click on the **Open command** from the File menu. This entry has the same effect as entering a URL next to Address.

ACTIVITY

1. Access *Learning Online* at http://www.mhhe.com/cit/net/learning.
2. Select Site by Site.
   Scroll down and notice all the available links (Image 2-6).

Image 2-6

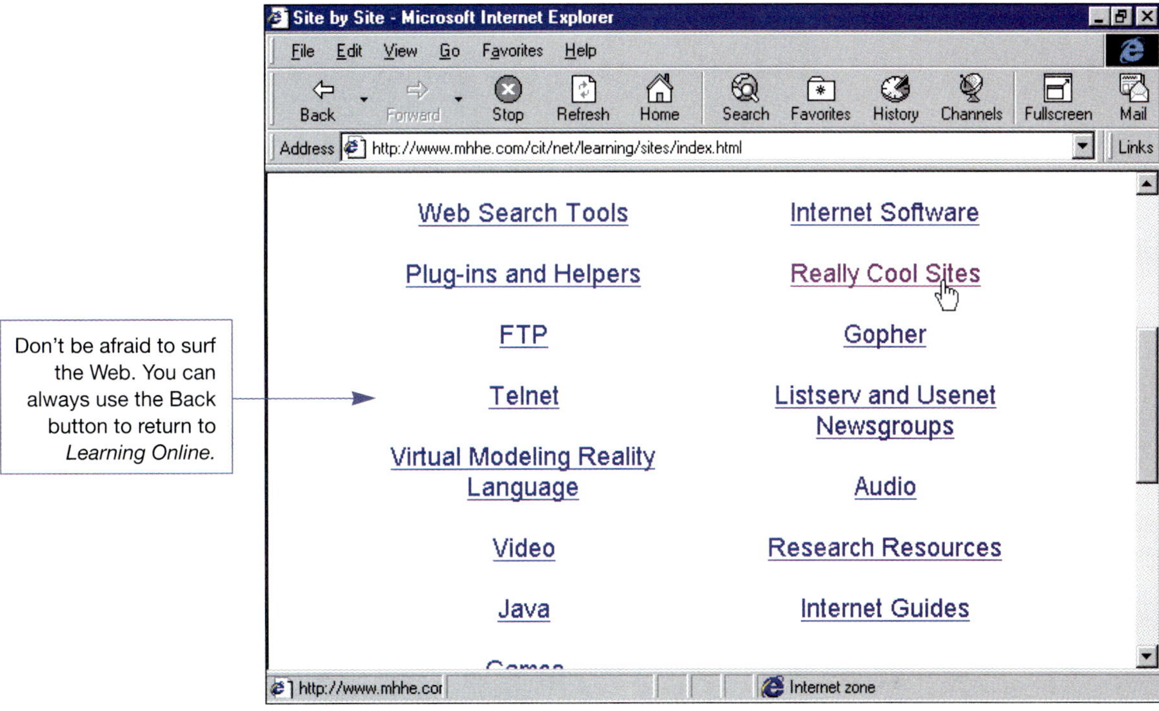

Don't be afraid to surf the Web. You can always use the Back button to return to *Learning Online*.

3. Click on the link Really Cool Sites.
   A new URL is located and opened. It appears next to Address (Image 2-7).

Image 2-7

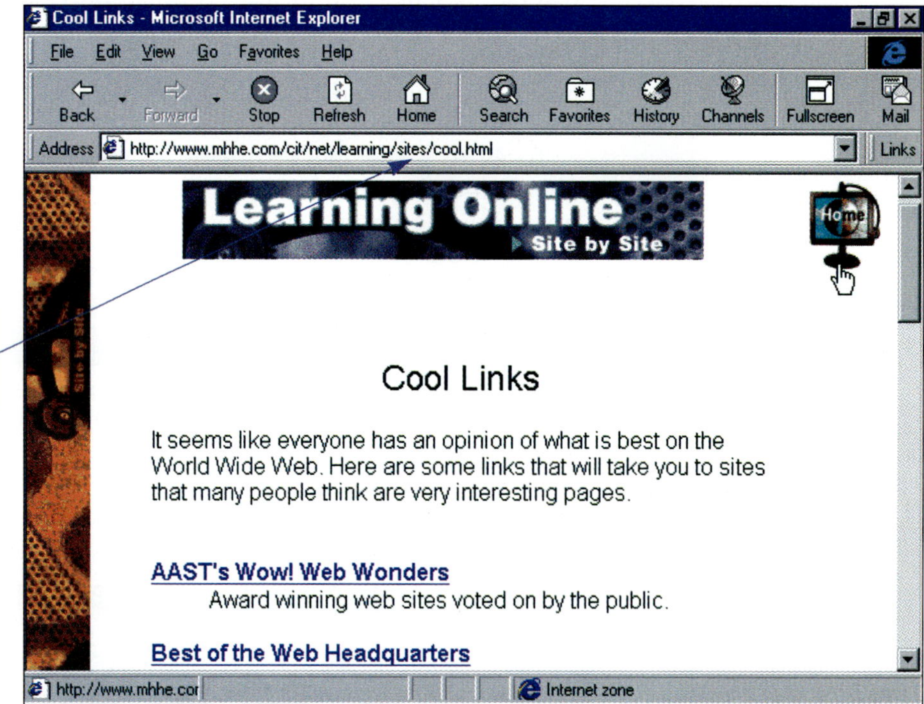

4. Click on Club Web Platinum 100.
   Another Web site is opened.
5. Click on the Back button.
   The Cool Links site Web page reappears.
6. Click on the Back button again.
   Learning Online appears again.
7. Select any link you desire from the Cool Links site.
   A new Web site appears.
8. Click on the Home button.
   Your original Web site reappears.

Tips, Tricks, and Ideas 2-5

Add-ons and Plug-ins

One of the strengths of Internet Explorer and other browsers is the ability to interpret audio and video files. However, Internet Explorer cannot do this job alone. It needs add-on programs for various types of documents. These are known as add-ons or plug-ins. You may need to download these tools and install them before you can access some of the information on the Web. For example, if you want to access RealPlayer files, you need to download and then install RealPlayer into Internet Explorer. The same holds true for QuickTime Video, Java, and many other applications. These are discussed in length later in this book.

A QUICK TOUR OF THE WEB

Now that you have some idea of how to use Internet Explorer, it is time to begin examining some interesting information on the Web. This guided tour is intended to give you a quick sample of the type of information available.

Surfing the Web can be a lot of fun. So much information is available that just exploring can lead to information that is fascinating and useful. To begin surfing, you need a starting point. To help you, we have created the *Learning Online* Web site. This site is filled with links to interesting and informative Web pages.

The *Learning Online* Web site is structured to help you sample information about a variety of multimedia. One of the big advantages of using the Web is that you can access text, graphics, images, audio files, animation, video clips, and a host of other interesting elements that are also fun. The issue that most users face is not what to access, but whether the browser has the capabilities to use these features.

Because so much is available in so many different forms, it is impossible for one browser, including one as powerful as Internet Explorer, to do everything. For this reason, and because the Web is changing so rapidly and new features are being added on a regular basis, Internet Explorer provides a means for adding capabilities. These added capabilities are referred to as **plug-ins.** To use a plug-in, it must be installed within Internet Explorer. For example, many audio files require a special set of audio enhancements to Internet Explorer. If you do not download and install these enhancements, the information available on the Web page may not appear within your browser.

It is beyond the scope of this book to teach you about each and every plug-in, although many of the most popular are presented in Chapter 5. For now, you only need to know that plug-ins exist. If you access multimedia information that will not run, it is probably because you need the plug-in. For example, if you select from the POP-I Audio link on the *Learning Online* Web site and then select riff of the day, which is a RealPlayer/Real Audio sound clip, you need the RealPlayer plug-in installed within Internet Explorer. If the plug-in is not installed, you cannot hear the sound. Fortunately, Internet Explorer comes preconfigured with several plug-ins, so you should always try to listen. You can always use the Back button if the sound clip doesn't work.

ACTIVITY

1. With your Internet connection established, launch Internet Explorer and go to http://www.mhhe.com/cit/net/learning.
   The Site by Site link on *Learning Online* offers several links to interesting and exciting resources on the Internet.
2. Scroll through this Web site and notice all of the links.
3. Click once on the Research Resources link.
   Notice that a new HTML document opens.
4. Scroll down and notice the various links (Image 2-8).

Image 2-8

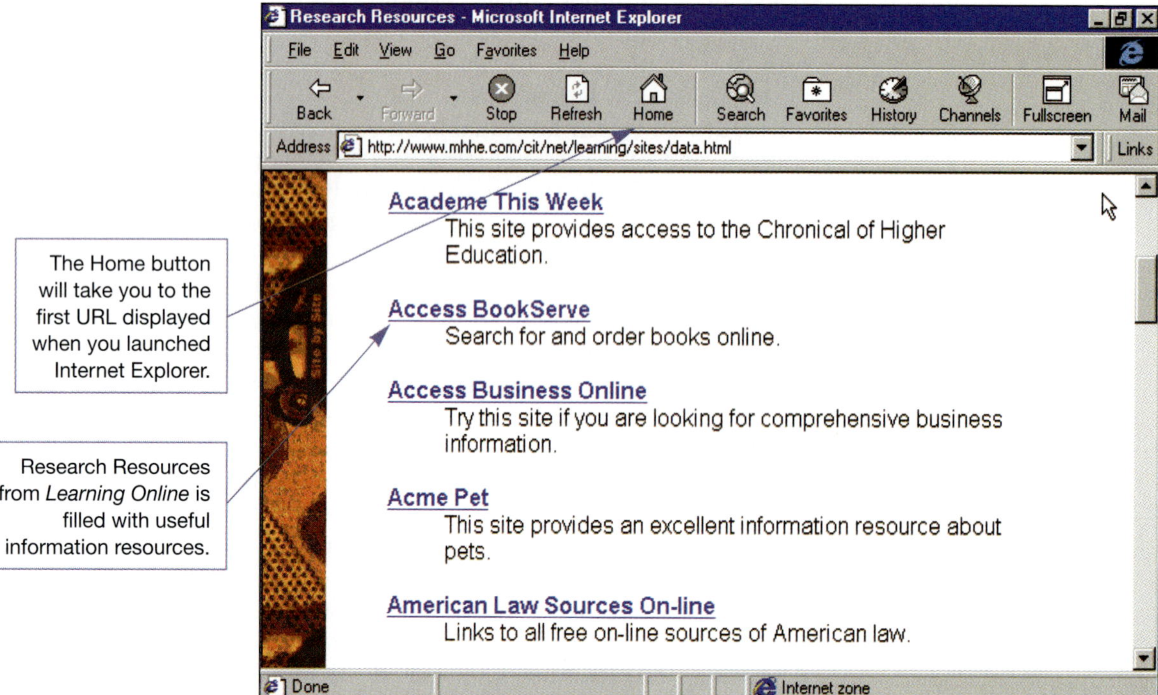

5. Click on any of the existing links on this Web site.
6. Click on the Back button.
   Notice that the previous link returns.
7. Click on the Forward button.
   Notice the Web site.
8. Take a few minutes to explore the sites available through all the links on *Learning Online.*

EXERCISE 2-1

The best way to learn what the Web has to offer is to take some time and explore links. This type of freeform browsing, although inefficient, is popular because it allows you to go where your interest takes you. As you explore, you may want to keep a notebook ready to record interesting URLs so that you can return to these locations.

KEY POINTS

- The World Wide Web (WWW), or as it is commonly called, the Web, has quickly become the most popular way to access and use the Internet.
- The World Wide Web was conceived by the European Laboratory for Particle Physics as a means for linking objects (text, graphics, sound, etc.) together.
- The foundation of the World Wide Web is the millions of Web pages created with a special language called HTML. HTML enables anyone to create Web documents that consist of several objects.
- HTML is a computer language that provides a computer with instructions in much the same manner as BASIC, Pascal, C, or many other computer languages.
- The documents that most users create with HTML are called Web pages. However, documents can also be sound, pictures, graphics, animation, and video.

- HyperText Transfer Protocol (HTTP) is the standard communication protocol for sending and receiving HTML documents over the Web.
- A URL identifies both HTML and HTTP when accessing Web pages. A URL is a standard that allows you to enter the name and location of information, as well as the method for transporting that information over the Internet.
- Each HTML document has its own URL made up of a specific Domain Name System.
- One requirement for using the Web is that you must have a browser. A browser is software that supports HTTP.
- In most cases the first step in using Internet Explorer (after you make the connection to the Internet and launch Internet Explorer) is to activate an HTML document identified through its URL.
- The Address text box in Internet Explorer identifies the location of a Web page or other document.
- When you make a connection to an HTML document, the Internet Explorer—letter *e*—changes into a globe. The spinning globe means that Internet Explorer has sent out a request to locate, load, and interpret a document.
- The status bar displays any link to a URL address.
- Underlined text or text in a different color represents links.
- A link may be an internal link to the HTML document or an external link to another URL.
- To go to a URL, you can type the URL address in the Open Location dialog box that appears when you click on the Open button.

KEY TERMS AND COMMANDS

Back button
bookmarks
Domain Name System (DNS)
Forward button
History button
Home button
HyperText Markup Language (HTML)
HyperText Transfer Protocol (HTTP)
link
Open command
plug-in
Source
status bar
Stop button
Uniform Resource Locator (URL)
Web pages
Web sites

STUDY QUESTIONS

1. Describe the World Wide Web. How is it different from the Internet?
2. Explain the difference between internal and external links.
3. What are plug-ins and why are they important?
4. What type of information is displayed on the status bar?
5. What is HTML?
6. What is HTTP?
7. What is a URL?
8. What is the purpose of the Home button?
9. How would you use the History button?
10. What is the purpose of the Back and Forward buttons?

PRACTICE TEST

1. To create a document for inclusion on the Web, you must use a type of programming language called
   a. HTTP c. URL
   b. HTML d. HTPL
2. The documents that most people create are called
   a. Web browsers c. Web documents
   b. Web sites d. Web pages
3. Anyone accessing and using the Web is accessing and displaying which type of documents?
   a. HTTP documents c. URL documents
   b. HTML documents d. HTPL documents
4. To access and display documents on the Web, you must have a communication standard called
   a. HTTP c. URL
   b. HTML d. DNS

5. The standard that allows you to enter the name and location of information and the method for transporting that information over the Internet is called
   a. HTTP   c. URL
   b. HTML   d. DNS
6. Uniform Resource Locators are limited to using HTTP.
   a. True   b. False
7. A listing of all the Web pages you have visited during a single session is referred to as
   a. Location index   c. Web list
   b. History   d. Site list
8. As you scroll through a Web page, it is likely you will see some underlined text or text in a different color. These represent
   a. Text markers   c. Graphics images
   b. Links   d. FTPs
9. Which button is used to return you directly to the initial URL identified when you launched Internet Explorer.
   a. Forward   c. Home
   b. Back   d. Stop
10. Internet Explorer provides a means for adding capabilities for sound, video, and other features. These added capabilities are referred to as
    a. Sound apps   c. Plug-Apps
    b. Plug-Help   d. Plug-ins

FILL-INS

1. By using ____________________, anyone can create documents consisting of several objects for inclusion on the Web.
2. Most documents created with HTML are called ____________________.
3. ____________________ is the standard communication protocol for sending and receiving HTML documents over the Web.
4. If you want to access an HTML document or any other type of information on the Web, you must identify its ____________________.
5. A ____________________ is software that supports the HyperText Transfer Protocol (HTTP).
6. ____________________ are URLs you can save so that you can return to these sites quickly and directly.
7. Internet Explorer displays a ____________________ at the bottom of the screen.
8. Underlined text or text in a different color represents ____________________.
9. The ____________________ button returns you directly to the initial URL identified when you launched Internet Explorer.
10. Adding capabilities in Internet Explorer is called ____________________.

PROJECTS

1. Surf the Web. The best way to learn to use the Web is to spend time exploring. By wandering from page to page, you are likely to come across a great deal of interesting information. Of course, *Learning Online* at http://www.mhhe.com/cit/net/learning should be your starting point. See what you can find in areas that interest you. Keep a handwritten record of interesting and useful URLs. Your list will help you find these locations again.

2. Use the *Learning Online* Web site as a starting point to visit some game sites. Explore several of the links that are presented on that page. Keep a handwritten record of some of the game sites that interest you.

3. From *Learning Online,* visit some of the Really Cool sites. Keep a record of the Web sites that were most attractive to you.

4. Use the History button of Internet Explorer to revisit the sites that were most attractive to you in the previous activity. Keep in mind that once you turn off the computer, Internet Explorer's record of history is erased. Use the bookmarks in the Favorite menu to identify one or two of the most interesting game sites.

INTERNET AT WORK

Edith is impressed with the amount of information that is available on the World Wide Web. However, she has heard that many people surfing the Web spend countless hours playing games. She is very concerned with the probability that her employees will spend time while they are at work playing games. She wants to know how she can check up on her employees to be sure they are working and not playing games. Your job as the resident expert on Internet Explorer is to write her a memo describing the History button of Internet Explorer. You must caution her that once the employee has left the Web, all traces of history are erased. Emphasize that she must catch her employees while they are surfing the Web. If you want to really impress Edith with your knowledge of Internet Explorer, show her how bookmarks work and how she can use them to determine whether her employees are visiting game sites.

3 Effective Search Tools and Techniques

OUTCOMES

When you complete this chapter you will be able to . . .

- Identify popular search tools and search engines.
- Use search tools for elementary categorical searches.
- Use search engines for keyword searches.
- Use meta directories for expanded search capabilities.
- Use the WWW Virtual Library and Galaxy for Web searching.
- Examine pay service search processes available on the Web.
- Use advanced search techniques including Boolean logic.
- Create and edit bookmarks in the Favorites menu for efficient Web navigation.

SEARCH TOOLS AND TECHNIQUES

The Web is only as valuable as the information you encounter. While it can be a great deal of fun visiting one Web site after another, browsing like this is not very efficient for locating specific information. In fact, if you cannot locate useful pages or meaningful information, the Web will be of little value. The trick, then, is to be able to find Web sites and pages with the information you want. To locate particular information, there are a variety of search tools and search techniques.

Effective Web users are skilled at using the considerable search opportunities that present themselves on the Web. These include numerous subject directories, search engines, meta search engines, the WWW Virtual Library, TradeWave Galaxy, and others. The process and technique you employ for searching will directly affect the type of results you find. Therefore, one of the most important features for learning to use the Web is to learn to use as many of the search processes as possible.

USING SEARCH TOOLS AND ENGINES

A few years ago a number of sites were developed to provide a mechanism for locating information on the Web. These sites, collectively known as **search tools,** gather information on other Web sites, organize and categorize this information, and then provide a tool for users to locate the sites that contain specific information. Some search tools provide users

NETIQUETTE 3-1

Do Not Assume That Information Is Accurate

Simply because information is presented on the Web, do not assume it is accurate or even up-to-date. Anybody can place information on the Web, but not everyone recognizes the importance of truth or accuracy.

Tips, Tricks, and Ideas 3-1

Broad First

Whenever you begin a search, you should start with a broad keyword. This approach allows you to determine the extent of the sites available. You can always go back and add narrower, or more specific, keywords to the search.

with organized lists of sites by subject matter. For example, they may provide a detailed listing of Web sites related to art, education, science, business, games, and a number of other categories. These categorical lists can be most helpful. However, categorical lists often do not provide the complete level of detail that many people need. As the number of categorical lists grew, it became more and more important for these search tools to provide a search engine (software for searching data) to locate Web pages based on specific criteria.

YAHOO! is one of the most popular search tools. Several other search tools, including WebCrawler, Infoseek, Excite, and Lycos, work in much the same manner. You can consider a series of predefined categories, or enter keywords, and the search engine looks at Web sites for word matches. The result is a list of Web sites that contain the word you want. You can browse through this list by clicking on the desired site. When you click on a desired site listing and you go directly to that Web site, the process is called **linking.**

One major strength of a search engine is also a major limitation. Search tools provide matches based on **keywords.** Consequently, any Web site that contains the keyword you identified will be listed. In many cases this approach results in a list of sites that are only marginally related to your search. For example, if you use YAHOO! to search for the keyword *education,* you will receive a list of several thousand sites that contain the word *education.* Web sites that deal with corporate training and education may be listed when you were looking for elementary education. The term *education* is too broad. One easy solution is to use multiple, specific keywords. In fact, the more specific the keyword, the more specific the search outcome.

It is important to note that all Web sites are not available in any single search. In fact, YAHOO!, WebCrawler, Excite, Infoseek, and others search only Web sites listed in their database. Therefore, many sites that you might find useful do not show up on a single search. Unless the creators of a Web site submit a request, or the Web site was added by an electronic process to any of the search tools, the site will not be in the search database. Also, if a Web site is, for some reason, not included in any search database, a search will never return that Web site. Fortunately, YAHOO! and the other search tools add thousands of new sites weekly.

Tips, Tricks, and Ideas 3-2

Try Several Search Tools

If you do not find what you want using one Web search tool, try another. Search tools, such as YAHOO!, Lycos, WebCrawler, Excite, and others, sometimes list different sites.

ACTIVITY

1. Make sure you are connected to the World Wide Web and Internet Explorer is up and running.
2. Go to the *Learning Online* site at http://www.mhhe.com/cit/net/learning.
3. From either Chapter by Chapter or Site by Site, select the Web Search Tools link. Scroll down and notice that a Web site, listing links to several search tools, appears (Image 3-1).

Image 3-1

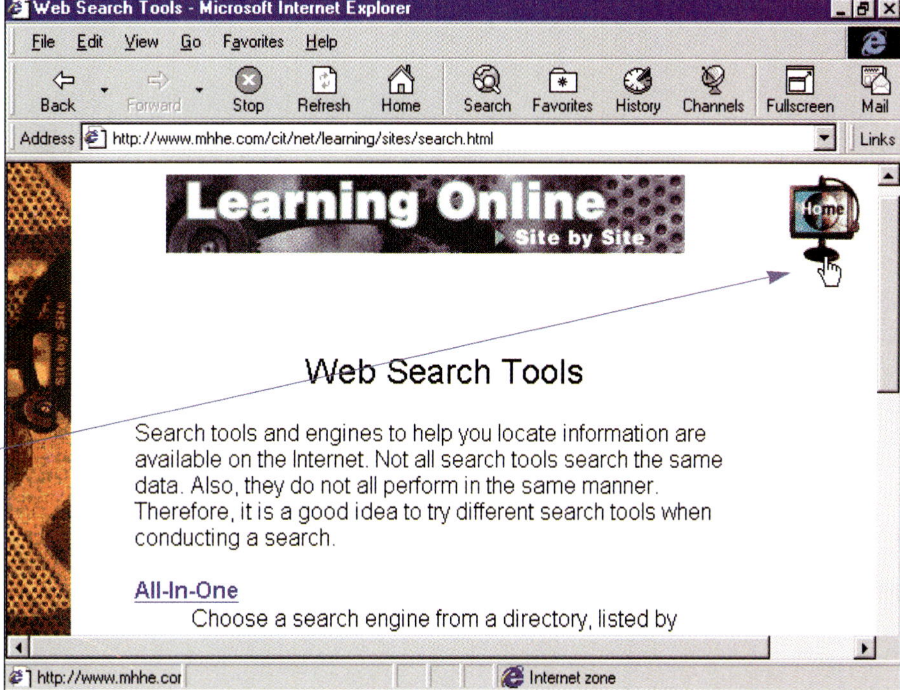

Click here to return to *Learning Online.*

4. Select YAHOO!.
   Notice the YAHOO! Web site (Image 3-2).

Image 3-2

5. Scroll down through the various categories provided by YAHOO!.
6. Select Entertainment and then on the next Web page select Music.
7. Select Artists.
   Notice that you can locate an artist by letter (Image 3-3).

Image 3-3

These links will take you to lists of various musical artists.

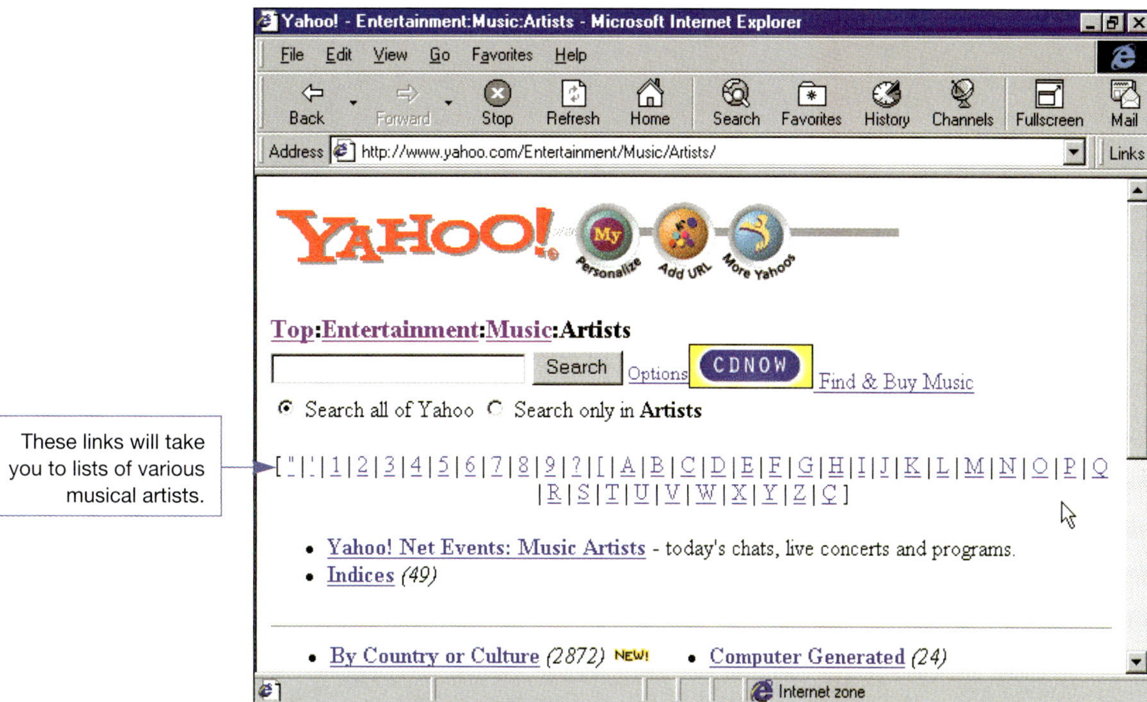

8. Select any letter you desire and try to locate a Web site for a particular music artist.
9. Use the Back button in Internet Explorer to return and see whether you can locate a different artist.
10. Take a few minutes to explore the listed Web sites.
11. Return to the beginning of YAHOO!.
12. In the text box, type Nanci Griffith (Image 3-4).

Image 3-4

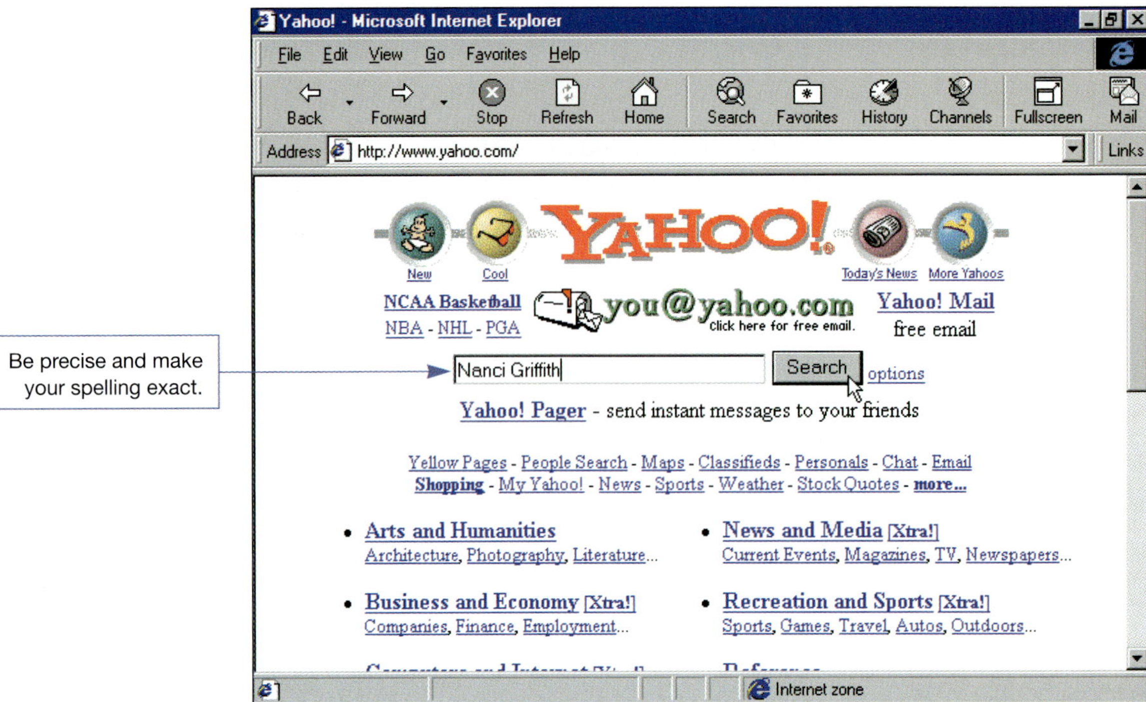

13. Click on the Search button.
    In a few moments a listing of Web sites related to Nanci Griffith will appear (Image 3-5).

Image 3-5

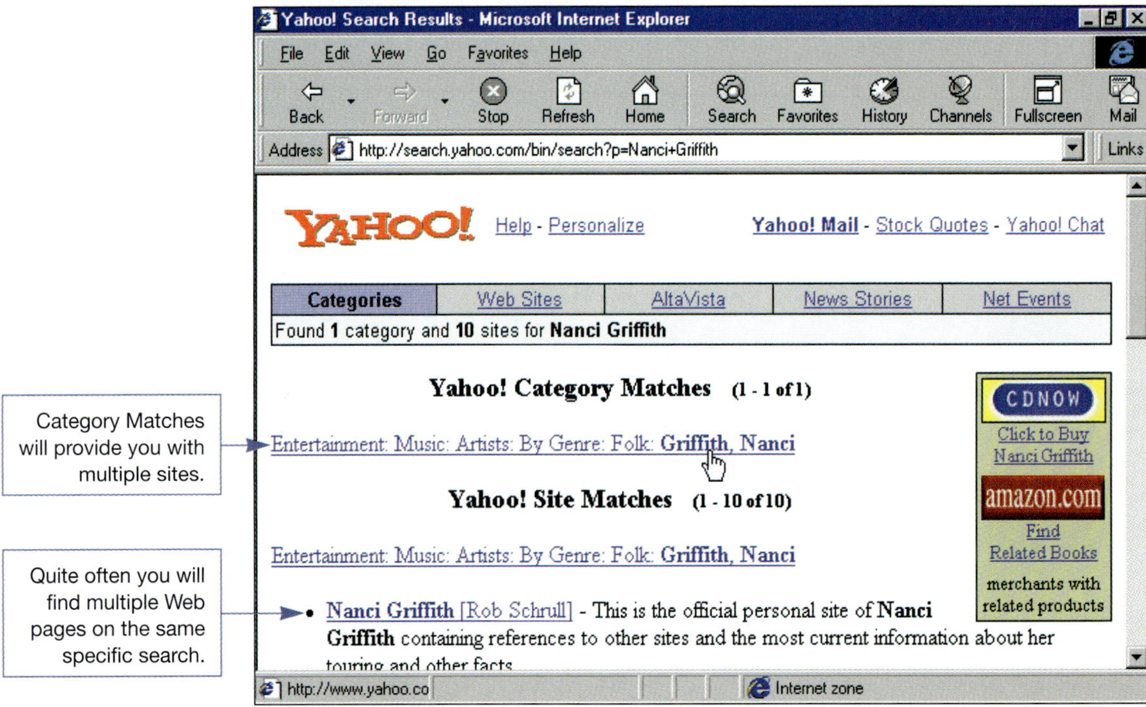

14. Click on the Back button and search for any other artist you desire.

EXERCISE 3-1

Learning to use search tools is very important. It frequently takes a bit of practice to learn how to enter the best keywords. Use YAHOO!, WebCrawler, and other search tools available through *Learning Online* to search for various topics. Take time to refine your search skills by using more specific keywords.

USING META DIRECTORIES

One very popular method for locating a specific Web site is to use a directory of directories, commonly called a **meta directory.** Some of the most popular meta directories are InterNIC, Mamma, All-in-One, and MetaCrawler. When you access a meta directory, you are able to browse through a directory of directories or use a variety of search engines, much as you would with YAHOO! or any other search tool.

One of the major advantages with using a meta directory is that the Web site listings frequently contain very useful descriptions of the sites. This feature means that you do not have to search through a list of titles to determine whether a particular Web site will be useful to you. Descriptions used in the meta directories help you quickly decide which Web sites are most closely related to the topic of your search.

Tips, Tricks, and Ideas 3-3

Don't Be Afraid to Browse

One of the most successful methods of locating valuable information on the Web is by browsing from one site to the next. If you enter a site that has useful information, look for links in that site. Often these links will take you to other sites with more useful information.

ACTIVITY

1. Make sure you are connected to *Learning Online.*
2. Get to the Web Search Tools link.
   Scroll down and notice that a Web site, listing links to several search tools, appears (Image 3-6).

Netiquette 3-2

Use Off-Peak Hours

Whenever possible, try to search during off-peak hours. This practice helps to reduce the enormous load on the system, especially at popular sites.

Image 3-6

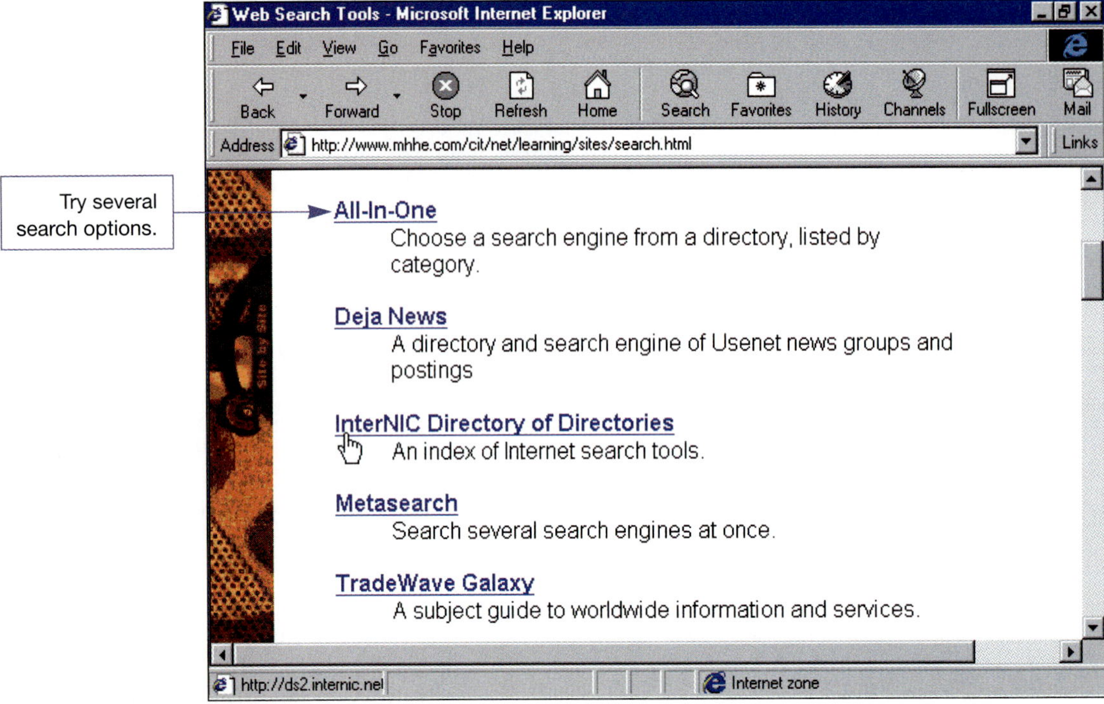

3. Click on Metasearch
4. Enter Jazz (Image 3-7).

Image 3-7

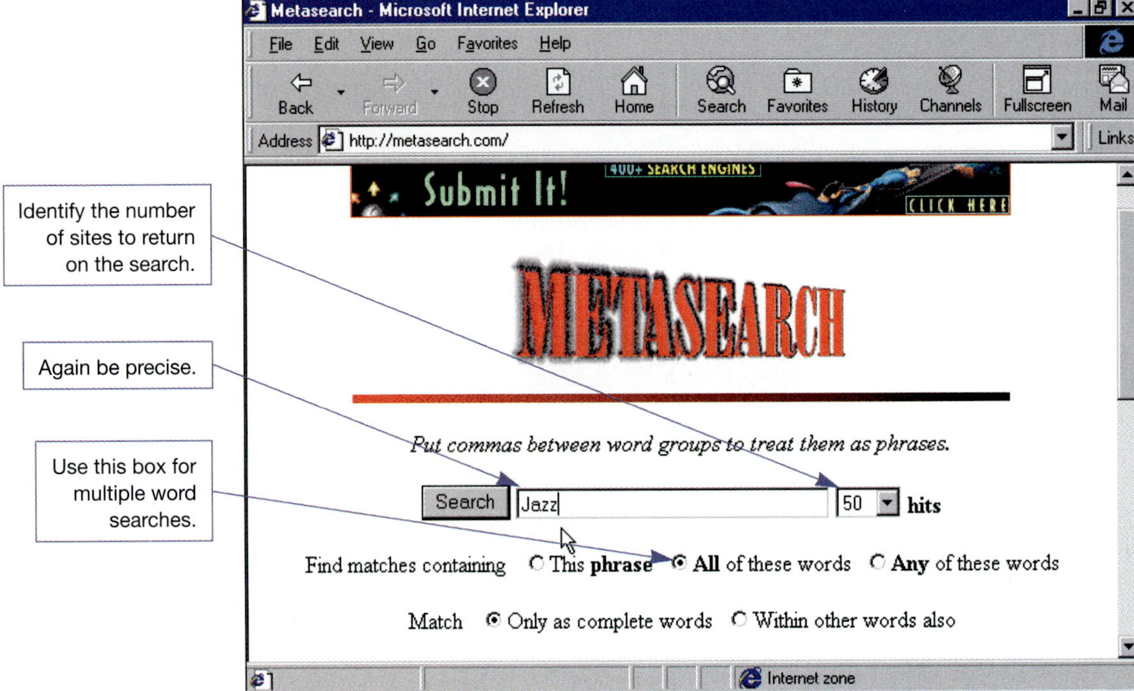

5. Click on Search.
   Notice that +Jazz appears for several popular search tools (Image 3-8).

Image 3-8

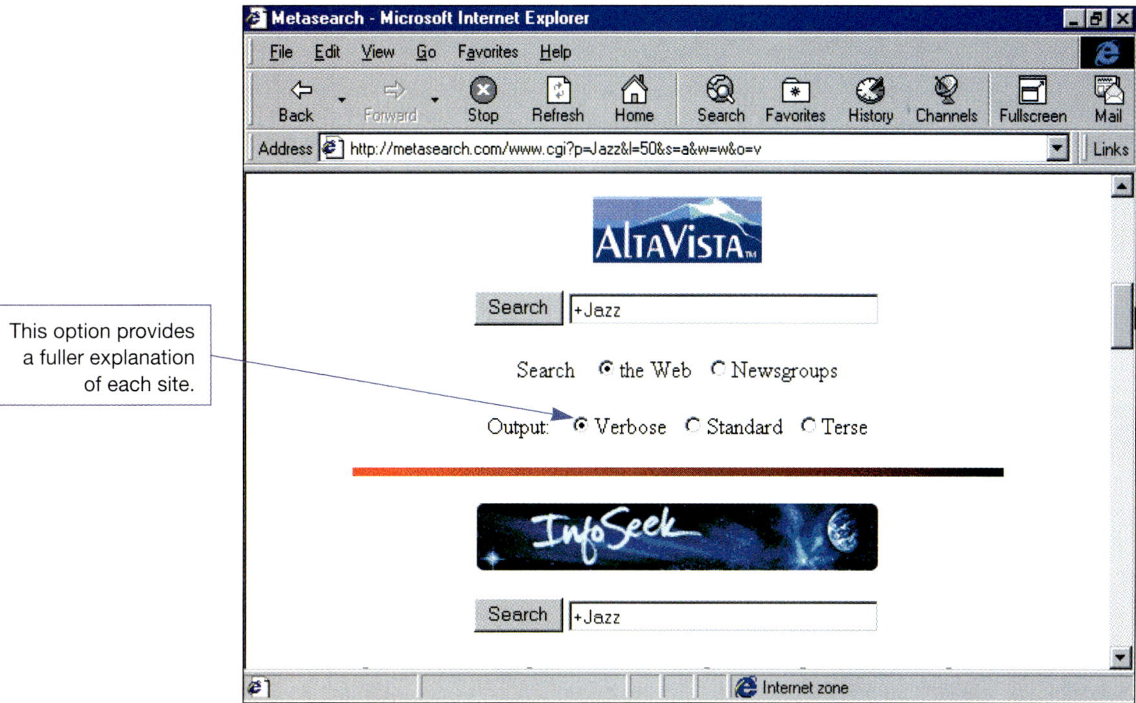

6. Select any search tool and then take a few minutes to browse through the various sites related to Jazz.
7. Click on the Search button on the Internet Explorer toolbar.
   Notice that the screen splits and a search tool appears (Image 3-9).
8. Click on Choose a Search Engine.
   Notice that a listing of search engines and tools appears (Image 3-9).

Image 3-9

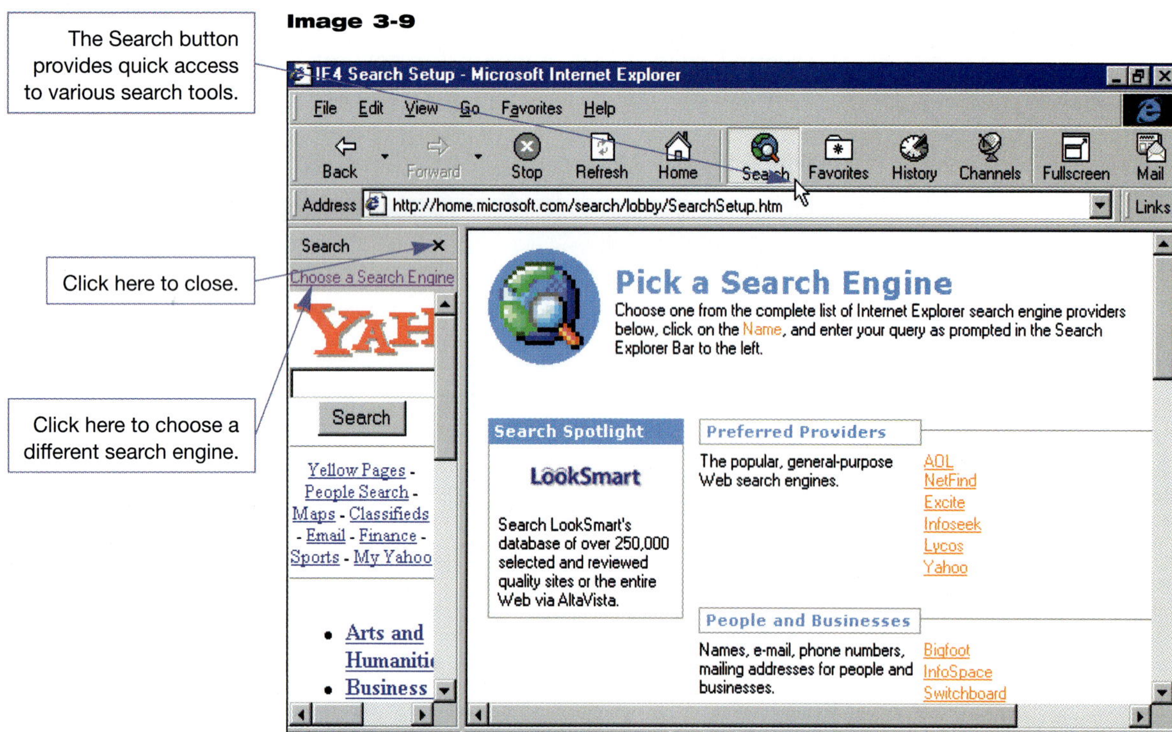

9. Click on the close button for the search window and then return to *Learning Online.*

EXERCISE 3-2

Exploring a meta directory can take a bit of time. Select any one topic and then perform a thorough search on any meta directory. Can you compare the successful sites you receive with a meta directory to those you receive with a search tool such as YAHOO!?

Tips, Tricks, and Ideas 3-4

Internal Search Engines

In addition to the daily increase in the number of Web sites, the content of individual Web sites is also on a steep rise. Because so many Web sites now contain so much information, it is very common for an individual Web site to have its own search engine. Often these are driven by other search engines such as Infoseek, but internal search engines perform keyword searches limited to information within a specific Web site. You should use these very useful tools regularly.

USING WEB GUIDES

Just finding lists of sites may not always be particularly useful. If your keyword produces many matches, you might have to spend a lot of time analyzing which Web sites will provide the most useful information for you. To save time, more and more Web users are turning to **Web guides** as a means for selecting the highest quality sites. Web guides perform a very useful service by evaluating a Web site or by providing lists of particularly good Web sites based on both content and design. Through Web guides such as CNET, Microsoft's Best of the Web, WWWomen, and others, you can get information on high-quality Web sites and you can find these sites by category.

ACTIVITY

1. From *Learning Online* select the Web Search Tools link.
2. Select Web Guides.
3. Select Start Exploring: Microsoft's Best of the Web.
   Notice the categories and search tools available within this Web site (Image 3-10).

Image 3-10

4. Select Computers & Internet (Image 3-11).

Image 3-11

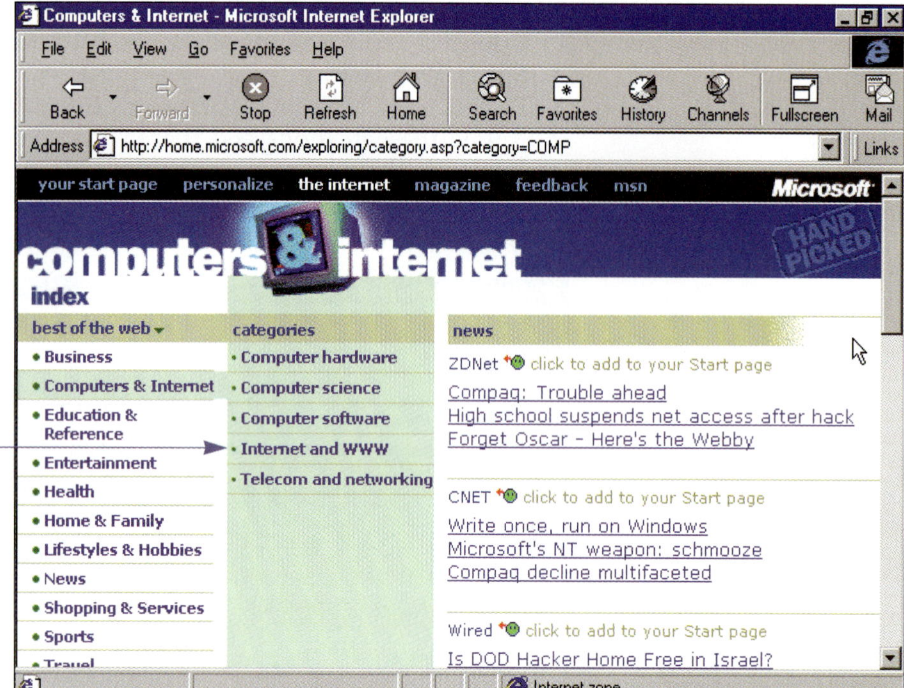

Try Internet and WWW; it contains links to some valuable learning resources.

5. Take a few minutes to browse through the recommended sites by Microsoft.

EXERCISE 3-3

The best of the best is certainly a subjective opinion. Your task is to make your own list of 10 best of the best sites. On a sheet of paper, write down 10 sites identifying your personal best of the best list. Be prepared to share these with the rest of the class.

SEARCHING WITH THE WWW VIRTUAL LIBRARY

Searching for Web sites is easily accomplished by using any of the search tools, meta directories, or search engines described previously. However, what if you are looking for specific information that is organized by subject or category? You may want to consider using a controlled-vocabulary search resource such as the WWW Virtual Library.

The **WWW Virtual Library** is a collection of information resources by specific subjects. There is no single WWW Virtual Library. Instead, it is a collection of information resources by subject or discipline maintained by various institutions or individuals. For example, if you are interested in anthropology, locate the anthropology virtual library. The anthropology virtual library contains some of the most valuable information resources on anthropology on the Internet.

One of the most valuable features of the WWW Virtual Library is that the links and information resources are maintained by an individual or organization. Maintenance of the links and information resources usually means that the information you find is reliable to the subject you are searching. In other words, when you get to a WWW Virtual Library, you can generally be assured of finding high-quality information about the subject.

There are a number of ways to locate a WWW Virtual Library for a specific topic. One of the easiest methods is to use the WWW Virtual Library guide available through Stanford University. You can find the link to this site at *Learning Online.*

ACTIVITY

1. From *Learning Online* select the Web Search Tools link.
2. Select Web Guides.
3. Select WWW Virtual Library.
   Notice the directory of available WWW Virtual Libraries within this Web site (Image 3-12).

Image 3-12

The WWW Virtual Library is organized by category.

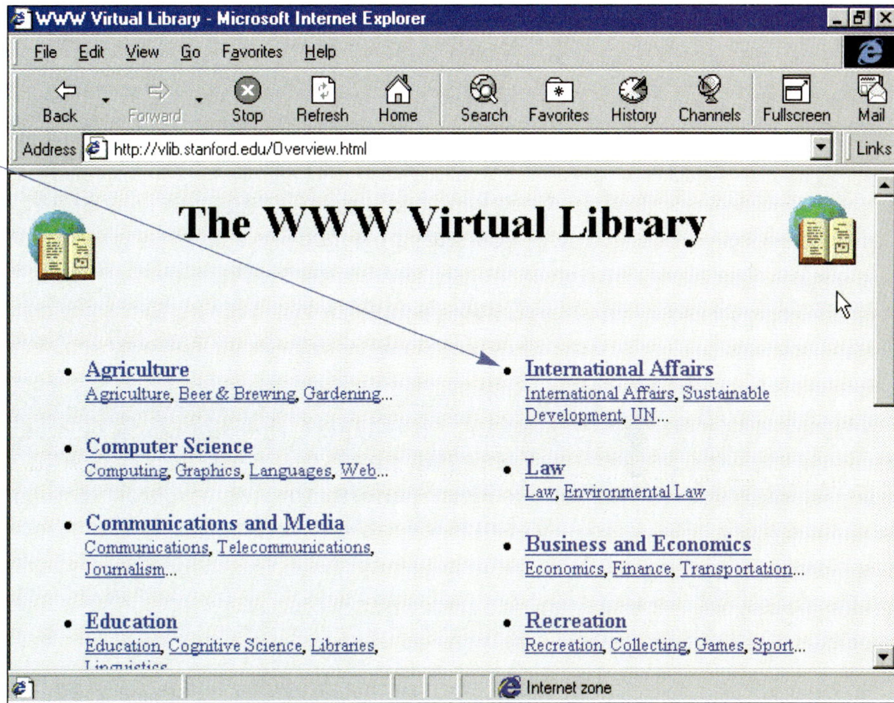

4. Select Science and then select Physics.
   Notice that a new URL appears for the WWW Virtual Library on this topic (Image 3-13).

Image 3-13

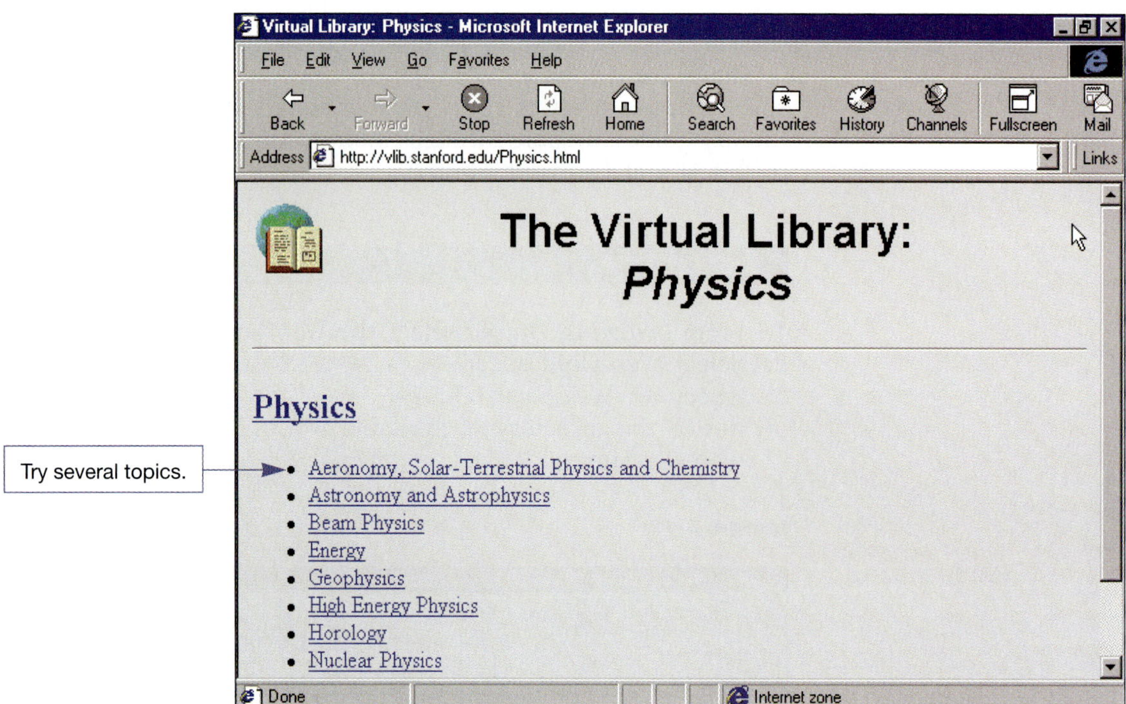

5. Select any link of interest to you and then browse through the various sites provided by this or any other WWW Virtual Library.

EXERCISE 3-4

As with other search processes, using the WWW Virtual Library requires practice. To compare the difference between WWW Virtual Library and other search processes, perform a search in YAHOO! or any other search tool. Then perform the same search through the WWW Virtual Library. Are there any differences in the type and quality of information located?

USING TRADEWAVE GALAXY

Galaxy is another subject controlled–vocabulary search resource. **Galaxy** uses search procedures similar to the WWW Virtual Library. Because subject controlled–vocabulary resources are maintained by individuals and organizations, it is not a very good idea to rely on only one.

You use Galaxy by navigating through the lists of subjects provided. You can also use the search engine provided with Galaxy.

ACTIVITY

1. From *Learning Online,* select the Web Search Tools link.
2. Select TradeWave Galaxy.
   Notice the structure of this search site (Image 3-14).

Image 3-14

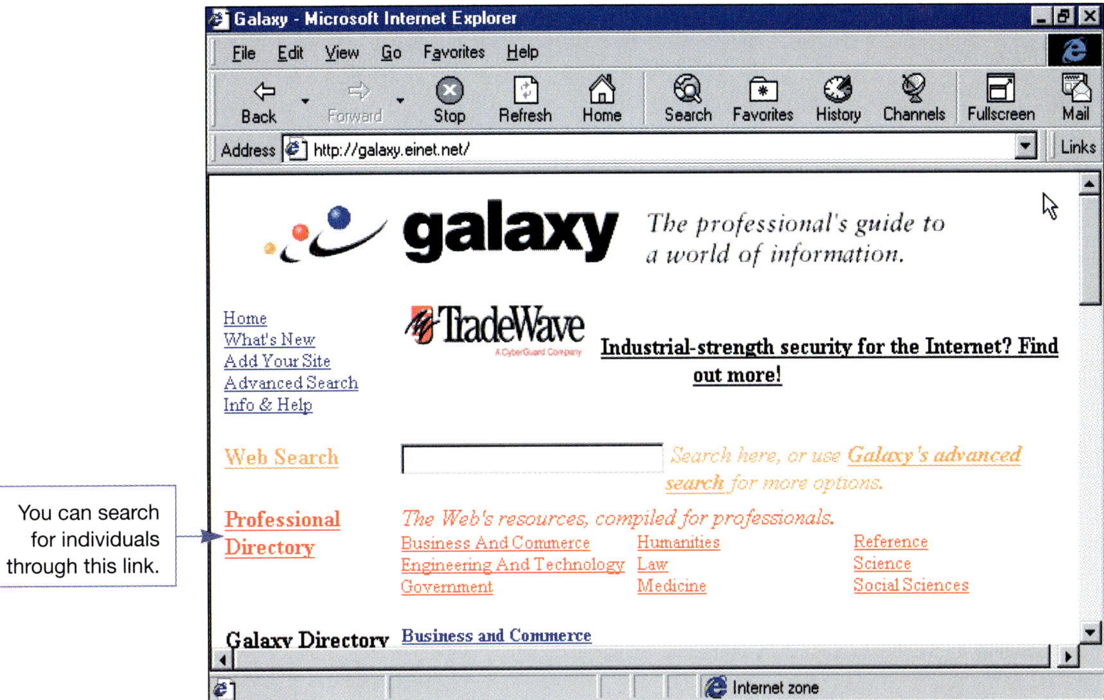

3. Select Government and then select Government Agencies. Notice that the list reflects your selection (Image 3-15).

Image 3-15

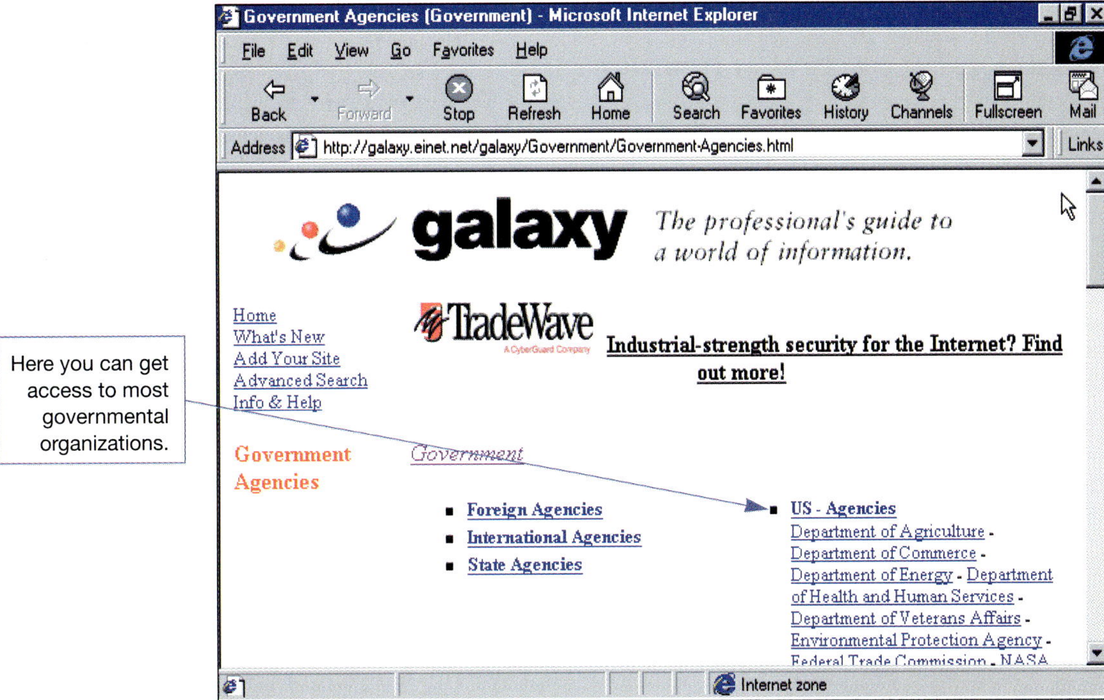

4. Select any link of interest to you and then browse through the various sites.

ADVANCED SEARCH TECHNIQUES

All the sites described in this lesson allow you to perform keyword searches. In most cases these search tools allow you to enter one or more keywords and locate all matches. The downside of this procedure is that in many cases you get far more *hits,* or returns of listed links, than are useful. Even worse, you may get a large number of hits that are not specific to your search. For example, if you do a keyword search for Jerry Lewis you are going to get back all sites with Jerry and all sites with Lewis. The listing would include sites for Jerry Seinfeld and Lewis and Clark. Not very useful. The solution is to learn to use the advanced search features common to most search engines.

One of the most important advanced search features is called **Boolean logic.** Boolean logic enables you to include the terms AND, OR, and NOT as part of your search. The operator **AND** allows you to combine two words. For example, Jerry AND Lewis requires that the match have both the terms Jerry and Lewis. In this case it would eliminate Lewis and Clark. In general, AND narrows the search. By default, many search engines use AND.

In contrast, the **OR** operator broadens a search. For example, Jerry OR Lewis would return all sites with the term Jerry and all sites with the term Lewis. The OR operator returns Jerry Seinfeld and Lewis and Clark. In other words, if your search for Jerry Lewis returns Jerry Seinfeld and Lewis and Clark, what you are really entering is Jerry OR Lewis.

The **NOT** operator can be very useful for eliminating certain hits. For example Jerry AND Lewis NOT Telethons would eliminate all sites as hits that contained the word Telethons. This technique might be useful if you were searching only for comedy sites about Jerry Lewis.

Another important search issue is searching based on **proximity.** To search based on proximity, enclose the keywords in quotation marks. For example, Jerry OR Lewis along with Jerry AND Lewis will also return Jerry Lee Lewis the singer. If you want Jerry Lewis, you may opt to enclose Jerry Lewis in quotes, that is, "Jerry Lewis". The quotes tell the search to locate Jerry Lewis as one word. In other words, only the entire name would find a match rather than just the first or last. The downside to this approach happens when a middle name is used in a site. For example, "Jerry Lewis" would not return Jerry John Lewis, Jerry J. Lewis, G. Jerry Lewis, or any other variation. Some sites use the **NEAR** proximity operator as an alternative to quoted search strings.

Tips, Tricks, and Ideas 3-5

+, -, and Other Tips

Different search engines provide enhanced keyword searching options. With Excite and others, you can use the + sign to indicate that the search results must have that keyword. For example, +baseball+rules means that all returned sites will have both baseball and rules as identifier words. For each search tool that you use, you may want to examine the advanced search options available and find one that fits your needs the best.

ACTIVITY

1. From *Learning Online* select the Web Search Tools link.
2. Select Excite.
3. Enter Jerry OR Lewis in the search box (Image 3-16).

Image 3-16

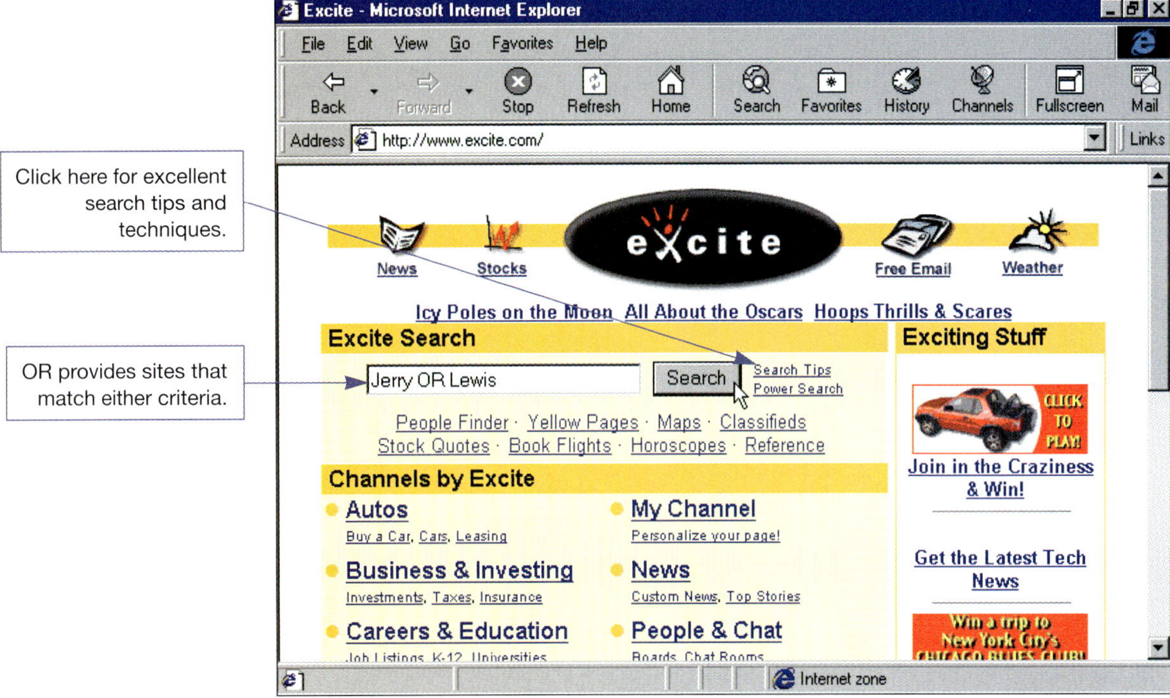

4. Click on Search.
   Notice that the hits include Jerry Lewis and Jerry Lee Lewis (Image 3-17).

Image 3-17

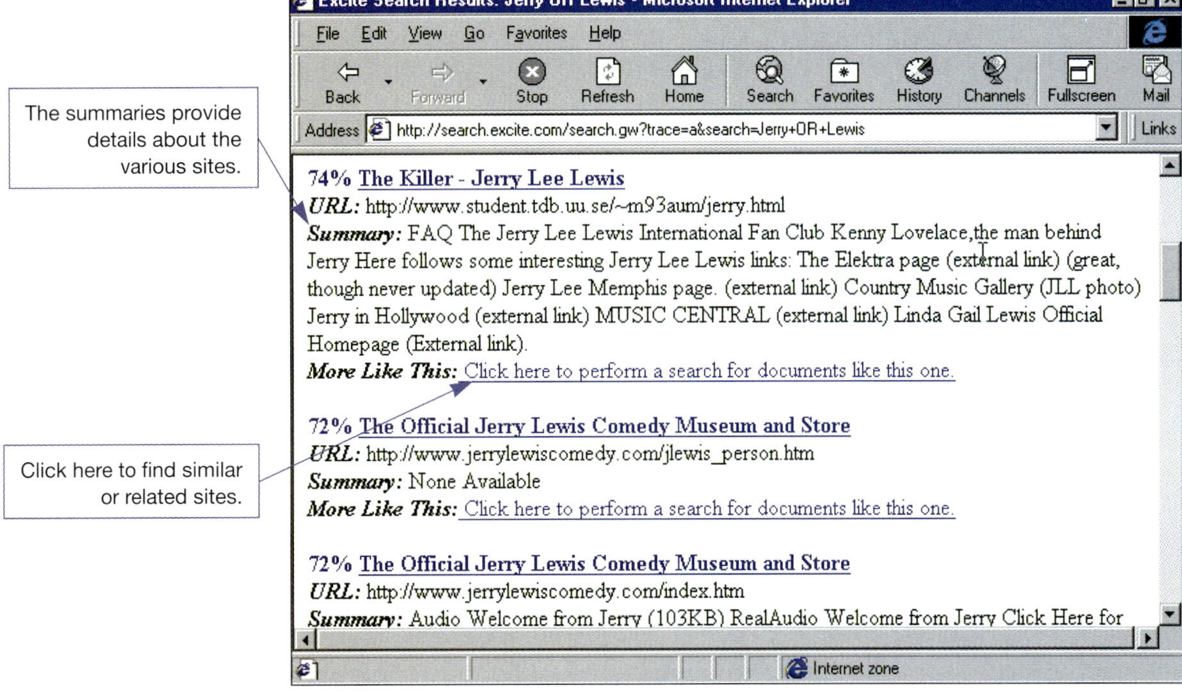

5. Click on the Back button.

6. Enter Jerry AND Lewis
   Notice that the results differ from the OR results.
7. Click on the Back button
8. Enter Jerry AND Lewis NOT Lee
   Notice that this search produces another set of hits.
9. Click on Back to return to Excite's home page.
10. Click on Search Tips.
    Notice the list of tips that are available for this search tool (Image 3-18).

Image 3-18

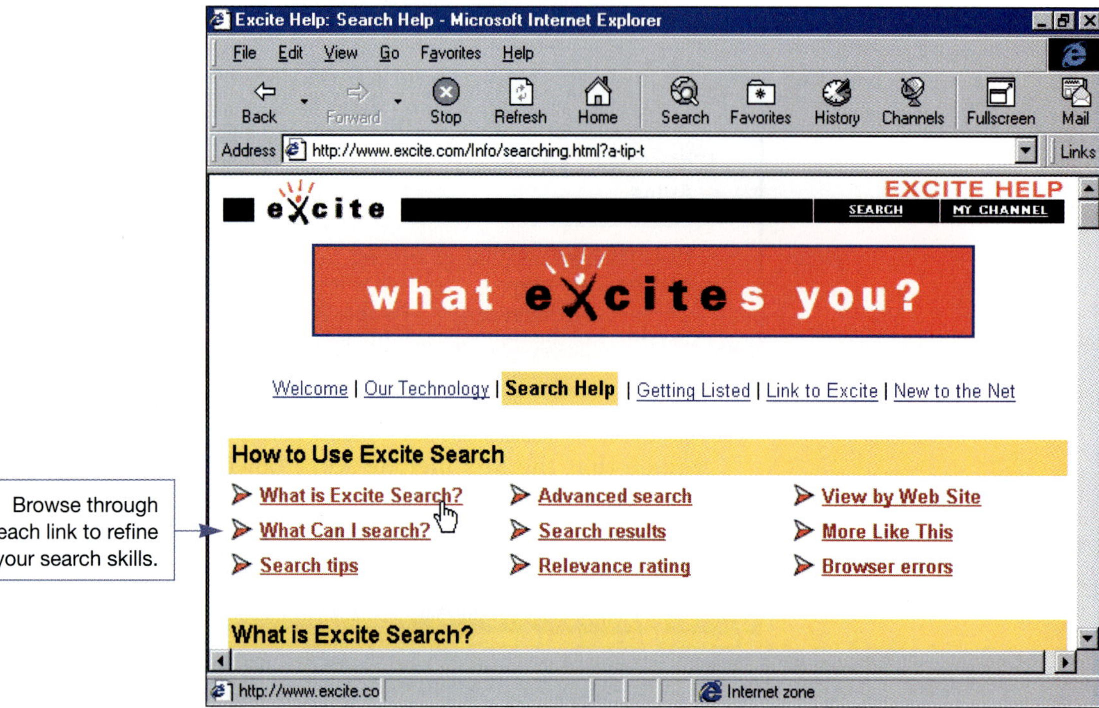

Tips, Tricks, and Ideas 3-6

Costs

UnCover and Dialog, as well as other services, do charge. You may want to consider visiting your college or university library, where these services or an equivalent service may be available at no charge to students. However, even if you do have to pay, the time you save may be well worth the cost.

ADDITIONAL SEARCH CAPABILITIES

Locating Web sites may not be enough. For example, if you are searching for articles on various subjects, journals, or any other information that is commonly found in university libraries, you may want to consider using some of the many document resource search processes that are available. Two popular information resources are UnCover and Dialog.

Netiquette 3-3

Check First

Some information on the Web is free. But some is not. Be sure you check before copying information.

Both **UnCover** and **Dialog** maintain searchable databases that enable you to seek out articles on various subjects. They are very similar to what you would find at a college or university library. Dialog provides access to more than 450 online databases and more than 45 CD-ROM titles. UnCover provides access to nearly 17,000 English-language periodicals and these databases continually expand.

One nice feature about these sites is you are able to access information from almost anywhere. You don't have to be at your college library. The downside is that you must pay. In many cases you must pay for an actual document to be produced and distributed to you. Although these services can be somewhat costly, many users opt to use UnCover and Dialog because they are very fast and efficient.

ACTIVITY

1. From *Learning Online* select the Web Search Tools link.
2. Select UnCover.
3. Click on Search UnCover database (Image 3-19).

Image 3-19

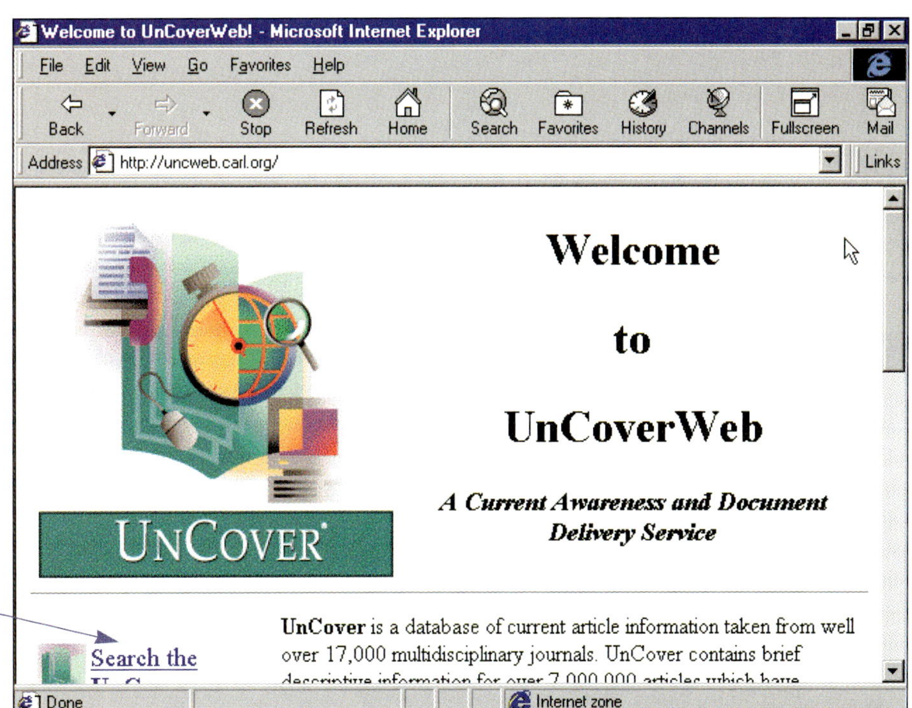

If you have access to UnCover, you can search thousands of journals and millions of articles.

4. Take a few minutes to explore UnCover. Be sure to locate the pricing information for this service.

USING FAVORITES

Among the most powerful search tools are lists of sites that you create for your own use. If you keep your own list of URLs for important information, this information will be very valuable when you return to the Web. Of course, there are millions of Web pages, and each day thousands of Web pages are added. Keeping track of which ones are most useful to you can be a bit daunting. There are, however, a number of solutions to help you remember.

> **Tips, Tricks, and Ideas 3-7**
>
> *Using Favorites*
>
> It is worth a little bit of time to keep your favorite bookmarks organized and updated. After you add a bookmark, use Organize Favorites from the Favorites menu to keep your bookmarks organized.

With Internet Explorer, one of the most popular methods for remembering Web locations is to use the **Favorites** feature. The Favorites feature is simply a list of **bookmarks** that provide a way to store URLs for quick and easy access. Selecting the Favorites button produces the listing of all of the bookmarks you have stored. Selecting the Favorites menu also displays the listing of favorite sites and includes additional commands.

The **Add to Favorites** command from the Favorites menu produces the Add Favorites dialog box. This dialog box has several options, including the option of subscribing to a page. If you select No, just add the page to my favorites, then a bookmark of the current URL is added to your list of favorites. For example, if the Address is http://www.mhhe.com/cit/net/learning and you activate the Add to Favorites command, *Learning Online* will be added to your list of favorites and will appear when you click on the Favorites button. Once a bookmark is added, you can go immediately to the URL by selecting that bookmark from your list of favorites.

The other options in the Add to Favorites dialog box are for subscribing to newsgroups. They are discussed later in the book.

The **Organize Favorites** command from the Favorites menu allows you to modify the organization of your bookmarks. Select this command to open the Organize Favorites window. The options here include the ability to move, rename, and delete an existing bookmark.

One of the most critical organization tools for favorite bookmarks is folders. **Folders** are for storing related bookmarks. This feature is especially important because the number of bookmarks you see in any one screen of the Favorites menu is limited. If you have more bookmarks than can be shown in the Favorites menu, you can put bookmarks in folders that will be displayed in the Favorites menu.

To add a folder, click on the Create New Folder button. You can change the name from New Folder to something more meaningful. After you create a folder, you can click and drag bookmarks into that folder. Folders should always contain related bookmarks. For example, you can create a folder called Games to contain all your bookmarks for games on the Web.

You can also use the Favorites menu to set the order of your bookmarks by clicking and dragging the bookmark to a new location. This technique allows you to place your most important or frequently visited bookmarks high on the favorites list.

If you right-click on a bookmark in the Favorites list, a menu will appear. If you select the **Properties** command, you can modify bookmark titles, URLs, and the description of a selected bookmark item. Most of these features are very easy to use, and with a little experimentation you can create a set of bookmarks to meet your individual needs.

If you are working in a computer laboratory, you may not be able to create or modify favorites because you may have to work on various computers. Therefore, using a single favorites file stored on one computer may not be very practical. There are, however, other options for keeping track of URLs.

Keeping your own Internet notebook can be a valuable technique for keeping track of URLs. When you come across a URL for a Web page that you would like to access again, write the URL in your notebook. It only takes a few seconds to write it down and can save you considerable amounts of time if you want to locate a URL again.

Another technique is to create your own Web page. This process is discussed later in this book. Creating Web pages with HTML is not all that difficult. With a few basic skills, you can generate a Web page that contains all your links to other pages. Having a personal Web page is becoming very popular. To create one you need to have access to storage on a computer connected to the Internet. Many college and university computers provide students with computer space for storing Web pages. Most Internet providers also provide places for personal Web pages. You should check with your instructor or computer center for details.

ACTIVITY

1. Make sure you are connected and Internet Explorer is up and running.
2. Go to the *Learning Online* Web site.
3. Click on the Favorites menu.
   Notice the Add to Favorites and Organize Favorites commands (Image 3-20). Your favorites are likely to be different, since each computer user generates individual Internet Explorer bookmarks.

Image 3-20

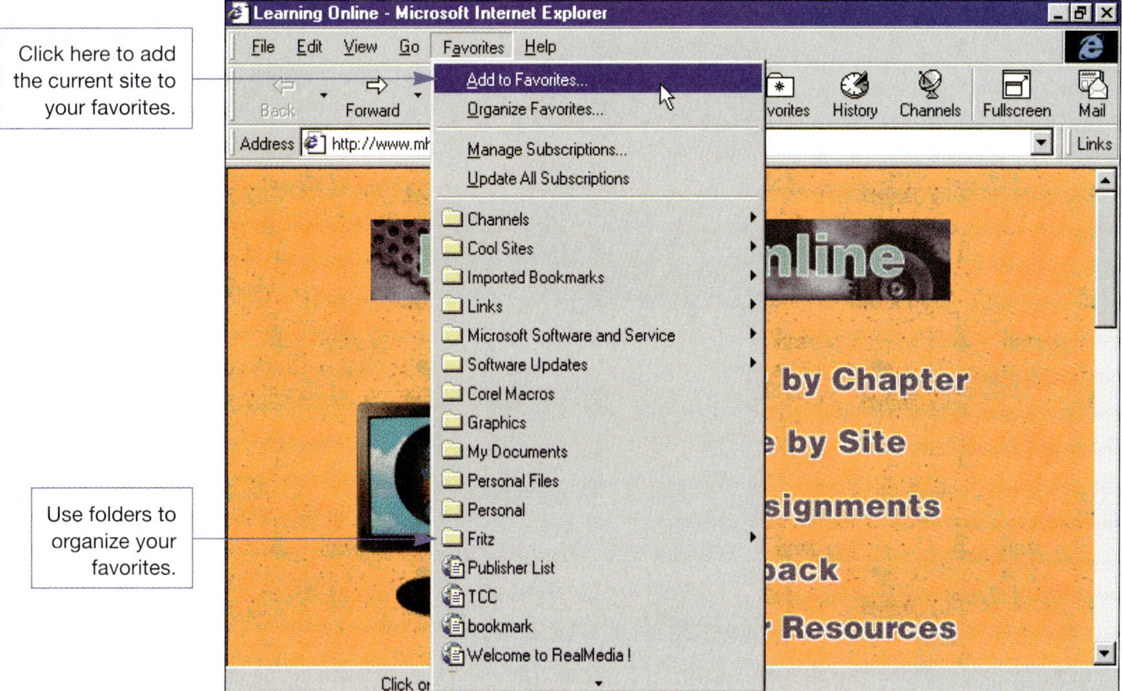

4. Click on the Add to Favorites command.
   Notice the Add Favorite dialog box (Image 3-21).
5. Select No, just add the page to my favorites (Image 3-21).

Image 3-21

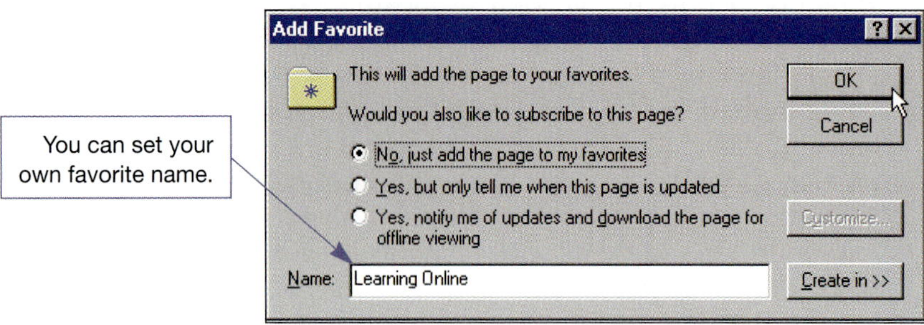

6. Click on OK.
7. Click on the Favorites button.
   Notice that the Learning Online bookmark has been added to the list (Image 3-22).

Image 3-22

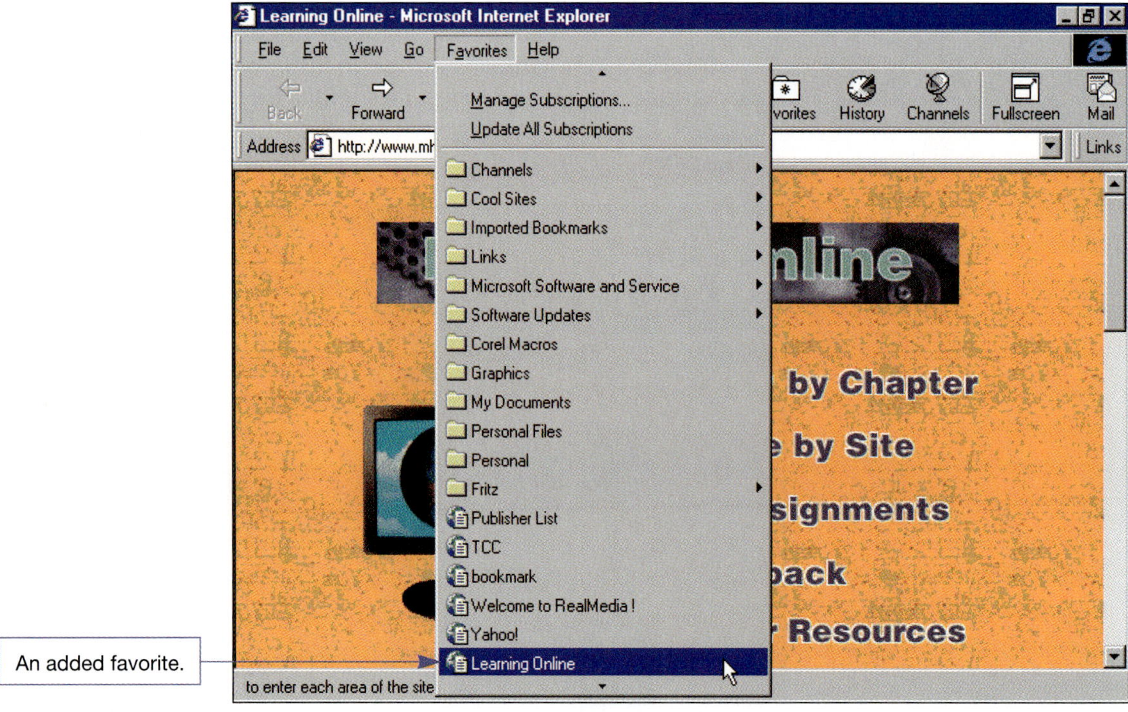

8. Select the Organize Favorites command from the Favorites menu.
   Notice the Organize Favorites window (Image 3-23).
9. Click on the Create New Folder button.
   Notice that a new folder appears.
10. Change the Name to Learning Online Folder (Image 3-23).

Image 3-23

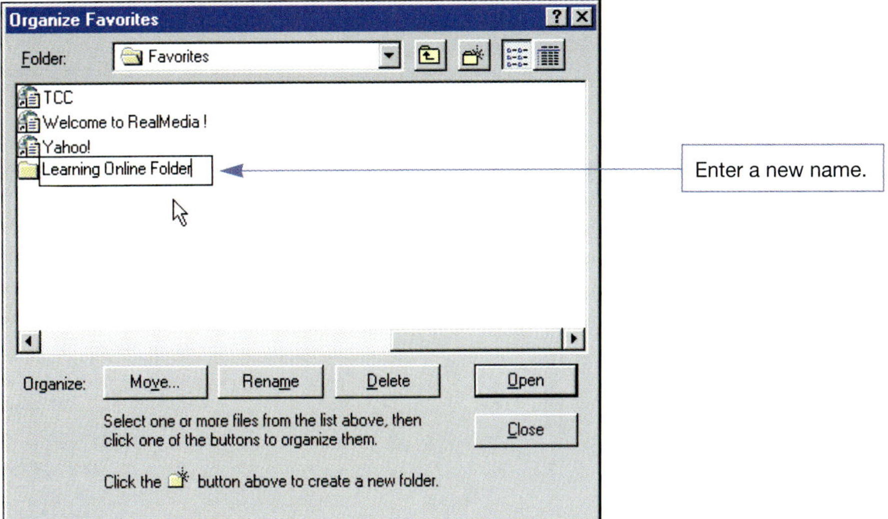

11. Drag the Leaning Online bookmark into the Learning Online Folder.
12. Close the Organize Favorites dialog box.
13. Activate the Learning Online Folder bookmark.
    Notice that *Learning Online* appears (Image 3-24).

Image 3-24

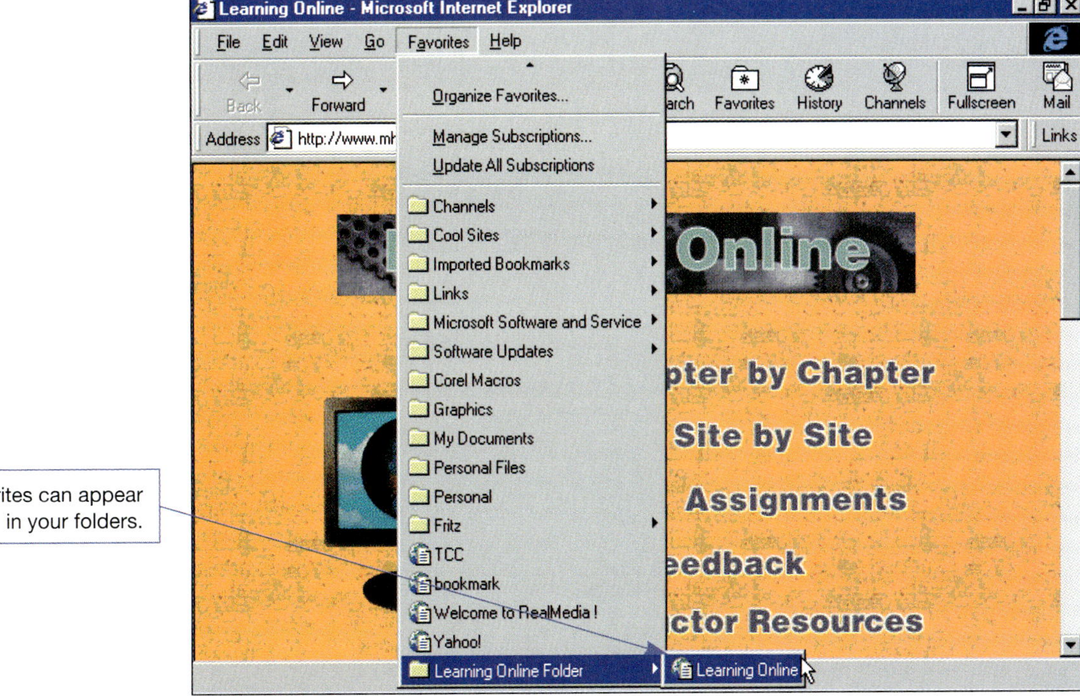

14. Again, select the Organize Favorites command from the Favorites menu and select the Learning Online Folder.

15. Right-click on the Learning Online bookmark (Image 3-25).

Image 3-25

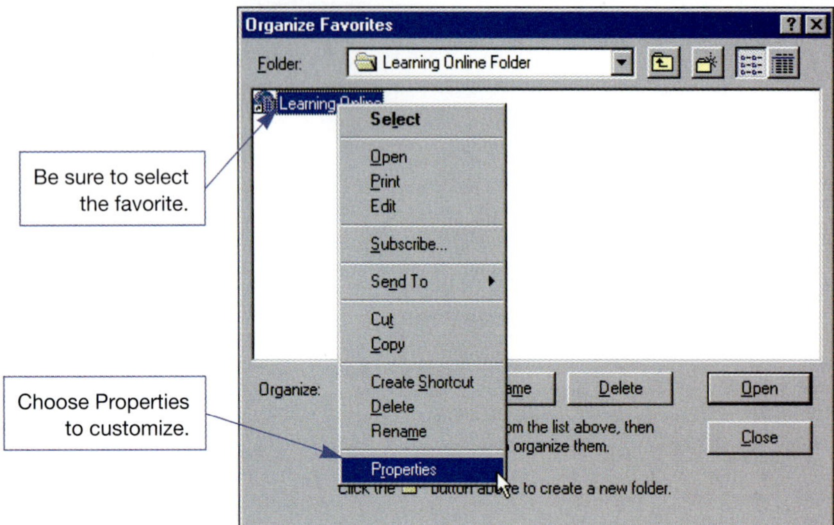

16. Select Properties.
    Notice the Properties dialog box (Image 3-26).
17. Select the Internet Shortcut tab.
    Notice the URL for the bookmark (Image 3-26).

Image 3-26

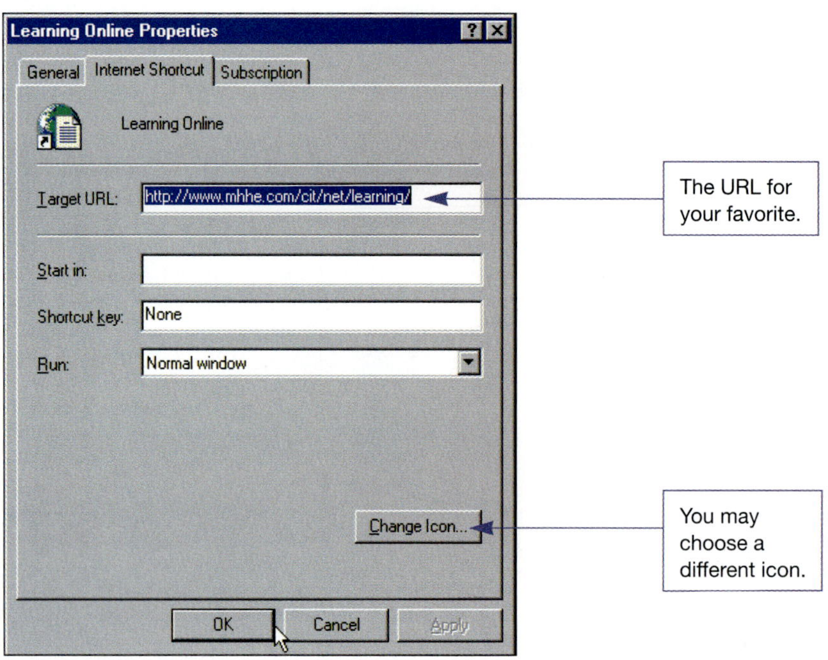

18. Click on OK.
19. Click on the Favorites button on the toolbar.
    Notice that a split window appears with a list of Favorites (Image 3-27).

20. Click on the Learning Online Folder.
    Notice that the Learning Online bookmark appears (Image 3-27).

Image 3-27

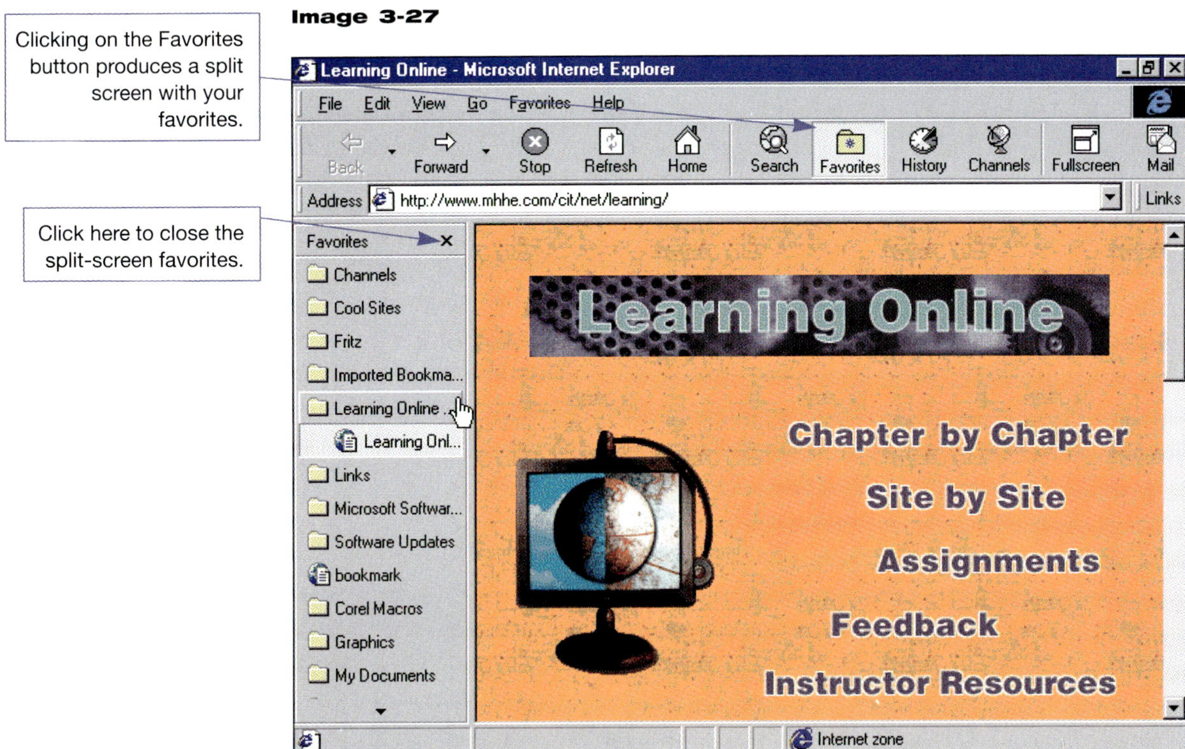

21. Click on the Close button on the Favorites window.

EXERCISE 3-5

If you have access to favorites in Internet Explorer, add five new related bookmarks. Then use the Favorites menu command and customize and reorder the bookmarks. Place your new bookmarks in a single folder.

KEY POINTS

- Search tools provide matches based on keywords.
- YAHOO!, WebCrawler, Excite, and others search Web sites that they have listed in their databases.
- Meta directory is a directory of directories.
- One of the major advantages with using a meta directory is that the Web sites listed often contain very useful descriptions of Web sites.
- Web guides provide a very useful service by providing an evaluation of a Web site or lists of particularly good Web sites based on both content and design.
- The WWW Virtual Library is a collection of information resources by specific subjects. There is no single WWW Virtual Library.
- One of the most valuable features of the WWW Virtual Library is that the links and information resources are maintained by an individual or organization.
- One of the easiest ways to locate a WWW Virtual Library for a specific topic is to use the WWW Virtual Library guide available through Stanford University.
- Galaxy is another subject controlled–vocabulary search resource. Galaxy uses search procedures similar to the WWW Virtual Library.
- You use Galaxy by navigating through the lists of subjects.
- One of the most important advanced search features is called Boolean logic. Boolean logic

allows you to include the terms AND, OR, and NOT as part of your search.

- In general, AND narrows the search.
- The OR operator broadens a search.
- The NOT operator can be very useful for eliminating certain hits.
- Another important search issue is searching based on proximity. To search based on proximity, enclose the keywords in quotation marks or use the NEAR command.
- If you are searching for articles on various subjects, journals, or any other information that is commonly found in university libraries, you may want to use a document resource search. Two popular information resources are UnCover and Dialog.
- Both UnCover and Dialog maintain searchable databases that enable you to seek out articles on various subjects. The databases are very similar to what you would find at a college or university library.
- A powerful search tool is a list of sites that you create for your own use.
- With Internet Explorer, one of the most popular methods for remembering Web locations is to use the Favorites feature.
- Selecting the Add to Favorites command from the Favorites menu creates a bookmark for the current URL.
- The Organize Favorites command allows you to modify the organization of bookmarks.
- In addition to changing the order of favorites, you can also create folders for storing related bookmarks.
- Keeping your own Internet notebook can be a valuable technique for keeping track of URLs.

KEY TERMS AND COMMANDS

Add to Favorites	**Galaxy**	**Organize Favorites**
AND	**keywords**	**Properties**
bookmark	**linking**	**proximity**
Boolean logic	**meta directories**	**search tools**
Dialog	**NEAR**	**UnCover**
Favorites	**NOT**	**Web guides**
folders	**OR**	**WWW Virtual Library**

STUDY QUESTIONS

1. Identify four of the most popular search tools.
2. Explain the difference between a search engine such as YAHOO! and a meta directory.
3. Why is it so important to learn how to use Web search techniques?
4. Why are keywords both a strength and a weakness of search engines?
5. Describe the process of linking.
6. Describe a virtual library.
7. How would you use Boolean logic to make a search more precise?
8. Which searchable databases are very similar to what you would find at a college or university library?
9. Describe the options Internet Explorer provides for organizing a large set of favorite bookmarks.
10. Explain the process for creating folders as a way of organizing bookmarks.

PRACTICE TEST

1. You can use any of the search tools because they all work the same way and will return the same results.
   a. True
   b. False
2. Which search tools often provide very useful descriptions of Web sites?
   a. Links
   b. Meta directories
   c. Beta directories
   d. Web guides
3. In general, which Boolean command is used to expand a search?
   a. AND
   b. NOT
   c. OR
   d. PROXIMITY
4. The Favorites menu in Internet Explorer displays a list of all current bookmarks along with two commands. These commands are
   a. Add to Favorites and Edit Bookmarks.
   b. Add to Favorites and Create Folder.
   c. Edit Bookmarks and Create Folder.
   d. Add to Favorites and Organize Favorites.
5. Which service are users turning to as a means for selecting sites that are of the highest quality?
   a. Web guides
   b. Proximity searches
   c. Meta directories
   d. Keyword searches
6. Which of the following search resources uses search procedures similar to the WWW Virtual Library?
   a. YAHOO!
   b. Galaxy
   c. Infoseek
   d. InfoNet
7. Which of the following commands is similar to the AND command in Boolean logic?
   a. &
   b. OR
   c. +
   d. NOT
8. Which of the following operators is used as an alternative to quoted search strings?
   a. PROXIMITY
   b. NEAR
   c. LIKE
   d. NOT
9. The NOT operator can be very useful for eliminating certain hits.
   a. True
   b. False
10. Two of the most popular meta directories are
    a. TradeWave and Galaxy
    b. InterNIC and MetaCrawler
    c. UnCover and Dialog
    d. UnCover and Galaxy

FILL-INS

1. Two of the most popular meta directories are InterNIC and ______________.
2. ______________ provide an evaluation of a Web site or provide lists of particularly good Web sites based on both content and design.
3. ______________ uses search procedures similar to the WWW Virtual Library.
4. With Internet Explorer one of the most popular methods for remembering Web locations is to use the ______________ feature.
5. A ______________ is a way to store URLs for quick and easy access.
6. ______________ gather information on other Web sites, organize and categorize this information, and then provide a tool for users to locate the sites that contain specific information.
7. ______________ means that you click on a desired site listing and you go directly to that Web site.
8. To search based on ______________, enclose the keywords in quotation marks.
9. Internet Explorer allows you to create ______________ as a means for storing related bookmarks.
10. The ______________ operator can be very useful for eliminating certain hits.

PROJECTS

1. From *Learning Online,* scroll down and select Web Search Tools. When you get to the search tools site, select YAHOO!. YAHOO! provides a list of categories that you can search for information on many different topics. Examine the list of categories available in YAHOO!. Select any category that interests you and look for specific information on that topic. Write down the URLs for 10 sites that you find on the category you selected.
2. Performing searches is an important part of using the Web. Return to the *Learning Online* Web Search Tools site and use any other search engine. Search for the same topic you did in project 1. Write down the URLs for 10 sites. Are any of these the same as you found in project 1? What are the differences?
3. Perform a meta directory search on the same topic you selected for projects 1 and 2. Again, are there similarities and differences between the searches? Of the three processes, which yielded the best search results?
4. Use the Favorites feature of Internet Explorer to create a new folder for the topic you identified in the preceding projects. Add at least 10 bookmarks to this folder. Be sure to select URLs that are particularly valuable and that you want to be able to re-

INTERNET AT WORK

Edith wants you to demonstrate that you know your way around the Web. She wants you to get her some information on candy, especially chocolate candy. Unfortunately, she didn't tell you what kind of information she wanted. Because she will be out of town for the next week, you have time to surf the Net for all types of information. Begin by using the Web Search Tools provided on *Learning Online.* Keep a log of the keywords you use in your search. Try different search tools. Keep a list of addresses of the best information you can get for Edith. Take this opportunity to make a good impression on the boss. If you are not successful, you will have to explain your failure to Edith when she returns to work, so get busy.

4 Upload/Download

OUTCOMES

When you complete this chapter you will be able to . . .

- Download files from various sources on the Internet.
- Describe the function of FTP.
- Identify various types of FTP software.
- Use FTP software.
- Download files directly from Web links.
- Download graphics files using the right mouse button.
- Activate FTP sites from within Internet Explorer.

WHAT ARE UPLOADING AND DOWNLOADING?

Would you like to have a new computer game, have access to updated software, obtain research articles in the form of text files, or acquire graphics files? Would you like to send your resume to a prospective employer, send a word processing document to a colleague who is working several hundred miles away, or send a graphics file that you have created to other computer users? You can do all of these things, and more, by **uploading** (sending) and **downloading** (receiving) these files on the World Wide Web.

Uploading and downloading are a multidimensional process and, as with many procedures on the Internet, there are multiple ways you can upload and download. In some cases, when you want to download a particular file, all that is required of you is to click on a download link. In other cases you need to access specific directories and follow a detailed set of instructions to successfully download a file. In many cases you can download graphics by pointing and clicking with the right mouse button.

What you do with a file that you have downloaded is another important issue. Some files that you download may be directly usable. Many others, particularly programs, must be installed on your computer. Other files, particularly those that are very large files, are downloaded in a compressed format. These must be uncompressed before you can use them.

Uploading is just as important as downloading because it provides a tool to share files with others. If you create a Web site, have a need to send a word processing document to a colleague, or want to make files publicly available for others, you need to know how to upload.

WHAT IS FTP?

On the World Wide Web you upload or download files through a procedure called **FTP** (file transfer protocol). As its name implies, FTP is a protocol or an agreed-upon standard by which information is transferred over the Web. **File transfer protocol** allows you to examine, send, and receive files to and from computers over the Web. It is an Internet resource that you can use in much the same way you use the Web, e-mail, Usenet, and other resources. It requires supporting software.

FTP is used in a variety of situations although it is not always obvious. For example, some downloading is accomplished by simply clicking on an FTP link. This evokes the protocol and the downloading process begins. At other times you need to access an FTP site as indicated by a URL that begins with **ftp://.**

DIRECT DOWNLOAD LINKS

For many people the major issue when using FTP is to locate the FTP links in a Web site. After locating a link, you may be able to click on the link to download the associated file. This relatively simple procedure enables anyone to have access to tens of thousands of data files, graphics images, and computer programs. In fact, many people who use the Internet obtain the software necessary to use the Internet directly from the Internet.

You can use a variety of techniques to download files using FTP on the World Wide Web. One of the easiest methods is through direct FTP links. An FTP link is identified by a URL that begins with ftp://. If you point at a link and the status bar indicates a URL beginning with ftp://, that link is an FTP link. To download the file from an FTP link, click the mouse button. When Internet Explorer asks where you want to save the file, you must specify a location. Then click on the Save button, and Internet Explorer will begin to download the file. Depending on the speed of

Tips, Tricks, and Ideas 4-1

Name and Location

Whenever you download a file, the Save As dialog box appears. In the Save As dialog box, there are two critical considerations—the name of the file you are going to download and the location on your disk where the file will reside. Make sure you select an appropriate disk drive and folder for saving the file before clicking on the Save button. You may use the Create New Folder button to create a new folder before downloading. This way you will know where the file resides after the downloading is complete.

Netiquette 4-1

Use a Server That Is Close

Sometimes popular files are available from a number of servers. If a list is provided, select a server that is geographically close to you. "Mirror" sites are identical to other sites, provide the same files as other sites, and help to reduce demand on the system at popular sites.

Tips, Tricks, and Ideas 4-2

Be Patient

Downloading files through FTP can take a long time, depending on several factors. One of the most critical factors is the time of day. During heavy Internet use times, downloading can take an excessive amount of time. You may want to consider downloading from FTP sites late at night or early in the morning to help speed up this process.

Tips, Tricks, and Ideas 4-3

Pay

Shareware is a great way to try out software before you commit to using the software. However, shareware is not free. Once you decide you want to keep and use a shareware program, it is important to register and pay the normally small fee for the software. This payment helps the software developers continue to improve software and provides them with the resources to continue to develop new software.

Tips, Tricks, and Ideas 4-4

Learning Online *Software Links*

Learning Online provides a large number of links you may use to access and download software. As you become familiar with the process of downloading software, you may want to explore the *Learning Online* links to find software that is useful to you.

your connection to the Internet and the size of the file, downloading a file may take a few seconds or it may take several hours.

Some software sites allow you to download files even if Internet Explorer does not directly support a particular type of file. For example, Internet Explorer does not directly support files that end with the .exe extension. When you click on a link that refers to a file that is not supported by Internet Explorer, you have the option of saving the file. The Save As dialog box is where you can specify the file name and, more important, the location where you will save the file on your disk drive. Again, after you determine where to save the file, the downloading process begins. The amount of time required to download the file depends on the size of the file and the speed of your connection to the Internet.

Learning Online provides several links to data files and software that you can download and use. Two of the most popular sites for downloading Internet software are The Ultimate Collection Of Winsock Software and The Consummate Winsock Apps List. You can access either of these popular sites through the Internet Software link on the *Learning Online* Web site. Selecting either of these sites takes you to pages describing software that is available for your use. These two sites also provide their own software ratings for specific Internet software.

Software available for downloading on the Web often falls into one of three categories—shareware, freeware, and commercial software. **Shareware** is software that is provided in either a full version or in a limited version for you to "try before you buy." In many cases the software developers ask you to send a relatively small amount of money if you want to continue to use the software. **Freeware**, as its name implies, means you can use it for free. **Commercial software** is software that generally requires an outright purchase. However, many commercial software companies offer limited demonstration versions over the Web, but you need to buy the full retail package to use all the features.

ACTIVITY

1. Launch Internet Explorer and activate the *Learning Online* Web site; then select Site by Site or Chapter by Chapter.
2. Select the Internet Software link.
   Notice that there are several sites for locating and accessing Internet software (Image 4-1).

Image 4-1

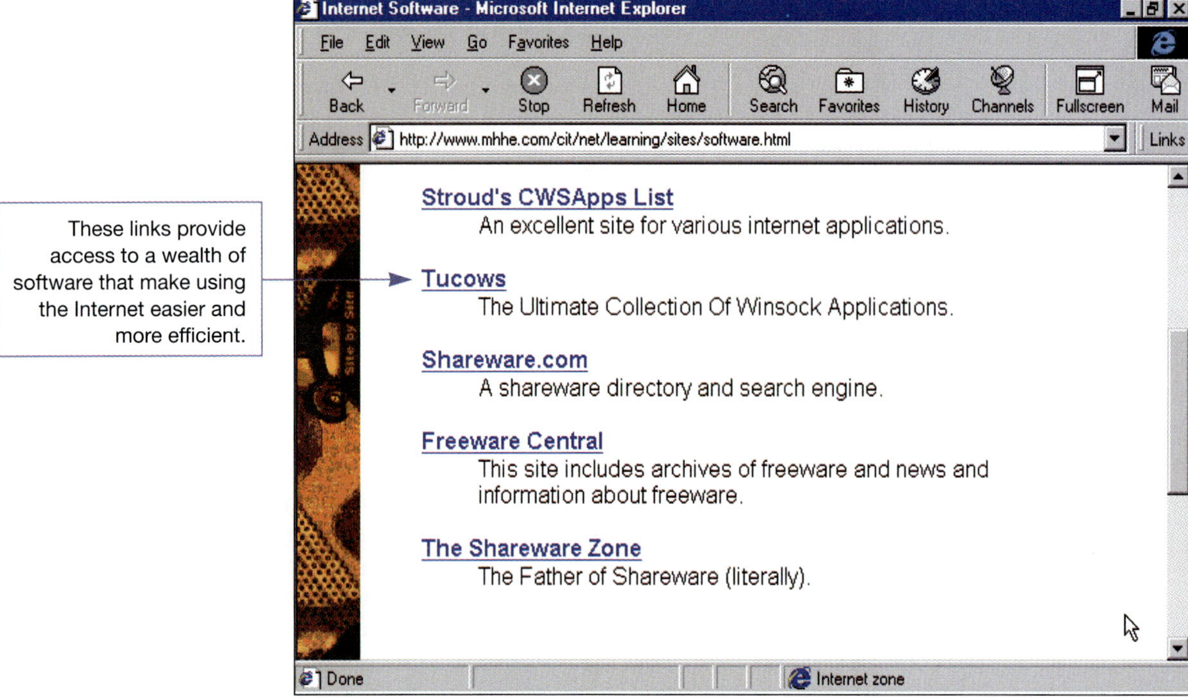

3. Take a few moments to browse through the various software categories in each of these sites.
4. Select Stroud's CWSApps List; then select the 32-bit Apps button. Scroll down and notice that the Menu of Apps is filled with download links for various categories of software (Image 4-2).

Image 4-2

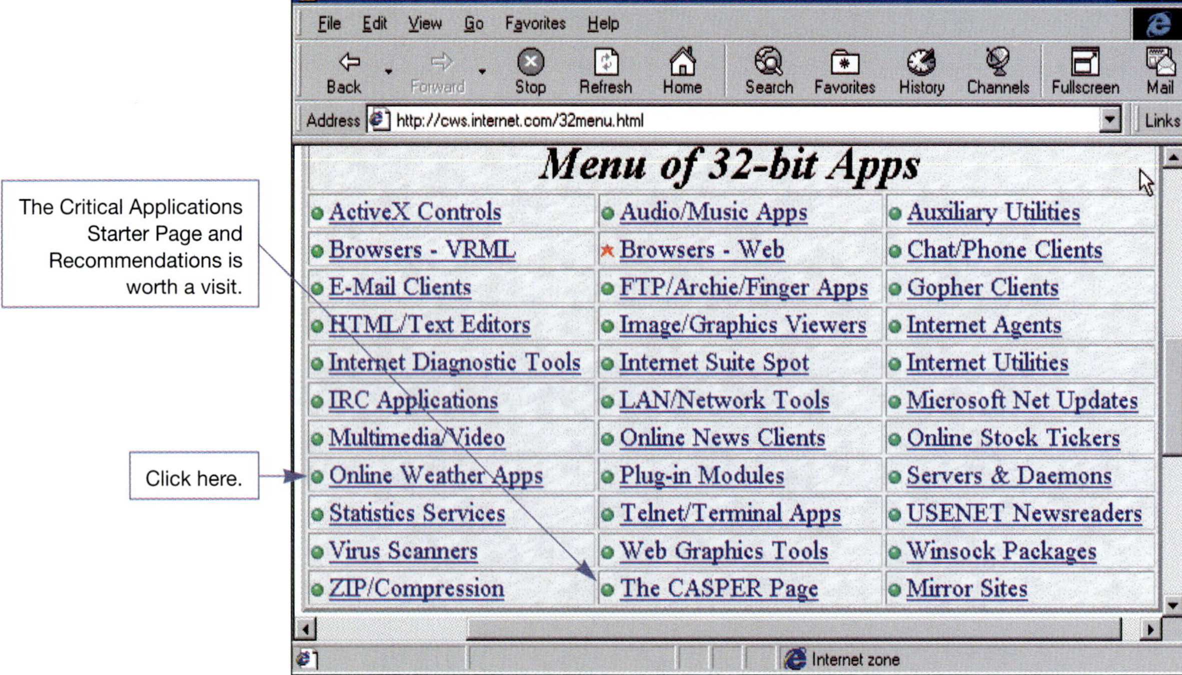

5. Select the Online Weather Apps link.
   Notice that a list of software appears with an FTP link for each piece of software (Image 4-3).

Image 4-3

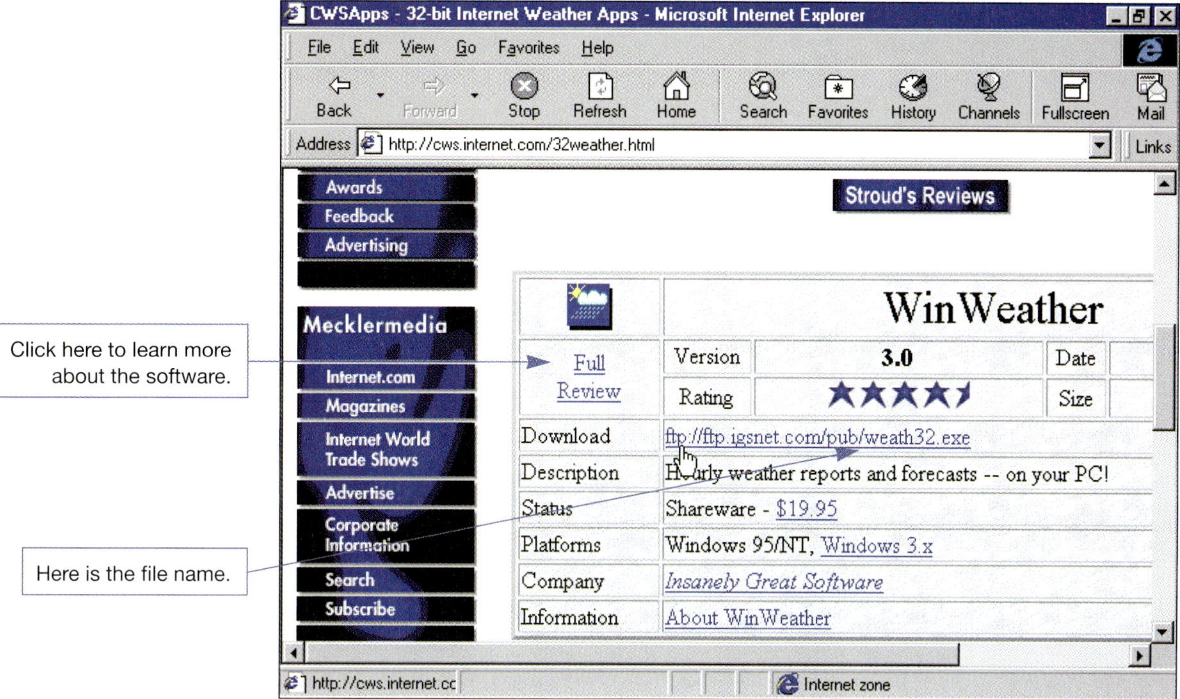

6. Select an Online Weather App by clicking on the download link.
   Notice that the File Download dialog box appears (Image 4-4).

Image 4-4

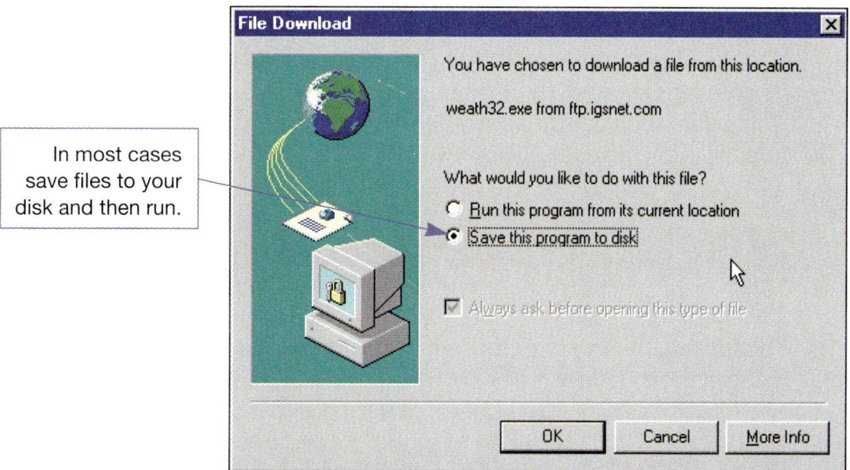

7. Be sure to select Save this program to disk; then click on OK.
   The Save As dialog box appears (Image 4-5).

Image 4-5

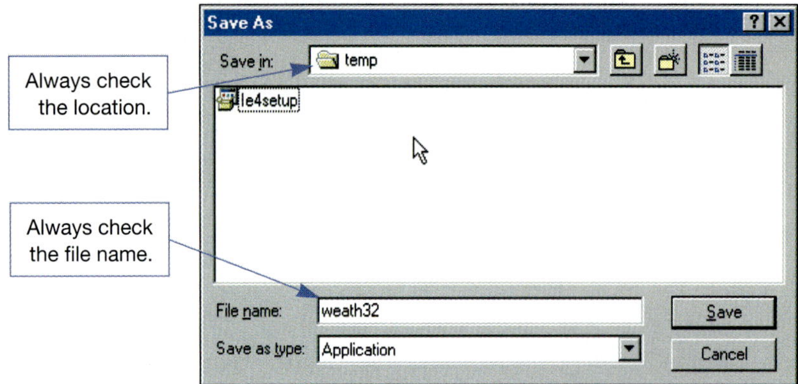

8. Set the location where you want to store the file and then click on Save.
   A new dialog box indicates the saving process (Image 4-6).

Image 4-6

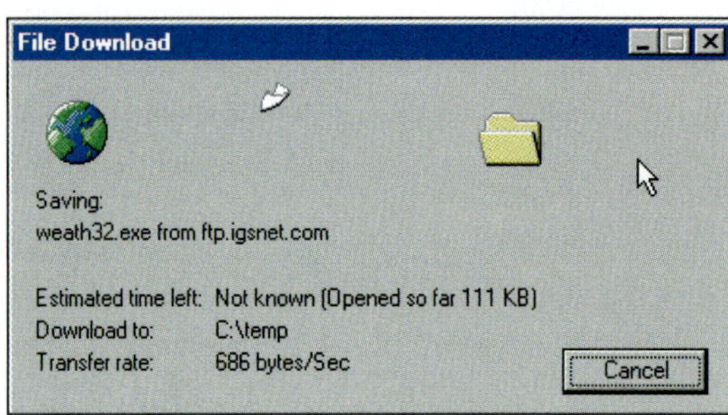

EXERCISE 4-1

The Game link in *Learning Online* has many downloadable games. To help you become familiar with the process of downloading software, select a game of your choice and then download it to your computer. You must download a .zip file such as those available from Happy Puppy Games Onramp. The next section discusses how to install the software you download.

EXERCISE 4-2

The *Learning Online* Web site also has numerous links to software sites. Take time to browse through the various sites. It is up to you to determine which, if any, files to download.

ZIP FILES AND INSTALLING SOFTWARE

If you download software from the Internet, you will need to install the software on your computer. Many of the programs available for downloading are stored in a compressed, or *zipped,* file format. Zipped files are not directly operable. They must be uncompressed, or *unzipped*, before they can be used. When a file uses the .zip extension, you need special software to decompress the software before installing it on your

Netiquette 4-2

E-Mail Address and Anonymous FTP

When an **anonymous FTP** site asks for your password, use your e-mail address. With your e-mail address, the site can assess the level of FTP use. If your e-mail address doesn't work, use the password *guest.*

computer. One of the most popular programs for this process is called **WinZip for Windows**. Similar programs are available for the Macintosh computer and for DOS. You can download these programs from the Internet as well. You might check some of the links from the Internet Software link on the *Learning Online* Web site. If you download a .zip file, you must also locate, download, and then install a decompression program such as WinZip.

Installing downloaded software is normally a very simple procedure. The first step is to use My Computer to open the folder that contains the desired file. If the file is a .zip file and you have a decompression program such as WinZip installed, simply double-click on the software icon. This action invokes the decompression program and decompresses the file. After the file is decompressed, you should go to the folder where the decompressed file is located. When you are in the correct folder, double-click on the Setup icon. At this point you should receive step-by-step instructions that explain how you can complete the software installation process.

If the software you download is directly executable, the installation process is even easier. To install this type of software, all that is required of you is to open the folder containing the program icon; then double-click on that icon. At that point you normally receive step-by-step instructions on the installation procedures.

ACTIVITY

1. Open the folder that contains the weather application you downloaded in the previous section. If you are not familiar with this process, open My Computer from the Desktop, open the disk drive where you saved the weather application, and then select the folder that contains the weather application (Image 4-7).

Image 4-7

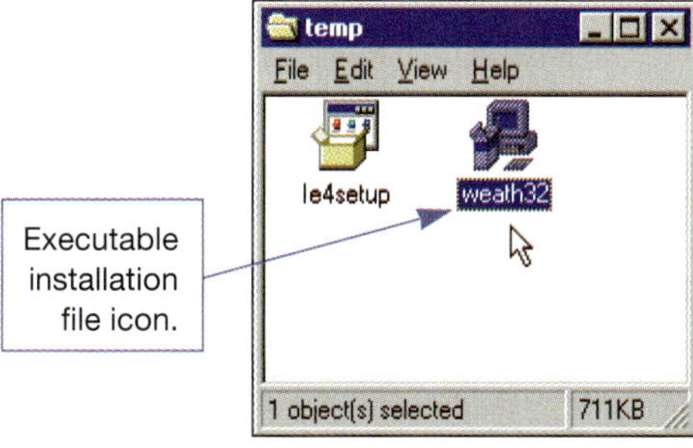

2. Double-click on the game icon you downloaded in Exercise 4-1 or the weather program you downloaded in the previous activity. If you did not download a file, make sure you do so to complete this activity. At this point you will go through a typical installation process (Image 4-8).

Image 4-8

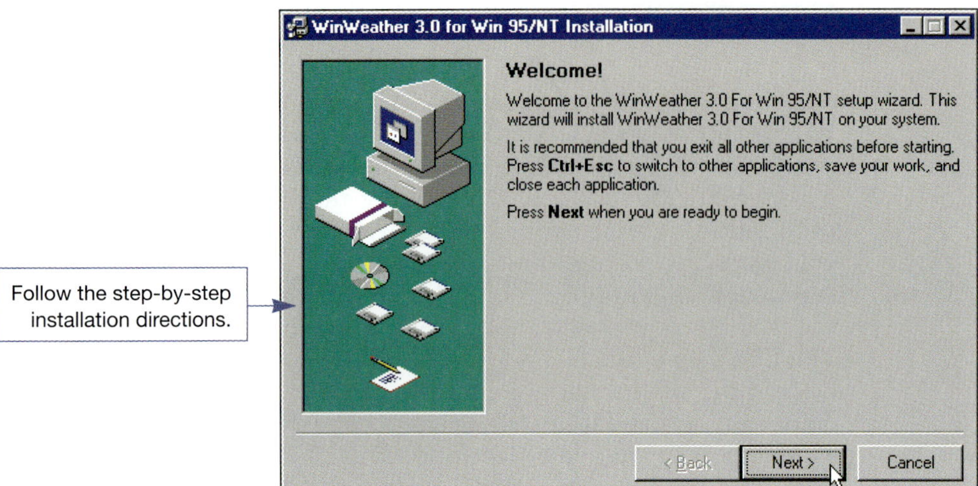

Follow the step-by-step installation directions.

3. Make sure the software functions correctly by taking a few minutes to use the software.

EXERCISE 4-3

Practice the process of downloading and installing a piece of software. Explore the various sites in *Learning Online* to determine which software you want to download. After you download the software, be sure to get permission to install the software from your instructor.

FTP SITES

An **FTP site** is a Web location that may contain files ready for you to download but it also may allow you to upload files. The major difference between downloading a file from a specific FTP site and downloading a file from any other Web site is that an FTP site includes a menu of files that you can download. The capability of uploading to an FTP site depends on the FTP site settings and whether or not it allows uploading.

Netiquette 4-3

Do Not Engage in Dumping

Using someone else's FTP site as a location for files you want other people to download is called dumping. Dumping is not acceptable behavior on the Web.

> **Tips, Tricks, and Ideas 4-5**
>
> *Passwords*
>
> You may find yourself at an FTP site that requires a password before you can upload or download files. This capability allows Web designers to create FTP links that are limited to specific access. If you want access to this site, try e-mailing the Web master to find out how to obtain a password.

> **Tips, Tricks, and Ideas 4-6**
>
> *Upload File*
>
> The only time Upload File is available from the File menu is when a valid FTP site has been selected.

Uploading requires you to have access to an FTP upload site. You will need to have the URL for the FTP upload site and permission (in some cases a password) for posting files. Check with your instructor for the specific permissions. After you obtain the permissions, select the Upload File command from the File menu. When this command is selected, the File Upload dialog box appears. From this dialog box select the file you want to upload and then select the Open button. If you have access privileges, the file will be uploaded to the FTP site. However, if you do not have access privileges, you will be denied permission to upload.

ANONYMOUS FTP SITES

It is easy to spot an FTP site. Rather than seeing the typical Web page, you will see a series of files and/or folders. **Anonymous FTP** sites are among the most popular types of FTP sites. Anonymous FTP sites are publicly available. To go to an anonymous FTP site you must know the full URL and anonymous directory. To get to the site, type ftp://ftpsite/ directory next to Address: and then press Enter. If the URL you enter is correct, you will activate an FTP site.

Anonymous FTP means that you may use anonymous as your user name. If the FTP site is an anonymous FTP site, you will receive instructions on what password to enter. Typically, for anonymous FTP the password is **guest** or your e-mail account name. After you enter this information, you will be able to up- or download files.

Most FTP sites severely restrict the number and types of files that are available for uploading and downloading. The reason is simple—an anonymous FTP is open to everyone on the Internet.

Logging on to an anonymous FTP site to download files, or programs, provides you with access to a wide variety of information. However, there is a danger. Some FTP sites allow users to upload files for public distribution. These are generally not secure sites, and some unscrupulous users may post files containing viruses or misleading information. Therefore, you need to use a bit of caution if you choose to download files from an anonymous FTP site.

> **Tips, Tricks, and Ideas 4-7**
>
> *FTP and Viruses*
>
> One of the most popular ways of spreading programs that can erase data from your computer system (viruses) is through FTP. Because so many people can download files, FTP is a perfect tool for anyone wishing to spread destructive software. It is a good idea to use some type of virus protection software if you plan to download files with FTP.

ACTIVITY

1. Connect to the Internet, launch Internet Explorer, and activate the *Learning Online* Web site. Select either Site by Site or Chapter by Chapter.
   Notice the FTP link
2. Select the FTP link.
3. Click on Microsoft Corporation.
   Notice the list of folders that contain files for downloading.

4. Click on the Products folder.
5. Click on the Windows folder.
   Notice that the current directory is /Products/Windows.
6. Activate the /Products/Windows/Windows95/CDRomExtras/FunStuff directory (Image 4-9).

Image 4-9

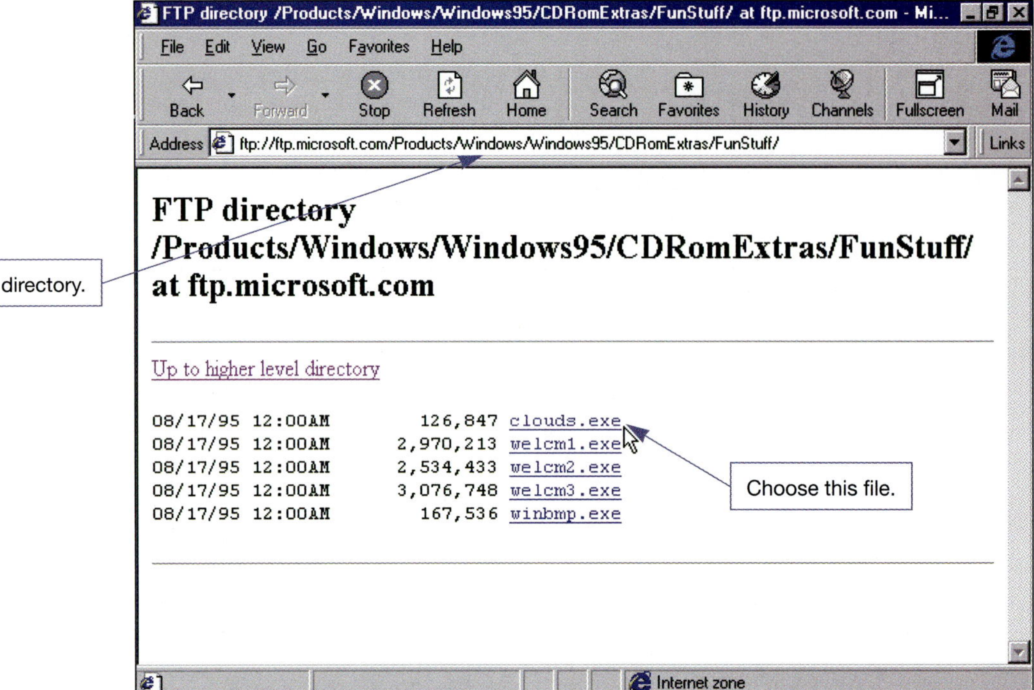

7. Click on clouds.exe.
8. From the Save As dialog box, click the C: drive and then click on Create New Folder to create a new folder called Clouds.
9. Make sure the Clouds folder is selected; then click on the Save button. At this point the clouds.exe file will be downloaded into the Clouds directory.
10. After the download, minimize Internet Explorer, open My Computer, open the C: drive, and then open the Clouds folder. The Clouds icon should appear.
11. Double-click to execute Clouds.
    Notice that this file is self-extracting (decompressed). Press Y to continue extracting only after you make sure the Clouds icon is in the Clouds directory (Image 4-10).

Image 4-10

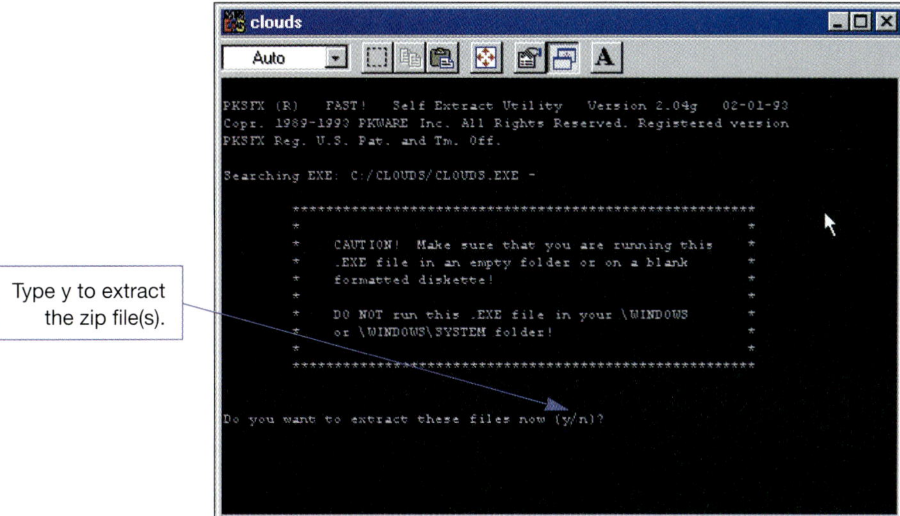

12. Close the decompression window.
13. The clouds.exe program is a wallpaper graphic you can use within Windows 95. If you want to use this wallpaper and are familiar with using the Display program from the Control Panel, go ahead and make the changes to use Clouds. Image 4-11 is a sample of the Clouds wallpaper in Windows 95.

Image 4-11

14. After you experiment with clouds, return your wallpaper to its original selection. Delete the Clouds folder and all of its contents from your C: drive.

Tips, Tricks, and Ideas 4-8

Using Windows 95

The Microsoft Corporation FTP site is filled with files for enhancing Windows 95. You are welcome to download and use the files as specified by Microsoft. However, you need to be familiar with the basic process and operations of Windows 95 before you attempt to use any of the available files. If you are not familiar with the operations of Windows 95, you might want to consult the *Effective Windows 95* text in this series or any other manual that explains the operation of Windows 95.

Tips, Tricks, and Ideas 4-9

Some Common Sense

Some of the files and programs available for downloading may be offensive to you. As it stands now, it is up to you to determine what to download.

Tips, Tricks, and Ideas 4-10

Ask

Never use a graphics file without permission. You may be violating copyright law. If you are downloading from a Web site, send an e-mail to the Web site to find out who you need to contact for permission to use a graphics file.

DOWNLOADING GRAPHICS FILES

There are other techniques for downloading files with Internet Explorer. One of the most popular procedures is to download any graphic that appears within Internet Explorer. You can use the right mouse button to download a graphic displayed on Internet Explorer. When you point at a graphic and then right-click on it, a menu of options appears. The **Save Picture As** option allows you to save the graphics file on your disk.

Saving graphics files can be very useful. For example, you can save graphics files off the Web and use them in your word processing files, spreadsheets, databases, or other applications. You can also use graphics files to create your own Web pages. Although downloading and using graphics files is very easy, you should be aware that graphics files are copyright protected. In other words, if you want to use a graphic created by someone else, you need to get permission before you use it. Many of the graphics file sites allow you free use of graphics. On these occasions the Web sites identify the permission requirements. Other sites may not expressly permit you to use their graphics. In these cases be sure to contact the Web developer and ask how you can obtain permission to use the graphic.

ACTIVITY

1. Go to the opening *Learning Online* site.
2. Point at the *Learning Online* title graphic and then click the right mouse button.
   Notice the menu (Image 4-12).

Image 4-12

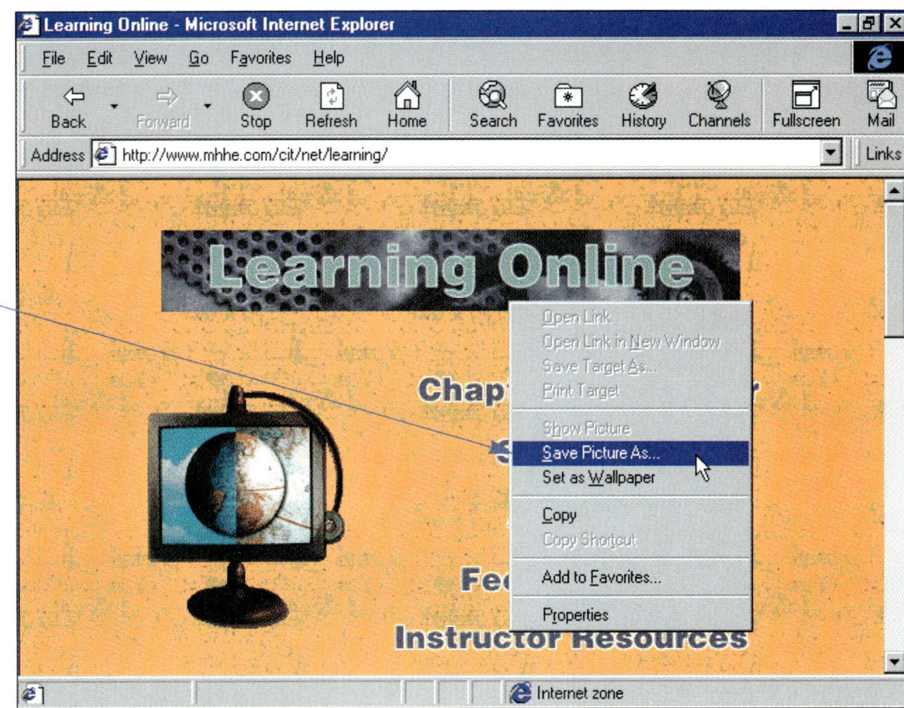

Use the right mouse button to select this menu.

3. Select Save Picture As.
   Notice the dialog box.
4. Select your disk and then click on Save.
   Notice the message that indicates a download is in progress. Depending on the speed of your Internet link, it may take some time to download the graphics file.

> ### Tips, Tricks, and Ideas 4-11
> *Multiple Browsers, Multiple Activities*
>
> One of the strengths of Internet Explorer is that you can perform multiple browser operations. This is especially useful when you are downloading files from an FTP site. After you have started a lengthy downloading process, you can minimize the download window and continue to use Internet Explorer. You can also select New and then Window from the File menu. This step allows you to run multiple copies of Internet Explorer.

EXERCISE 4-4

Browse the Web and download any three graphics (.gif, .jpg, or .tif) files. If any paint software is available on your computer, open that software and open any one of the downloaded graphics files. Try to make a few modifications and then print the graphic.

KEY POINTS

- An FTP link is identified by a URL that begins with ftp://.
- When you click on a link that directly refers to a file that is not supported by Internet Explorer, you have the option of saving the file.
- One of the most powerful applications of the World Wide Web is the capability to upload (send) or download (receive) files.
- On the World Wide Web, the process of uploading and downloading files is accomplished through a procedure called a file transfer protocol (FTP).
- FTP allows you to examine, send, and receive files to and from other computers over the Web.
- Software available for downloading on the Web often falls into one of three categories—shareware, freeware, and commercial software.
- Shareware is software that is provided in either a full version or in a limited version for you to "try before you buy."
- Freeware, as its name implies, means you can use it for free.
- Commercial software is software that generally requires a purchase.
- Many programs available for downloading are stored in a compressed, or zipped, file format.
- When a file uses the .zip extension, you need special software to decompress the software before installing it on your computer.
- An FTP site is a Web address that may contain files ready for you to download, but it also may allow you to upload files.
- Anonymous FTP means you may use anonymous as your user name. If the FTP site is an anonymous FTP site, you will receive instructions on what password to enter. Typically, for anonymous FTP the password is guest or your e-mail account name.
- Most FTP sites severely restrict the number and types of files that are available for uploading and downloading.
- You can use the right mouse button to download a graphic displayed on Internet Explorer. Be careful, however, about using the files you download; many graphics files are copyright protected.

KEY TERMS AND COMMANDS

anonymous FTP
commercial software
downloading
file transfer protocol (FTP)
freeware
FTP site
guest
Save Picture As
shareware
uploading
WinZip for Windows

STUDY QUESTIONS

1. Describe the process for downloading software from the Web. What are some of the concerns to be aware of when beginning the downloading process?
2. Describe the concept of "dumping."
3. Describe the process and the considerations involved when downloading a graphics file.
4. What is the purpose of anonymous FTP?
5. Discuss the dangers in using FTP.
6. Describe the process of using Internet Explorer to download an unsupported file.
7. Explain the distinction between shareware and freeware.
8. Describe the procedure for installing a compressed file with a .zip extension.
9. Describe the procedure for installing a compressed file with an .exe extension.
10. What is an FTP site?

PRACTICE TEST

1. When you want to provide a location for a friend to pick up some of your files, it is a good idea to store the files on someone else's FTP site.
   a. True b. False
2. Typically, when you use an anonymous FTP site, your password is
   a. Anonymous c. Host
   b. Visitor d. Guest
3. When you want to download a particular file, all that is required is to click on a download link.
   a. True b. False
4. Graphics files can often be downloaded by clicking the right mouse button.
   a. True b. False
5. An FTP link is identified by a URL that begins with
   a. http:// c. html://
   b. ftp:// d. www.ftp://
6. Which of the following terms is also used to describe a compressed file?
   a. FTP file c. Telnet file
   b. Packed file d. Zip file
7. Files that end with which of the following extensions are not supported directly by Internet Explorer?
   a. .zip c. .doc
   b. .exe d. .edu
8. Which dialog box has the option for saving files not directly supported by Internet Explorer?
   a. Save Unsupported File
   b. Uncompress File
   c. Unknown File Type
   d. Zip File
9. An FTP site generally permits you to download a file, but uploading is not possible.
   a. True b. False
10. Software that is provided in either a full version or in a limited version for you to "try before you buy" is called
   a. Shareware c. Commercial ware
   b. Freeware d. Tryware

FILL-INS

1. ______________________________ allows you to examine, send, and receive files from other computers over the Internet.
2. ______________________________ FTP means you may use anonymous as your user name.
3. An FTP link is identified by a URL that begins with ______________________________.
4. ______________________________ is software that is provided in either a full version or a limited version for you to "try before you buy."
5. ______________________________, as its name implies, means you can use it for free.
6. With an anonymous FTP site, you typically use ______________________________ or ______________________________ as your password.
7. Using someone else's FTP site as a location for files you want other people to get is called ______________________________.
8. One of the most popular programs for unzipping or decompressing a file is called ______________________________.
9. Many people who use the Internet obtain the software necessary to use the Internet directly from ______________________________.
10. One way to download a graphic displayed on Internet Explorer is to use ______________________________.

PROJECTS

1. The *Learning Online* Web site provides the FTP link that contains a variety of FTP sites for you to examine. Use FTP to visit a few of these anonymous FTP sites and explore what files are available. Select and download any one file of your choice.
2. Are you using the best Internet software for your application? *Learning Online* has an Internet Software link. This link can take you to some locations that specialize in reviewing Internet software. These sites also allow you to download software. Visit one or more of the Internet Software links and then decide whether the software you are using is the best for you.
3. Many hobbyist organizations create and maintain Web sites. Use a search engine of your choice to locate such an organization. You might look for a kennel club, a dog or cat breeders club, a bird-watching society, or a coin- or stamp-collecting organization. Visit any site of this type and locate a graphic that you can download (i.e., not copyright protected). Click on the right mouse button to download the graphics file.

INTERNET AT WORK

Even though Edith looks very businesslike, she is actually a computer-gaming geek. Various gaming sites on the Web enable you to download freeware, shareware, or demonstration versions of software products. Your task is to find a computer game that you think Edith might like, download the game, play the game, and then remove the game from your computer. Once you have identified the game, write Edith a brief memo describing the game, where it can be located, and any other pertinent information. You can then share this information with your coworkers (classmates).

5 Expanding Internet Explorer

OUTCOMES

When you complete this chapter you will be able to . . .

- Define add-ons, plug-ins, and ActiveX.
- Distinguish between an add-on and a plug-in.
- Identify the characteristics of ActiveX.
- Use *Learning Online* to locate appropriate add-ons, plug-ins, and ActiveX.
- Download an add-on, plug-in, and ActiveX.
- Install an add-on, plug-in, and ActiveX.
- Identify and use major add-ons and plug-ins and explain the role of ActiveX.

EXPANDING INTERNET EXPLORER

By now you should understand how to use several basic features of Internet Explorer. You should be able to enter a URL; use links; create, use, and organize favorites; use a variety of navigational tools; and perform searches using various search tools. Although these fundamental activities are very important, there is a lot more you can do with Internet Explorer to gain access to additional, and different, types of information.

Before you can use all the features and power of Internet Explorer, you need to be able to expand its capabilities. You should also be able to modify Internet Explorer for your own personal needs. One of the key benefits of Internet Explorer is that it allows you to add new features to your copy of the software. These features include the capability to access and use graphics, sound, video, and virtual reality. Add-ons (with some browsers these are referred to as helper applications or helper apps), plug-ins, and a special set of tools collectively known as ActiveX provide the additional features to Internet Explorer.

PLUG-INS

One of the most exciting features of the World Wide Web is the flexibility it has for incorporating new features. If there is one constant about the World Wide Web, it is the continuous state of very rapid change. New ways of presenting digital information are constantly being developed. For

Netiquette 5-1

Learn the Conventions for Extensions

Learn and use the conventions for file extensions. For example, use .exe for non-UNIX executable files, .txt for ASCII text files, .html or .htm for HTML files, and the correct file extensions for graphics files.

example, a few years ago it was unheard of for the World Wide Web to display and use three-dimensional animation. Today you can use **Virtual Reality Model Language (VRML)** documents to display and control three-dimensional images. In the past browsers were limited to displaying only basic text and graphics. Now you can use Internet Explorer to process live audio, full motion video, and a host of other multimedia applications.

Tips, Tricks, and Ideas 5-1

Status Bar and Links

In Internet Explorer, when you point at a link, the full URL including the file name and file type extension appears on the status bar. After you learn the appropriate file extensions, you can quickly identify the file type for the link.

When you access an HTML document, it is common for this type of document to contain links to other HTML documents. However, Internet Explorer is not limited to accessing only HTML documents and the links that are provided in these documents. You can also link to other types of files. For example, there are links to graphics files, links to audio files, and links to video files.

File extensions are used to identify document types on the World Wide Web. For example, all HTML documents use the .HTML or .HTM extension. Graphics links use .gif, .jpg, .pcx, .bmp, and many other extensions to identify graphics files that are available on the Web. Audio files, video files, and virtual reality files are all identified on the Web by a file **extension**.

Many **file types** are directly supported by Internet Explorer. If a file uses either the .gif (called gif files) or .jpg (called jpeg) extensions, you can directly view the file by pointing and clicking on the graphics file link. In other words, Internet Explorer displays these graphics files when you click on the graphics file links.

However, some file types are not directly supported by Internet Explorer. What happens if the link file type is not supported by Internet Explorer? In this case Internet Explorer may use an external viewer to display the file. An **external viewer** is a program that displays files that are not internally supported by Internet Explorer.

Very early in its development, the designers of Internet Explorer realized the need for their browser to be able to adapt and change to accommodate new types of information that would appear on the World Wide Web. Thanks to the foresight of these designers, Internet Explorer allows you to add features such as external viewers to support a specific type of file. For example, if you want to listen to audio files, you need an audio player (viewer). If you want to use VRML documents, you need a VRML viewer. However, the way that Internet Explorer uses the term *viewers* is a little confusing. You don't "view" an audio file—you listen to it. As Internet Explorer and the World Wide Web have evolved, these special software enhancements or viewers have come to be known as simply **plug-ins**. The reason for having a variety of plug-ins is that you can download a specific plug-in, install it within Internet Explorer, and then use

Internet Explorer to access and use the files supported by the plug-in. Some plug-ins are better than others for specific uses. The choice of a plug-in is often a matter of personal preference.

The way plug-ins work is actually very simple. All files, including HTML documents, are stored on a Web server. Each file is identified by the file name and the name of the Web server, that is, its URL. For example, the URL http://www.mhhe.com/cit/net/learning/loaudio.htm is for the loaudio.htm or .HTML file located in the /cit/net/learning directory on the www.mhhe.com Web server.

One of the most popular add-ons is called Shockwave for Director (or simply Shockwave). **Shockwave** files add animation to a Web page. When you access a Web site that uses Shockwave files, Internet Explorer automatically invokes Shockwave for you. As soon as you leave the Web site, the Shockwave plug-in terminates. You never need concern yourself about running a plug-in; it runs itself.

Image 5-1

Shockwave is a very popular plug-in that brings controlled animation to the Web.

If Internet Explorer does not understand, or support, the file type, the file type Registry in Windows is used. In other words, when Internet Explorer is unable to open a file, it checks with those file types registered in Windows. If a file type matches, the application for that file type is opened along with the file. In short, it works just as if you were to double-click on a document icon in Windows. The major difference is that you will be given the option to open the file or save the file to disk.

INSTALLING AND USING PLUG-INS

Installing and using plug-ins begins by locating and downloading the program. Many of the most popular plug-ins can be found on the *Learning Online* Web site. For example, if you click on the Audio link, the Audio Web site presents links for downloading RealPlayer and other audio

Tips, Tricks, and Ideas 5-2

TUCOWS and Strouds

There are some excellent sites in the *Learning Online* Web site for locating and downloading a full range of plug-ins and add-ons. TUCOWS and Strouds can be located through the Internet Software link of *Learning Online.* These sites are great sources for a full listing of available plug-ins and add-ons. You may want to visit these sites not only to locate plug-ins and add-ons but also to discover a variety of other Internet-related software.

Tips, Tricks, and Ideas 5-3

Locate Internet Explorer

The exact location of Internet Explorer on your computer depends on the computer. In some cases Internet Explorer is installed under the Program Files folder of the C: drive. In other cases it may be on a different network drive. In still other cases Internet Explorer may reside in the Internet Explorer folder on the C: drive. The only time the actual location of Internet Explorer really matters is when you need to determine where to save add-ons and other Internet Explorer–related files.

add-ons. The Video link from *Learning Online* has several video plug-ins you can use. The plug-ins link provides access to some of the most popular and useful plug-ins available. In addition, you can use the Internet Software link from *Learning Online* to access TUCOWS, Stroud's, and other sites for a full listing of plug-ins. To download a plug-in, follow the link and then download the file in the normal fashion. If you are having difficulty with downloading, refer to Chapter 4.

After you download a file, you need to install it within Internet Explorer. Most plug-ins have a simple installation procedure. Normally, from the My Computer icon, you locate the file icon, double-click on it, and follow the on-screen installation instructions. After a plug-in is installed, you can click on any of the links supported by the plug-in and use them within Internet Explorer.

ACTIVITY

1. Go to the *Learning Online* Web site and select the Audio link.
   Notice that there are several audio links including a link to download a copy of RealPlayer. RealPlayer is an important plug-in that most people using the World Wide Web should have.
2. Click on the download RealPlayer link.
   Notice that this action activates the RealPlayer Web site (Image 5-2).

Image 5-2

Click here to download the free version of RealPlayer.

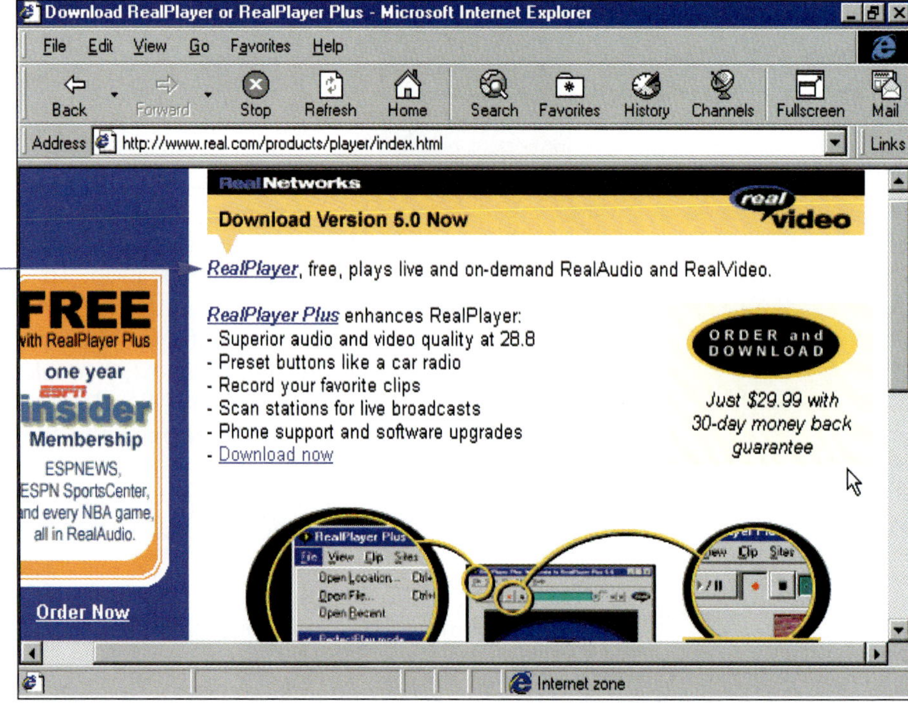

3. Follow the RealPlayer link. To download this helper, you will need to provide information about what you want to download and information about your system. If you are unaware of your operating system, processor type, and connection speed, consult your instructor. Be sure to include your name and e-mail address (Image 5-3).

Image 5-3

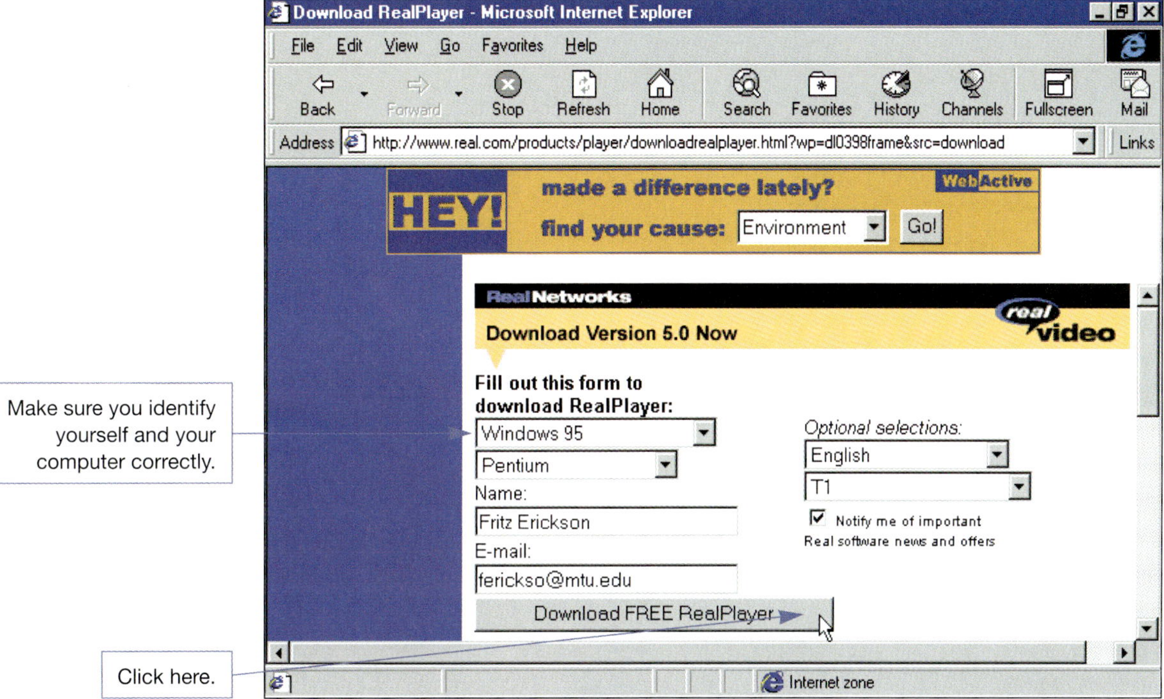

4. After completing the form for downloading, continue the downloading processes. Select a mirror site close to you. After you select a site, the Save As dialog box will appear. Be sure to save the RealPlayer file in an appropriate location on your computer. You may want to create a folder on your hard disk called plug-ins as a convenient place to save these types of files (Image 5-4).

Image 5-4

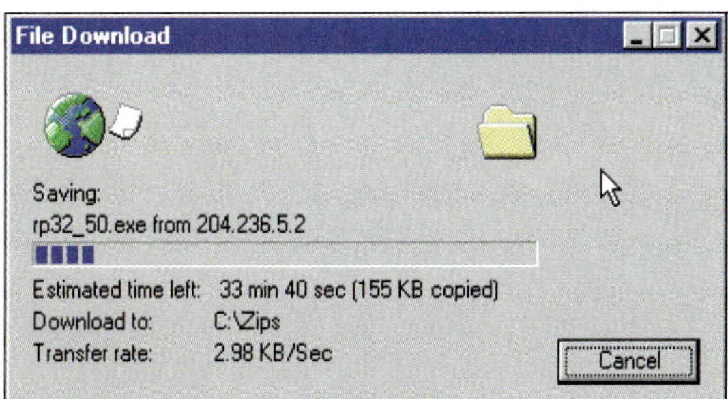

5. After the plug-in is downloaded, exit Internet Explorer.
   It is best to install plug-ins with Internet Explorer closed.
6. Open the My Computer icon from the desktop, open the C: drive, and open the folder containing the downloaded RealPlayer plug-in (Image 5-5).

Image 5-5

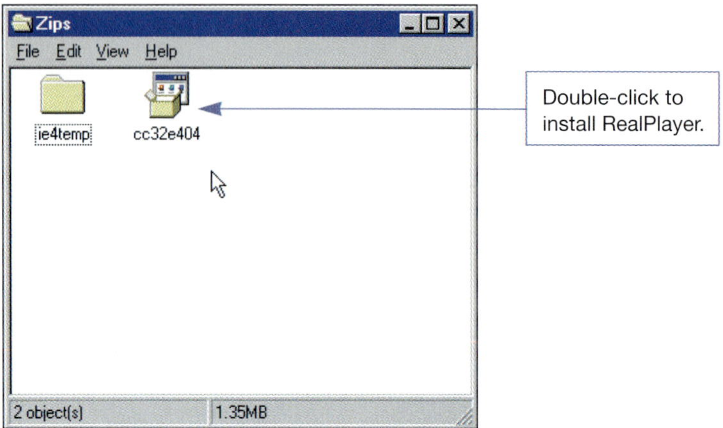

7. Double-click on the RealPlayer file. This is the same file name used to download RealPlayer.
   Notice that the setup procedure begins. Be sure to follow the instructions for installing RealPlayer (Image 5-6).

Image 5-6

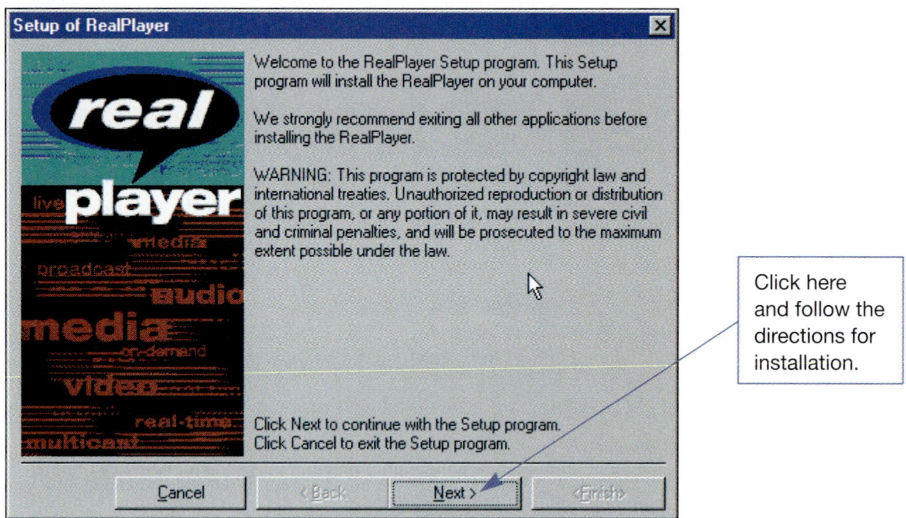

8. If necessary, close the RealPlayer window.
9. Select the Audio link from *Learning Online.*
   Select any audio link that looks interesting and listen to the audio files. Make sure you have turned on your speakers.

Tips, Tricks, and Ideas 5-4

Your Sound Card

It will not do you any good to download RealPlayer, or any other audio application, unless your computer has a sound card and speakers to hear sound files over the Web. In fact, RealPlayer may not even install unless you have these components.

EXERCISE 5-1

Now that you have downloaded and installed RealPlayer, experiment with some of the audio links located on the *Learning Online* Audio Web site. Many audio files are compatible with RealPlayer. However, other audio files such as .wav (called wave files) are also available. Try to execute these files to see whether Internet Explorer supports these .wav files. If not, download and install this plug-in in Internet Explorer.

ADD-ONS

Add-ons are very similar to plug-ins in that they both expand the functionality of Internet Explorer. However, add-ons tend to operate more like programs within Internet Explorer. The major difference between a plug-in and an add-on is that add-ons run with Internet Explorer and provide additional Internet tools. Some examples of add-ons are Microsoft NetMeeting, Outlook Express, Chat, and Netshow.

An application that uses an add-on is started within Internet Explorer. Add-ons tend to work directly within Internet Explorer. For example, you need to use Apple's QuickTime video add-on whenever you access a QuickTime video. This will enable the file to be displayed directly within Internet Explorer.

For most users, the distinction between a plug-in and an add-on is not very important. They both add features to Internet Explorer and allow you to fully access and use the Web. The process of obtaining and installing a plug-in is much the same as for an add-on. For example, if you want to add a real-time MPEG video player (one of the most popular on the Web), you will need to download the file and then run the installation or setup program from the appropriate My Computer folder. The install program will direct you through the process.

In most cases, using an add-on with Internet Explorer is **transparent** to the user. In other words, the add-on provides access to specific types of Web files, but you do not realize that it is operating. An add-on is activated whenever you access a Web page that calls for the use of the add-on.

How do you know which add-ons are installed and available on your computer? The answer is found by accessing the Microsoft Components Download page at microsoft.com. You can find the link to the Microsoft Components Download page by selecting the Plug-ins, Helpers, and Add-ons link in *Learning Online*. From this site, selecting Microsoft's Component Download link will analyze your copy of Internet Explorer and tell you which add-ons are included and which are not. In addition, you can find updates and download locations for add-ons.

Tips, Tricks, and Ideas 5-5

Plug-ins versus Add-ons

Most Web users prefer plug-ins to add-ons. The reason is that plug-ins operate seamlessly within Internet Explorer. Software developers are changing many add-ons to plug-ins. For example, RealPlayer is more like a plug-in than an add-on. If you have the choice, choose a plug-in over an add-on.

ACTIVITY

1. Launch Internet Explorer and activate the Plug-ins, Helpers, and Add-ons site from *Learning Online*.
   Notice the links to several popular plug-ins.
2. Select Microsoft Component Download.
   Notice the message box that asks permission to analyze the components currently installed on your computer (Image 5-7).

Image 5-7

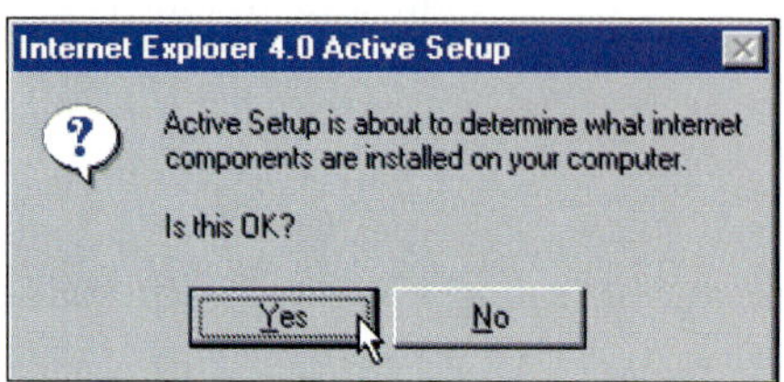

3. Click on OK.
   In a few moments a listing of all installed and yet-to-be-installed add-ons appears on the Web site (Image 5-8).

Image 5-8

Scroll down and examine which components are and which are not installed.

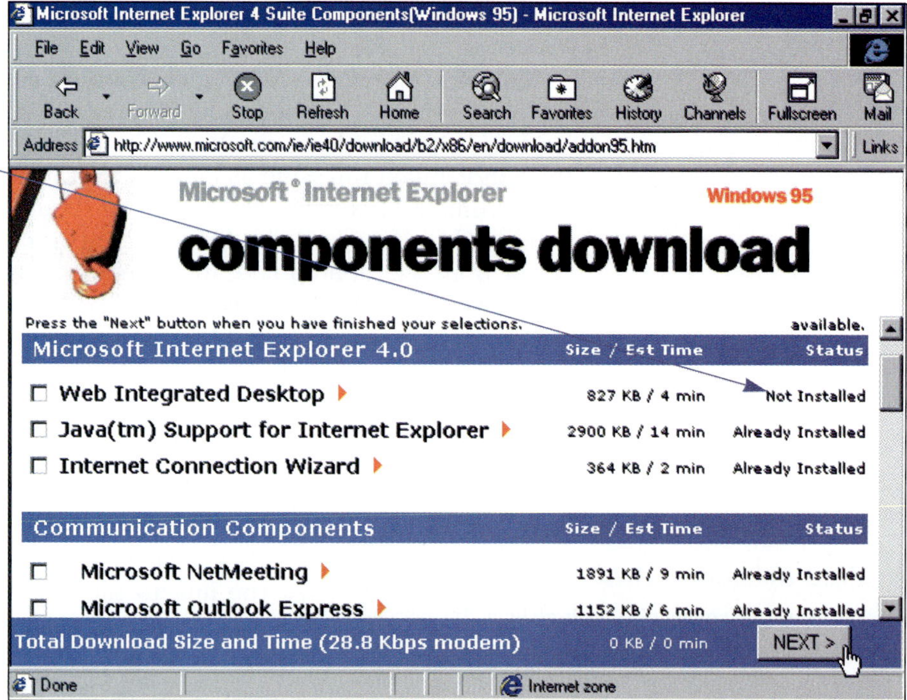

4. Click on the selection box next to Microsoft VRML 2.0 Viewer if it is not installed.
5. Click on the Next button.
6. Select a download site and then click on the Install Now button. Notice the add-on will download and install (Image 5-9).

Image 5-9

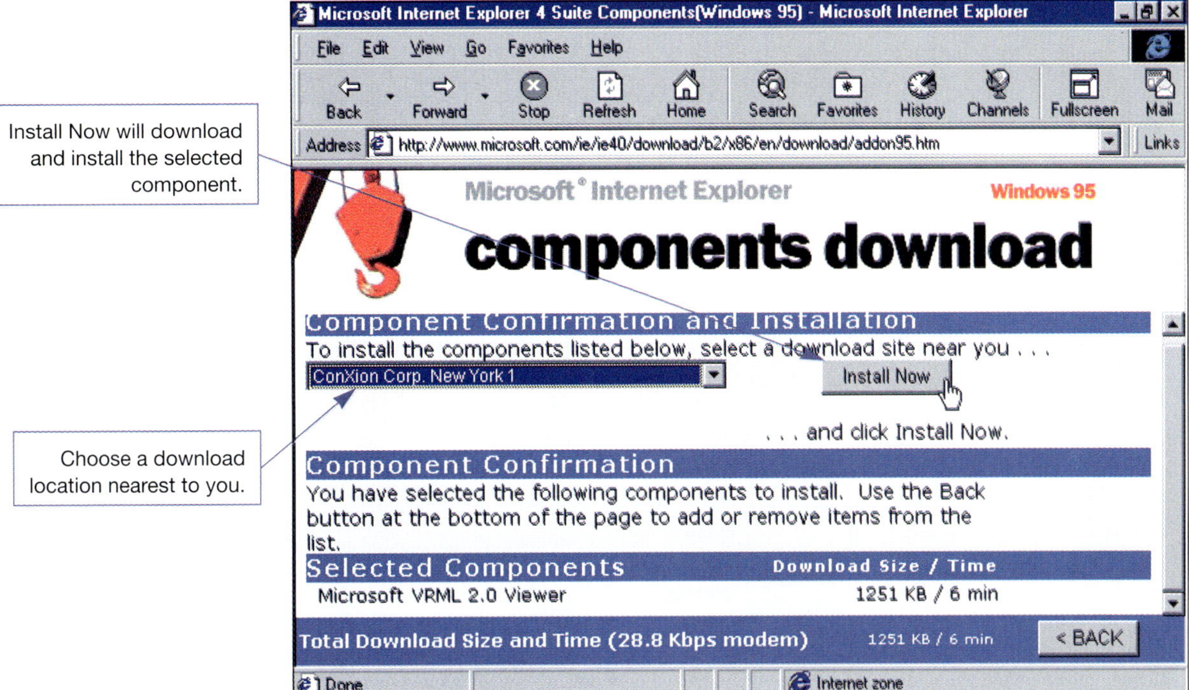

MUST-HAVE ADD-ONS AND PLUG-INS

Which add-ons and plug-ins do you really need? Ask any two Web users, and you will get two different answers. In general, you should have the add-ons or plug-ins for the types of files you intend to download or use. Following is a list of some of the more popular plug-ins and add-ons that you may want to add to your Internet Explorer. The list is by no means exhaustive. Several additional plug-ins and add-ons are discussed at length in subsequent sections and chapters.

Audio

Sound brings the Web to life, and many Web users prefer to be able to access and use audio files. Because of the importance of audio on the Web, Internet Explorer comes with add-ons and plug-ins that support .wav and .au audio files. Although these add-ons and plug-ins are nice, they are not sufficient. You may want to consider adding some of the following audio add-ons and plug-ins.

RealPlayer. RealPlayer is one of the most popular audio applications on the Web. If you do not

> **Tips, Tricks, and Ideas 5-6**
>
> *Learning Online*
>
> It seems that no two Web users can agree on which plug-ins and add-ons are really needed. The list provided here is only a sample. You may find that other add-ons and plug-ins work best for you. The Plug-ins, Helpers, and Add-ons site within *Learning Online* is a great place to begin looking for various plug-ins and add-ons, but you have to select those you think are most useful for you.

have RealPlayer, you should download and install it in Internet Explorer. Also, if the version of RealPlayer you are using is not the latest, obtain the latest version of RealPlayer and install it within Internet Explorer (Image 5-10).

Image 5-10

RealPlayer provides access to a wealth of audio information.

TrueSpeech TrueSpeech is a program that you can use to listen to files created in the TrueSpeech format. Several Web developers use True-Speech because they can record their voices using a simple microphone and the Sound Recorder in Windows 95. Then they convert the files to TrueSpeech and incorporate them into a Web site. You will need True-Speech to hear these files (Image 5-11).

Image 5-11

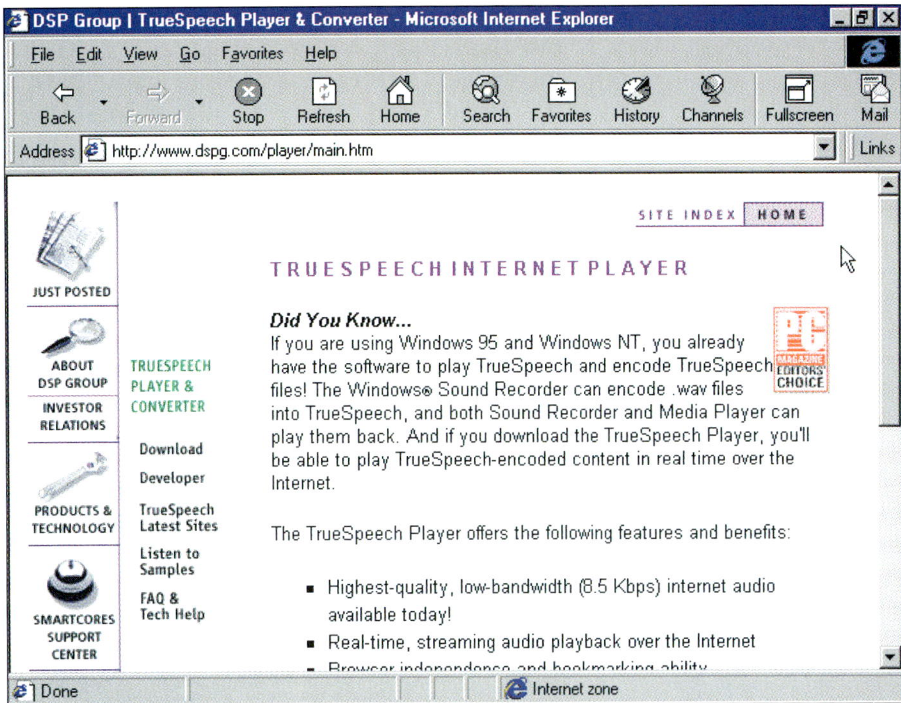

Crescendo If your computer has a Musical Instrument Digital Interface (MIDI) compatible sound card you can use Crescendo and Crescendo Plus to listen to Web sites that use a full music sound track. More and more Web sites are adding a MIDI soundtrack. When you access these sites, you can read the text, look at the graphics, and hear a great deal of music (Image 5-12).

Image 5-12

Graphics

If a picture is worth a thousand words, a graphic on a Web site is worth two thousand. Graphics images add style, interest, and excitement to any Web page. In fact, many people attribute the rapid success and growth of the World Wide Web to the use of graphics images. If you plan to use the Web for more that just reading text, you will need expanded graphics capabilities.

Because of the importance of graphics, Internet Explorer 3.0 and later versions have graphics image capabilities built in. These include .gif and .jpg graphics file formats. Although these formats are the two most popular, there are others.

Paint Shop Pro Paint Shop Pro is an outstanding graphics program that allows you to load, view, and manipulate a wide range of graphics images. It works much like a traditional draw or paint program but provides support for a full range of graphics file formats (Image 5-13).

Image 5-13

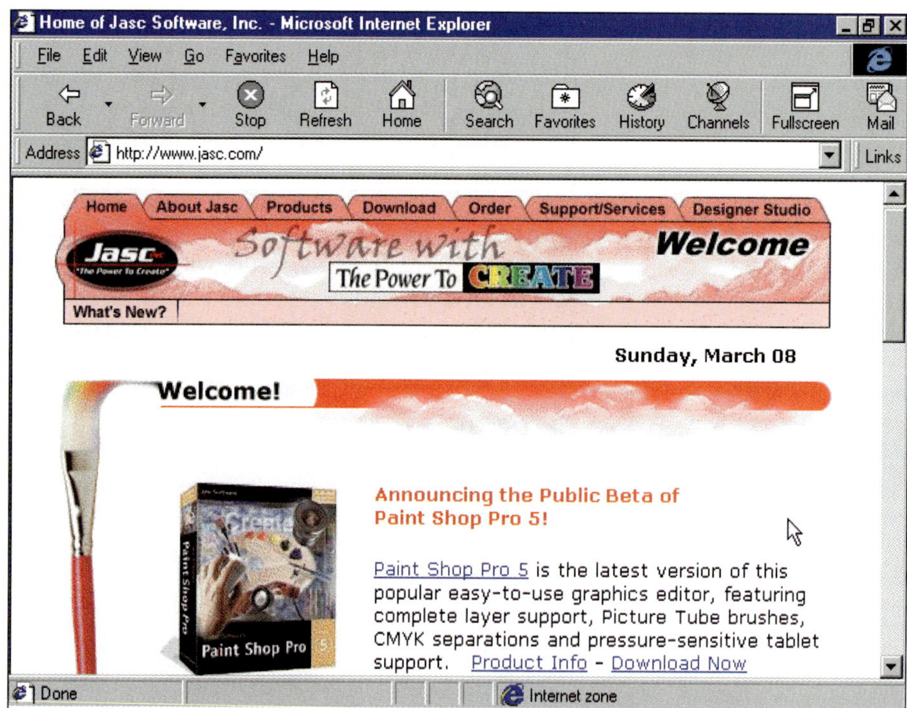

Thumbs Plus Thumbs Plus is another great graphics program that supports a wide range of graphics file formats. Among its other strengths, Thumbs Plus works well when you need to locate, view, edit, organize, and print files referred to as image, metafile, font, and multimedia files (Image 5-14).

Image 5-14

Video

Video plug-ins and add-ons are needed to bring the world of motion to Internet Explorer. Various video formats are available on the Web. Internet Explorer 3.0 and up include Microsoft Video for .avi video files.

QuickTime Apple's QuickTime video is important for all Web users. QuickTime may already be available in your version of Internet Explorer. If you cannot run QuickTime movies, then download, or obtain, a copy of QuickTime and install it so you can view .qt, .mov, and .moov videos.

MPEG No application of Internet Explorer can be complete without an MPEG plug-in. **MPEG** is one of the standards for creating and using video files on the Web. Many MPEG player programs are available. NET TOOB Stream is a popular MPEG viewer. So are StreamWorks and MPEG Movie Player for viewing .mpeg, .mpg, .mpe, .mpv, .vbs, and .mpegv. In addition, the viewer you use for MPEG should also support MPEG-2. **MPEG-2** is an advancement in compression of video. MPEG-2 files are smaller than equivalent MPEG files. For these files, you will want to install an MPEG viewer that supports MPEG-2 format for .mpv2 and .mp2v files (Image 5-15).

Image 5-15

Try the MPEG Store for video files.

Multimedia

Using multimedia on the Web is discussed in Chapter 8. However, it is a good idea to obtain some of the necessary multimedia add-ons and plug-ins to take advantage of the many multisensory Web sites. By definition, *multimedia* means for "more than one media." You may want to consider adding the following applications to Internet Explorer.

Shockwave Some people suggest that Internet Explorer is not Internet Explorer without Shockwave because Shockwave adds interaction to Web sites. Shockwave for Director allows animation, video, and audio created with Macromedia's Director to be viewed on a Web site. When you add Shockwave you are adding interaction.

VRML/VRML 2.0 Virtual Reality Modeling Language, or VRML, adds virtual three-dimensional space to the Web. With VRML you can move throughout 3-D Web pages, manipulate objects in a 3-D form, and develop 3-D modeling. VRML is in an early stage of development but shows great promise. As with other plug-ins, a variety of VRML viewers are available. Some of the more popular products include Live3D, VR Scout, and PLATINUM WIRL. For VRML 2.0, two of the most common plug-ins are SGI Cosmo and the Intervista WorldView viewer.

ACTIVITY

1. Go to the Plug-ins, Helpers, and Add-ons site in *Learning Online.*
2 Select the Macromedia's Shockwave (Image 5-16).

Image 5-16

3. Download Shockwave. You may want to download this file to your Plug-ins folder (Image 5-17).

Image 5-17

4. Complete the installation process for Shockwave.
5. From the *Learning Online* Web site, open the Plug-ins, Helpers, and Add-ons link and then open the Macromedia's Shockwave Web site.

6. Select Shockwave and then Explore Shockzone.
   Notice the list of available Shockwave sites (Image 5-18).

Image 5-18

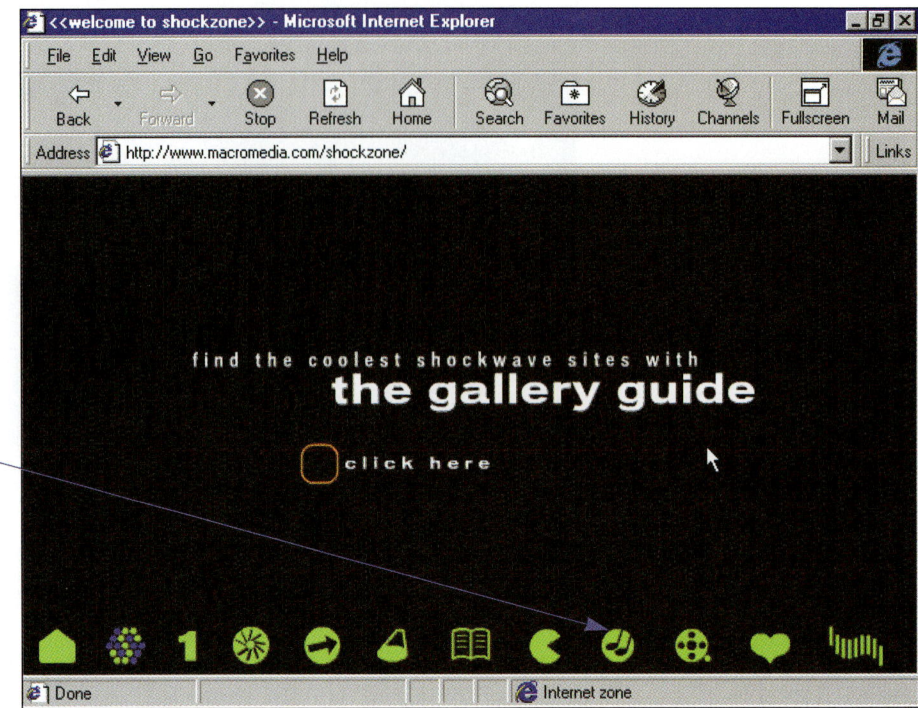

7. At the bottom of the screen, choose Jukebox.
   A list of Shockwave-supported sites will appear (Image 5-19).

Image 5-19

8. Make sure your speakers are on and select any site you want.
9. Take a few minutes to explore this Shockwave site. Then go back and select other Shockwave sites from Macromedia's Shockwave listing.

EXERCISE 5-2

Now that you have installed Shockwave take some time to experiment with several Shockwave sites. Shockwave is one of the most exciting additions to the World Wide Web. Be prepared to demonstrate a Shockwave site to the rest of the class.

ACTIVEX

ActiveX is a series of mini-applications that operate inside Internet Explorer. These applications provide access to even more specialized Web files. With ActiveX you have additional controls for special Web content. For example, Adobe Acrobat is a popular file format that allows you to view formatted text on a Web site. Adobe Acrobat files use the .pdf extension. With ActiveX controls you can view and read Adobe Acrobat–formatted files.

ActiveX is used for a variety of applications. For example, ActiveX controls are used with VRML to enable you to move through VRML 3-D worlds. You can use ActiveX controls for a host of other activities. In fact, the number of ActiveX controls is rapidly growing.

You can download ActiveX controls from a wide range of sources, many of which are listed in the ActiveX link on *Learning Online.* You can also get access to a full range of popular ActiveX controls through both TUCOWS and Stroud's.

ACTIVITY

1. Select the ActiveX site from *Learning Online.*
2. Choose Platinum WIRL ActiveX.
   Notice the Platinum WIRL site (Image 5-20).

Image 5-20

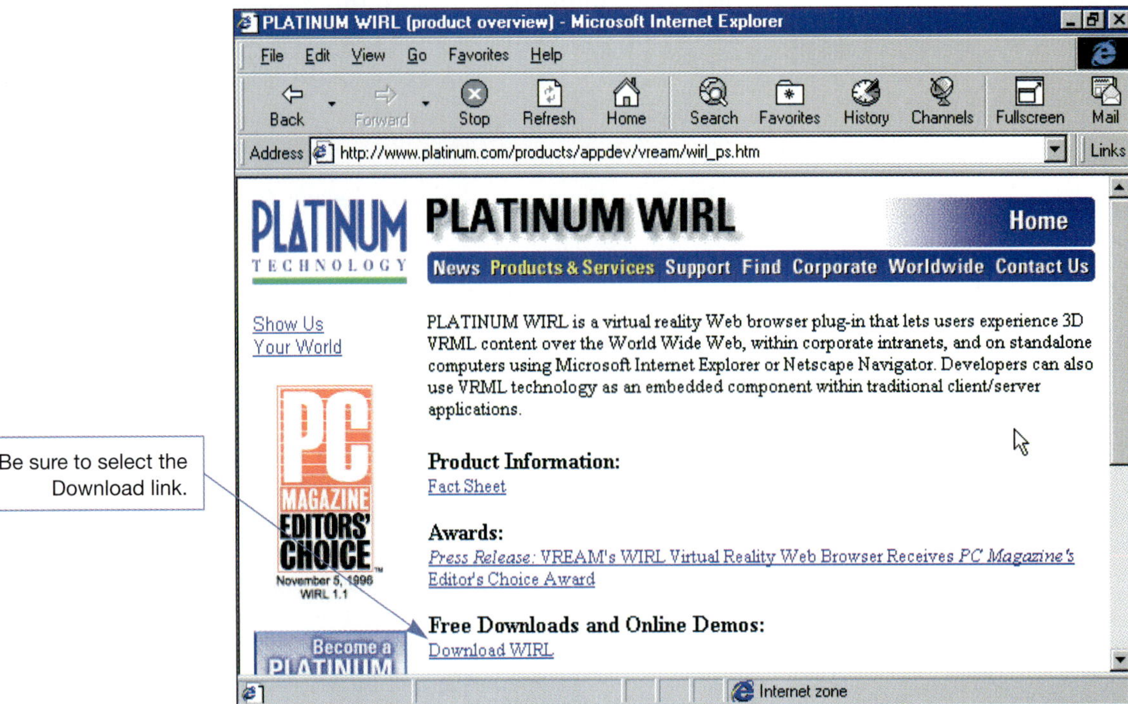

3. Click on Download WIRL and follow the process for downloading and installing Platinum WIRL. Be sure to download the ActiveX version for Internet Explorer.
4. From the Platinum WIRL site select WIRL Demos (Image 5-21).

Image 5-21

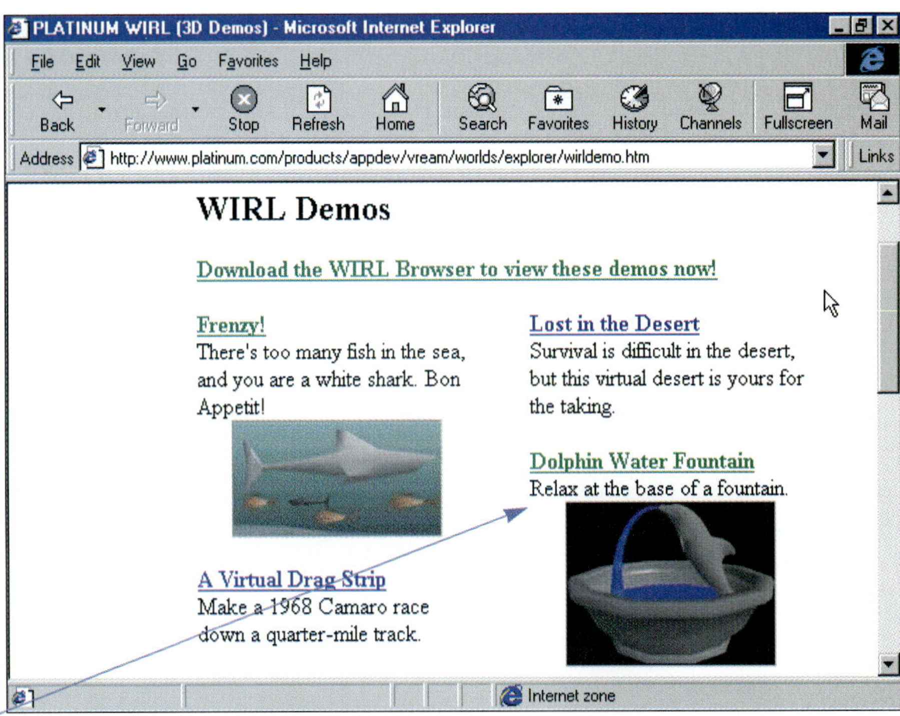

Try these WIRL demos.

5. Try the Dolphin Water Fountain and several other VRML sites with ActiveX controls.

EXERCISE 5-3

It is up to you to decide which ActiveX controls, plug-ins, and add-ons to install with Internet Explorer. Your assignment is to add at least three ActiveX controls, add-ons, or plug-ins to Internet Explorer. After you add an add-on, plug-in, or ActiveX control, select a Web site that it supports and view that site. Using the Print button, print a copy of the three sites you visit that represent files supported by the new add-ons, ActiveX controls, or plug-ins.

KEY POINTS

- Before you can use all the features and power of Internet Explorer, you need to be able to expand its capabilities.
- One of the key benefits of Internet Explorer is the ability to add new features to your copy of this software with add-ons, plug-ins, and a special set of tools collectively known as ActiveX.
- One of the most exciting features of the World Wide Web is the flexibility it has for incorporating new features.
- New ways of presenting digital information are constantly being developed.
- You can use Internet Explorer to process live audio, full motion video, and a host of other multimedia applications.
- Internet Explorer is not limited to accessing only HTML documents and the links that are provided in these documents. You can also link to other types of files.
- File extensions identify document types on the World Wide Web.
- Internet Explorer supports a wide range of files. However, some file types are not directly supported by Internet Explorer.
- You can download a specific plug-in, install it within Internet Explorer, and then use Internet Explorer to access and use the files supported by the plug-in.
- Installing and using plug-ins begins by locating and downloading them.
- After you download a file, the next step is to install it within Internet Explorer. Most plug-ins have a simple installation procedure.
- Add-ons are very similar to plug-ins. They both expand the functionality of Internet Explorer. However, add-ons tend to operate more like programs within Internet Explorer.
- For most users, the distinction between a plug-in and an add-on is not very important.
- In most cases, using an add-on with Internet Explorer is transparent to the user. In other words, the add-on provides access to specific types of Web files, but you do not realize that it is operating.
- Microsoft's Component Download link analyzes your copy of Internet Explorer and tells you which add-ons are included and which are not.
- ActiveX is a series of mini-applications that operate inside Internet Explorer. These applications allow you to access even more specialized Web files.
- You can download ActiveX controls from a wide range of sources. Many of these are listed in the ActiveX link on *Learning Online*.

KEY TERMS AND COMMANDS

ActiveX
add-ons
extension
external viewer
file types
MPEG
MPEG-2
plug-ins
Shockwave
transparent
Virtual Reality Model Language (VRML)

STUDY QUESTIONS

1. Explain the difference between add-ons and plug-ins.
2. Describe the function of an external viewer.
3. What does it mean when something is *transparent* to the user?
4. Describe the process for downloading add-ons and plug-ins.
5. List three popular add-ons or plug-ins.
6. Why do Web browsers need add-ons and plug-ins?
7. What type of add-on or plug-in would you use to display and control three-dimensional images?
8. Describe the importance or significance of ActiveX.
9. What are the benefits of an MPEG viewer?
10. What is an audio viewer?

PRACTICE TEST

1. The file name and the name of the Web server are known as the
   a. HTTP c. MIME
   b. URL d. VRML
2. With MPEG-2 controls you can view and read Adobe Acrobat–formatted files.
   a. True b. False
3. The process of obtaining and installing a plug-in is much the same as obtaining and installing a helper app.
   a. True b. False
4. Which of the following is among the most popular graphics file formats on the Web?
   a. .gif c. .fif
   b. .pif d. .jig
5. What type of plug-ins and add-ons are needed to bring the world of motion to Internet Explorer?
   a. Video c. Graphics
   b. Audio d. Multivideo
6. Which of the following is an advancement in the compression of video data?
   a. JPEG c. JPEG-2
   b. BPIG d. MPEG-2
7. What type of plug-in would you use to add virtual three-dimensional space to the Web?
   a. MIME c. HTML
   b. VRML d. HTTP
8. Add-ons are preferred over plug-ins.
   a. True b. False
9. All HTML documents use the .HTML or .HTM extension.
   a. True b. False
10. Some graphics links use which of the following extensions?
    a. .HTM c. .MIM
    b. .HTML d .GIF

FILL-INS

1. All files on the World Wide Web are identified by the file name and the name of ________________.
2. ____ identify document types on the World Wide Web.
3. If a file uses either the ________________ or ________________ extension, you can directly view the file by pointing at the graphics file link.
4. When you use an add-on that is ________________ to the user, the user does not realize that it is operating. (However, the add-on does provide access to specific types of files on the Web.)
5. An ________________________ is a program that displays files that are not internally supported by Internet Explorer.
6. All HTML files or documents use the ____________ or ____________ file name extension.
7. You can use ________________________ documents to display and control three-dimensional images.
8. For those files not internally supported by Internet Explorer, you must install a ________________ to use the file.
9. With ActiveX controls you can view and read ____ - formatted files.
10. ____ files add animation to a Web page.

PROJECTS

1. Use *Learning Online* to download a new audio, graphics, and video add-on or plug-in to the computer you are using. After downloading, install the add-on or plug-in on your computer. (You may have to obtain permission from your instructor before installing the application.) Use a sheet of paper to record all the steps you used to download and install each of these add-ons or plug-ins.
2. If Shockwave is not installed on your computer, obtain permission to download and install it. After installation, prepare a presentation of a Web site containing animation, video, and audio for the rest of the class. Be sure to examine several Web sites and select a site that demonstrates the strengths of Shockwave.
3. Now that you have downloaded and installed Shockwave, download and install VRML. Visit several sites that use 3-D Web pages or objects. Create a log of the 3-D sites you visit. You may also want to include information on other multimedia sites you would like to visit.

INTERNET AT WORK

Edith has heard that you can use Internet Explorer to listen to music, hear people give speeches or make announcements, display animation, and view different types of files. She wants you to demonstrate these features for her office staff. Your job, should you decide to accept it, is to prepare a presentation of multimedia Web sites. First show sites that use music. Next demonstrate several Web sites that incorporate speech. Perhaps you can show the staff how speech can be incorporated in a site in different ways. Don't forget to include Web sites that employ different graphics as well as video. Good Luck.

6 Outlook Express

OUTCOMES

When you complete this chapter you will be able to . . .

- Define e-mail.
- Identify the structure of e-mail.
- Use an e-mail address.
- Identify various types of e-mail software.
- Use Outlook Express.
- Locate various e-mail addresses.
- Use address books.
- Use mailing lists.
- Identify e-mail security techniques.

WHAT IS E-MAIL?

Electronic mail (**e-mail**) is a method of composing, editing, sending, and receiving messages (i.e., mail) electronically. It is not much different from writing a letter and using the post office to mail it. E-mail is just faster and easier.

E-mail was one of the first applications on the Internet. In fact, e-mail remains one of the primary reasons that so many people use the Internet. The Internet gained wide acceptance, in large part, because it provided an easy system for sending messages from one computer to another.

E-mail systems consist of two programs—user agents and mail delivery systems. You interact with a **user agent**, also known as an **e-mail client**, as a means of generating, sending, and receiving mail. The mail **delivery system**, or **mail server**, routes your mail to its intended destination. With the Internet, mail delivery within the system is controlled by a program called **Simple Mail Transport Protocol (SMTP)**. In most cases you will never need to be concerned with SMTP (although it is a good idea to know that it exists). Most users interact with electronic mail through the e-mail client. Therefore, the term *e-mail* usually refers to the e-mail client.

Outlook Express is the user agent for Internet Explorer. You activate this user agent by selecting the Mail command from the Go menu. Outlook Express operates as an add-on to Internet Explorer. When you launch Outlook Express, it opens in a separate window. This distinct window is useful because it allows you to work on your e-mail while you are browsing the Web.

E-MAIL SOFTWARE

To use e-mail you need a user agent, or in more common terms, e-mail software. As with many other features of the Internet, various e-mail software products are available. One of the easiest e-mail programs to use is Outlook Express. Several other excellent e-mail programs offered independently from Internet Explorer are Pegasus, E-Mail Connection, Eudora, Mail-Check, and Ladybird, to name just a few. These e-mail programs allow you to access your e-mail if your provider (or college or university) supports these types of mail software. You can use Outlook Express as long as your provider supports this software with POP3 (an e-mail routing system), you set up Internet Explorer to use Outlook Express as your user agent, and you set up Outlook Express to access your e-mail account.

Tips, Tricks, and Ideas 6-1

Most E-Mail Software Are Similar

Regardless of whether you use Outlook Express or another e-mail package to access, read, and send e-mail, the process is somewhat similar. Keep in mind that the command structure of individual software packages can vary. Here you will learn Outlook Express. However, you may end up using another e-mail program, possibly a program that you download through *Learning Online* and Internet Software.

SETTING UP OUTLOOK EXPRESS

Before you can use Outlook Express, you need three things. First, you must have a valid e-mail address. Second, you must have the e-mail address for those to whom you want to send messages. Finally, you must set up Outlook Express to access your e-mail account. The process of setting up Outlook Express begins by selecting the **Internet Options** command from the View menu and then selecting the Programs tab. To use Outlook Express as your user agent, Outlook Express must appear next to Mail.

After you have instructed Internet Explorer to use Outlook Express for e-mail, you must tell Outlook Express where to look for your e-mail. The easiest way to configure Outlook Express is to use the configuration wizard that appears the first time Outlook Express is loaded. However, in some cases, especially in computer labs, you may need to set the configuration manually.

To set the configuration, you must access the Accounts command from the Tools menu. From this dialog box, you need to select the Mail tab and then select Properties. Properties allows you to identify the name and location for your e-mail account. The name of your provider should be entered in the General tab. You then must select the Servers tab to identify the SMTP or Outgoing Mail Server and the Post Office Protocol (POP) or Incoming Mail Server. This information is required, and you will not be able to send or receive e-mail without these settings (Image 6-1).

Tips, Tricks, and Ideas 6-2

Computer Lab E-Mail

If you plan to use Outlook Express in a computer laboratory, there may be some special requirements. If necessary, check with your instructor for setup instructions or the procedures for using Outlook Express in your computer lab.

Tips, Tricks, and Ideas 6-3

Multiple Providers

When you select the Accounts command from the Tools menu in Outlook Express, you have the option of adding a new Internet account. Select this option if the account you want to use is different from the one displayed. If your account is the same as the display, select the Properties button to set all of your account information.

Image 6-1

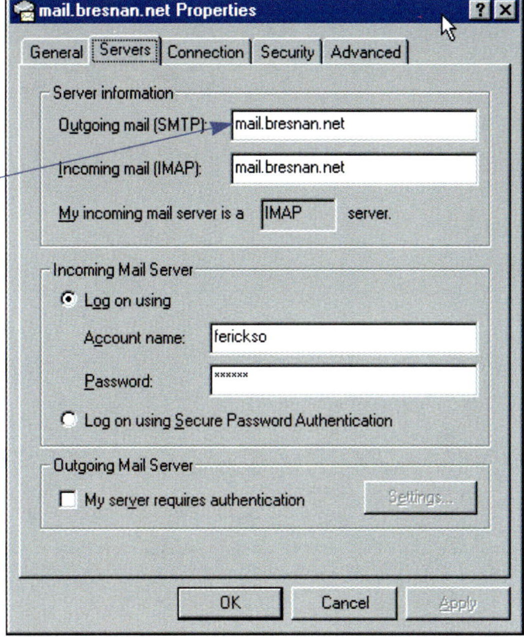

Table 6-1
Your SMTP and the POP Internet addresses and your user name

SMTP (Outgoing Mail Server) ______________________
POP (Incoming Mail Server) ______________________
POP User Name ______________________

Tips, Tricks, and Ideas 6-4

Servers

Most Internet providers furnish you with the SMTP and POP servers' Internet addresses. The provider should also tell you the requirements for storing messages that have been read. Be sure to follow the provider's guidelines for settings in Outlook Express.

When you are setting the properties for your e-mail connection, you need to provide information about yourself in the General tab. The User Information section allows you to personalize outgoing messages. In this tab you should include your name, organization, and e-mail address. The **reply to address** is normally your e-mail address and is where people who respond to your e-mail will direct messages. However, you can insert a reply to address that is different from your sending address if you want to receive replies at another address.

Netiquette 6-1

Check Mail Frequently

When you are using a university e-mail account, it is especially important for you to check your e-mail frequently. Storage space is limited, and you should do your part to keep space available for others. Delete messages that you no longer need or want.

ACTIVITY

1. Launch Internet Explorer.
2. Select Internet Options from the View menu. Notice the various categories.
3. Click on the Programs tab.
4. Select Outlook Express next to Mail (Image 6-2).

Image 6-2

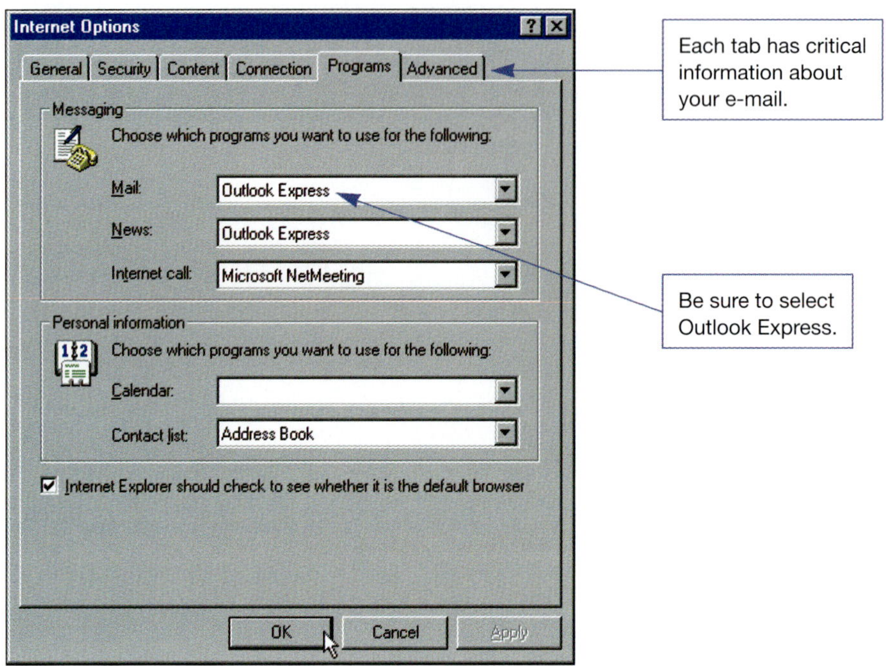

5. Click on OK.
6. Select Mail from the Go menu in Internet Explorer. Notice that Outlook Express appears in a new window (Image 6-3).

Image 6-3

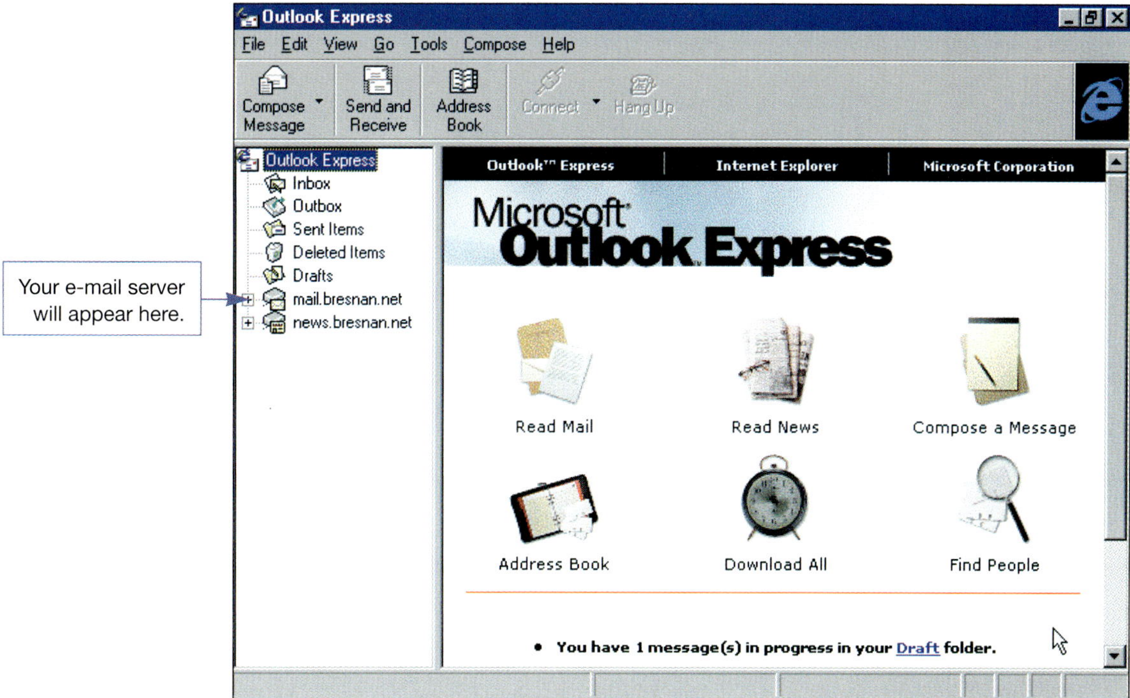

7. From Outlook Express select the Accounts command from the Tools menu.
   Notice the Internet Accounts dialog box (Image 6-4).
8. Select the Mail tab (Image 6-4).
   The name that your provider, or connection to the Internet, supplies you for connecting to an e-mail server appears (Image 6-4). If this name is not the server you are using for e-mail, check with your instructor.

Image 6-4

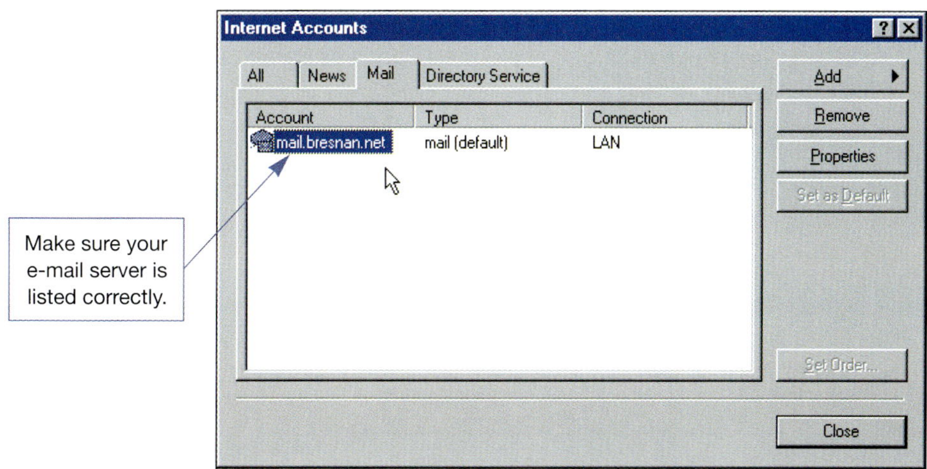

9. Click on the Properties button.
   Notice the Properties for your provider (Image 6-5).
10. Select the Servers tab (Image 6-5).
11. Either enter or make sure that the SMTP and POP servers are identified and correct along with your Account name (Image 6-5).

Image 6-5

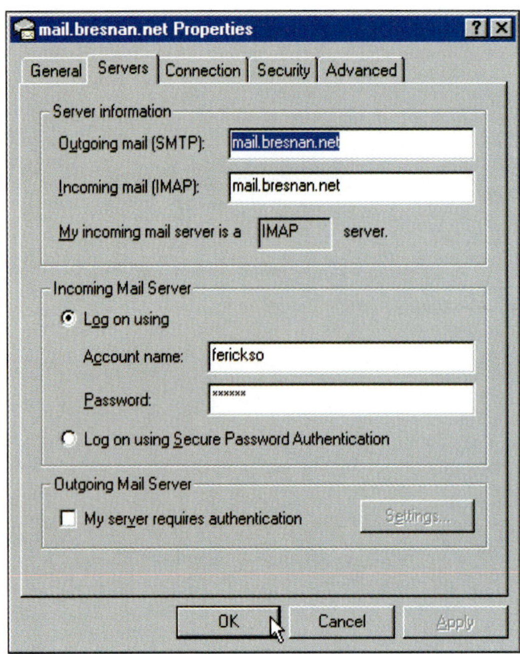

12. Click on the General tab.
    Notice the settings and make sure that your name and e-mail address are included (Image 6-6).

Image 6-6

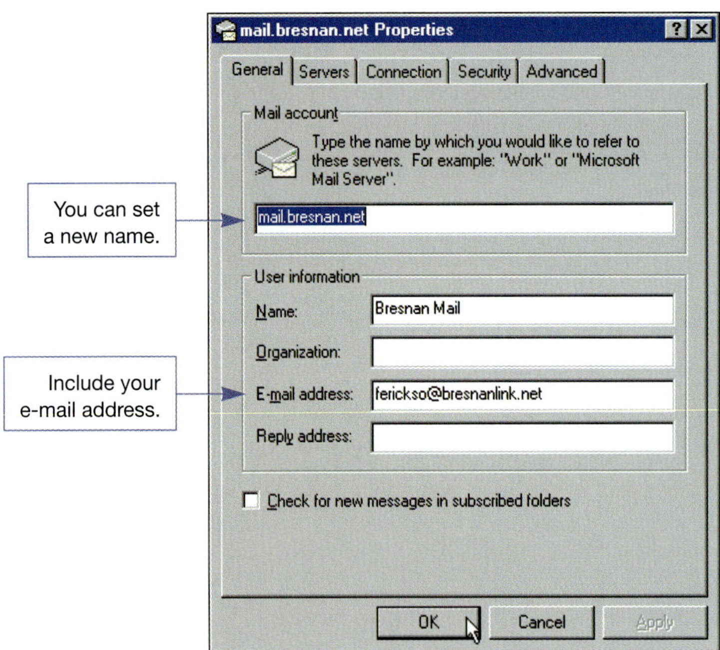

13. Click on OK.
    After you click on OK, the changes in each tab will take effect.
14. Click on Close to leave the Internet Accounts dialog box.

E-MAIL STRUCTURE

Before looking at the specifics of Outlook Express, it is important to understand the structure and process of using e-mail via the Internet. E-mail has two very important components—header lines and mail body. **Header lines** tell the computer where to send the mail (Image 6-7). Typically, there are four header lines; they are To:, Cc:, Bcc:, and Subject:. **To:** is very important because it is where you send e-mail. The To: determines who gets the mail. It must contain the valid address of a user. If you do not include a valid address, the mail cannot be routed. **Cc:** allows you to send a copy of the message to one or more other users. **Bcc:,** or blind carbon copy, allows you to send a copy of the message to someone without the other recipients knowing the copy was sent. To:, Cc:, and Bcc: are called **destination header lines** because they identify where the message is going. Finally, Subject: tells the recipient what the mail is about. The **Subject:** will appear in the recipient's list of mail. Subject: is referred to as an originator header line. The **mail body** is the message you create. Most e-mail systems have a variety of tools that simplify the writing process, including full editing capabilities and spell checking.

Image 6-7

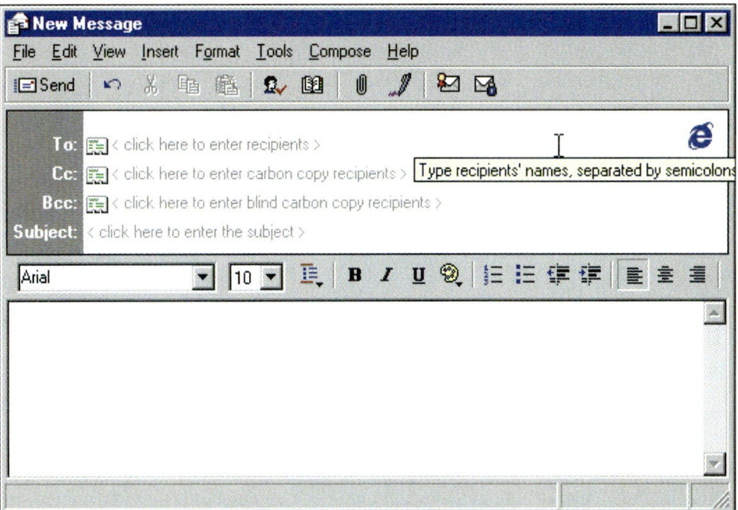

ADDRESSING

The most important element of an e-mail message is the address. If you want to send e-mail to someone, you must know his or her unique Internet address. If you do not address your mail correctly, it cannot be delivered. There is no room for error. If you miss someone's address by even one character, the mail will not be routed through the Internet.

In Chapter 1 we outlined the basic address structure. All e-mail consists of two primary components: the host name and the user name. These names are separated by the at (@) sign. The **host name** is the unique name of the recipient's computer. For example, bentley.unco.edu is a host name. The **user name** is the unique name on the host. For example, javonk is a unique user name on the bentley.unco.edu host. Therefore, the address javonk@bentley.unco.edu identifies one unique user on the Internet.

USING OUTLOOK EXPRESS

To launch Outlook Express you have two choices. One way is to click on the Mail icon located in the toolbar; the other is to select the Mail command from the Go menu. The Mail command provides access to all of Outlook Express, whereas the Mail button allows you to go directly to a specific Mail function. Both options activate Outlook Express, as a separate program. A separate icon will appear on the taskbar.

Tips, Tricks, and Ideas 6-5

Password

If you successfully launch Outlook Express, you may be required to provide your e-mail password. You may store your password within Internet Explorer by entering your password under Incoming Mail Server in the Servers tab of the Properties dialog box. If you are working in a lab, do not use this option. Keep your password private. Remember: Anyone who knows your password can read your mail and can send mail under your name.

When you launch Outlook Express, it is a good idea to check for e-mail messages. You can do so by clicking on the Send and Receive button on the Outlook Express toolbar. If you have mail, the new messages appear in a list that identifies From, To, and Subject. To read a message, click on it once. Then scroll through and read it. Of course, this procedure will work only if Outlook Express has been set up to receive messages.

After you read a message, you need to decide whether to save your message, delete the message, reply to the message, or forward the message. If you do nothing, your e-mail will remain in your list of messages. To reply directly to the person who sent you the message, click on the **Reply to Author** button on the toolbar. Clicking on this button allows you to specify whether you want to reply only to the sender or to all other recipients, including those listed for To: and Cc:, of the e-mail. When you select Reply to Author the same window used to compose a new message appears. In this case, however, the e-mail address of the sender has been entered automatically. With this window, all you need to do is enter a message; then click on the Send button.

Tips, Tricks, and Ideas 6-6

Delete or Save

Do not leave e-mail in your electronic mailbox. If you do, you will find that your e-mail box will become full rather quickly. As soon as you read or respond to a message, either delete it or save it. You can use the Save As command from the File menu to save a message as an independent file or, more commonly, to move the file to a folder other than your inbox.

You can also forward a message to any other person who holds a valid e-mail account by clicking on the **Forward Message** button on the toolbar. This action opens the same window used to create a message. However, in this case the To: line is left blank. You must enter the valid e-mail address of the person to whom you wish to forward the message.

Tips, Tricks, and Ideas 6-7

Print

You can use the Print button to print a copy of a message. When you select Print, the standard Print dialog box for Windows appears. Make certain the correct printer is selected and then click on the OK button.

Whether you reply to or forward a message, you should decide whether you want to save or delete the original e-mail you received. New users have a tendency to save all mail. However, it is easy to get buried in old e-mail. Therefore, you should save your incoming e-mail only if you really need to access the message again. Otherwise, it is a good idea to delete messages after you reply, forward, or read them.

To delete an e-mail message, read the message and then click on the **Delete** button on the toolbar. When you select Delete, you will be reminded that this option permanently deletes the message. Therefore, if you have any reason to save the message, move it to a folder away from your Inbox folder.

Netiquette 6-2

Spamming

It is unlawful to use a computer, and e-mail, to send an unsolicited advertisement. Usually, the fine for such junk mail is $500.00. Sending junk mail on the Internet is called *spamming.*

One advantage of using Outlook Express is the ability to organize your messages. Outlook Express has several internal windows: one for folders, one listing the messages within a folder, and, of course, one that displays a message. The Folders window enables you to organize your e-mail messages into various folders. In fact, whenever you receive an e-mail message, it goes into your Inbox folder. Saving e-mail is accomplished by putting messages into other folders. **Folders** allow you to store related messages in one location. In fact, **Deleted Items** is a folder that contains e-mail you wish to remove. You can create custom folders by selecting Folders and then selecting the **New Folder** command from the File menu. Selecting the New Folder command prompts you to enter a new folder name. To put e-mail in a folder, simply read your e-mail message and then drag the message into the folder of your choice.

ACTIVITY

1. Make sure that you are connected to the Internet and that Internet Explorer is up and successfully running.
2. From the Go menu of Internet Explorer, select Mail.
   Notice that Outlook Express launches (Image 6-8).
3. Select your mail server and then click on the Send and Receive button on the toolbar.
   Notice that all waiting messages are loaded and added to the list of messages.

Image 6-8

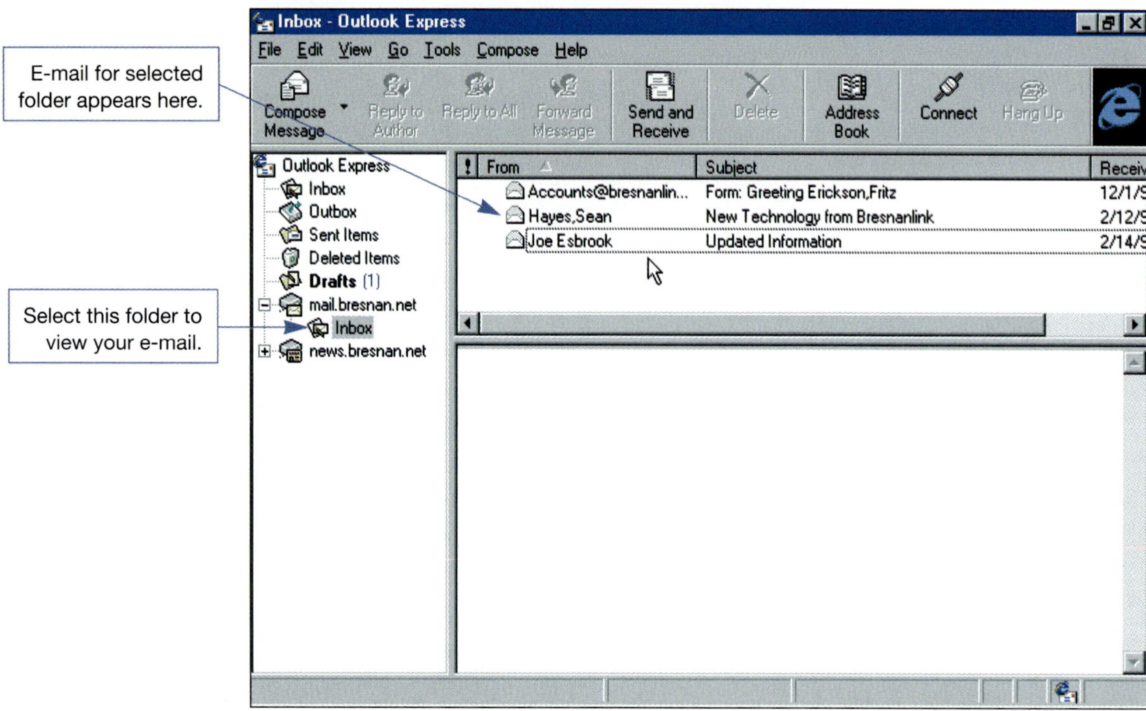

4. If any messages appear in your list of messages, click once on a message.
   The message appears at the message window.
5. Select Folder and then select New Folder from the File menu.
   A dialog box asks for the new folder name (Image 6-9).
6. Type Stuff for the new folder name (Image 6-9).

Image 6-9

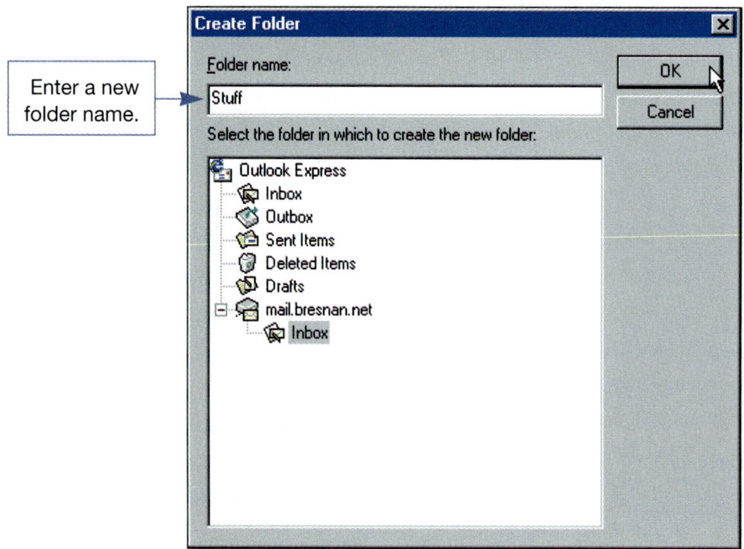

7. Click on OK.
   The new Stuff folder now appears in the list of folders (Image 6-10).

Image 6-10

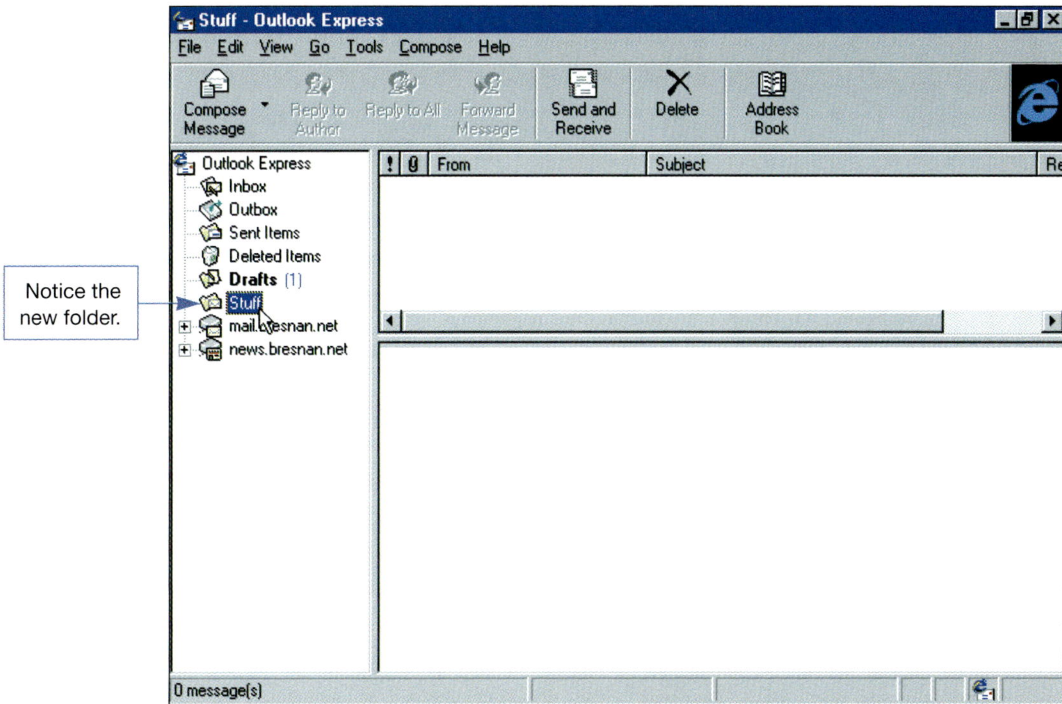

CREATING AND SENDING MESSAGES

Of course, receiving messages is only half the process of using e-mail. You also need to be able to create and send messages. The Compose Message, Reply to Author, Reply to All, and Forward Message buttons enable you to create a new message. Forward Message is a new message where the content of the message is automatically generated. With Reply to Author or Reply to All, the name of the recipient is automatically included. To create a completely new message, you use the Create Message button. In any of these situations, a message creation window appears.

The New Message window has two parts: a header and a body. In the header, next to To:, you must enter the valid e-mail address for the person to whom you want to send mail. This entry must be a full and complete e-mail address. You can then decide if you want to send a copy of the same message to anyone else; if you do, enter a valid e-mail address next to Cc:. After you have established to whom you are going to send a message, you should include a statement in the Subject: line. This information is important because it tells the recipient why you are sending the message.

After you establish the header, the next step is to create your message. With Outlook Express, creating an e-mail message is much like using a word processor. You can insert and delete text, check spelling, modify the e-mail, and perform a variety of e-mail creation tasks. When the

Tips, Tricks, and Ideas 6-8

Additional Features

Outlook Express has several useful features for controlling e-mail. Because this book cannot cover all the features of Outlook Express, it is up to you to experiment with this software.

Tips, Tricks, and Ideas 6-9

Was Your E-Mail Sent?

New users often ask, "Did my message go out?" The assumption is always yes. If your mail was not sent, you will receive a notice from your provider explaining the problem. Most failures are caused by an incorrect, or inaccurate, e-mail address. Every e-mail message you want to send must contain a valid e-mail address.

message meets your satisfaction, click on the Send button to send the e-mail to the addresses listed next to To:, Cc:, and Bcc:. After you send the mail, the New Message window terminates.

ACTIVITY

1. Click on the Compose Message button on the toolbar.
   The New Message window appears.
2. Type in the e-mail address for anyone in your class, or for anyone else you know who has a valid e-mail address, next to To: (Image 6-11).
3. Next to Subject:, type Hi (Image 6-11).

Image 6-11

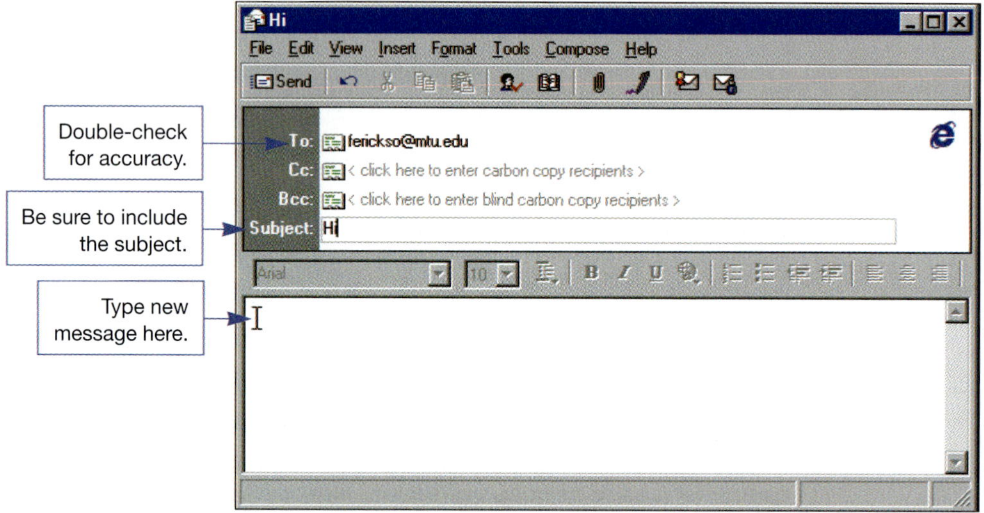

4. Click in the message box and type a message of your choice.
5. After you have completed your message, click on the Send button. In a moment your e-mail will be routed.
6. In the Outlook Express window, click once on any message.
7. After you read the message, click on the message title once with the right mouse button. This action produces a menu of message options. Click on Move To.
   Notice the list of all folders that appears (Image 6-12).

Image 6-12

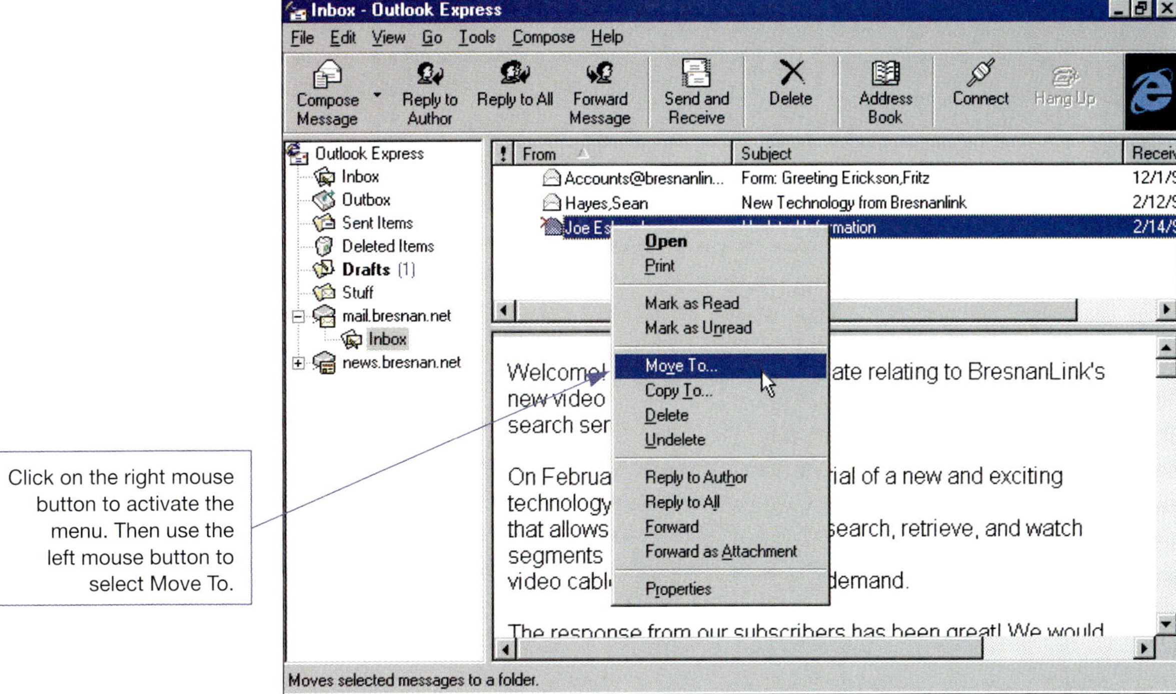

Select your Stuff folder. This step saves your message in the Stuff folder.

8. Click once on the Stuff folder.
   Notice that only messages in the Stuff folder appear.
9. Return to your Inbox. Click on any message in this folder and then click on the Delete button.
   A deletion mark (X) appears next to the message title (Image 6-13).

Image 6-13

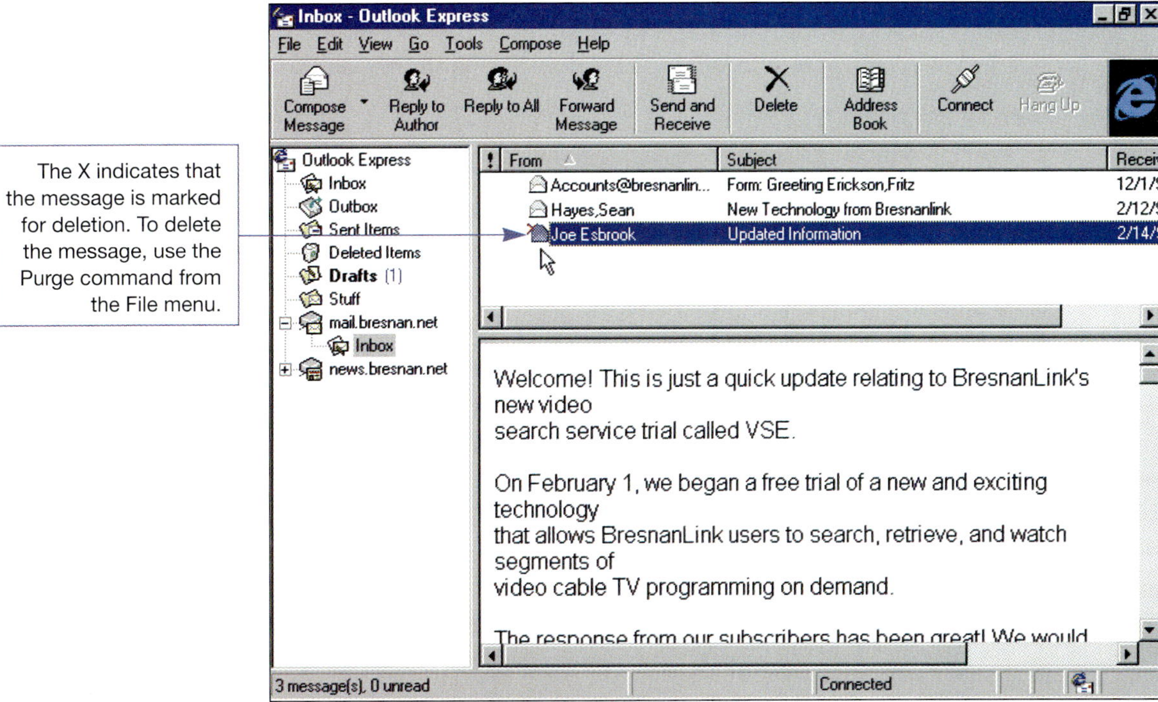

10. Select Purge Deleted Messages from the Edit menu.
    Notice that all messages marked as deleted are removed.
11. Delete all messages from the Stuff folder by clicking once on the Stuff folder and then pressing the Delete key.
12. If Outlook Express asks whether to remove the folder, click on Yes.

EXERCISE 6-1

It is very important to practice sending and receiving e-mail before you start to use e-mail as a regular communication tool. Send an e-mail message to any three individuals in your class. This exercise will help ensure that everyone has some e-mail to work with and that you know how to send e-mail messages in Internet Explorer.

ATTACHING FILES

One of the most useful features of e-mail is the ability to attach files to an e-mail message that you send. For example, if you want to send a formatted word processing file to a friend, you can attach the file to an e-mail message. When your friend receives the e-mail, he or she also receives a copy of the attached file.

To attach a file you need to know the name of the file and where it is located on your computer. Click on the File Attachment command from the Insert menu. The Insert Attachment dialog box allows you to specify which file to attach. When you locate the file, click once on the file and then click on the Attach button. The file will appear at the bottom of the New Message window in the list of attachments.

When you receive a message that contains an attached file, the file will appear as an icon at the bottom of the message as a link. Double-click on the icon to access the attached file. Then decide whether to open the file or to save it.

Tips, Tricks, and Ideas 6-10

Insert Text from File

Instead of attaching a file, Outlook Express allows you to insert the text of a file into a message. With this technique you can create all or part of a message with your word processor and then place it directly into a message. To use this feature you must save your word processing files as text or ASCII files.

Netiquette 6-3

Others May Read Your Mail

Do not assume that your e-mail is private. Many other people may be able to read your mail. Always assume that your mail can be read by everyone, and write your messages accordingly.

Netiquette 6-4

Download Files

Download files to a disk as soon as you receive them. Do not leave them on the computer where other users have access to them.

Tips, Tricks, and Ideas 6-11

Signature File

The **signature file** is a file that appears at the end of all e-mail messages you send. Quite often signature files contain your name, address, phone numbers, position, or anything about you that you want to appear at the end of each and every e-mail you send. You are welcome to create your own signature file, or as many people do, simply ignore this option.

ACTIVITY

1. Click on the Compose Message button in Outlook Express.
   Notice that the New Message window appears.
2. Enter your e-mail address next to To: and File Attachment Test next to Subject.
3. Type the following message:
   This is a test message.
4. From the Insert menu, select the File Attachment command.
   Notice the dialog box (Image 6-14).

Image 6-14

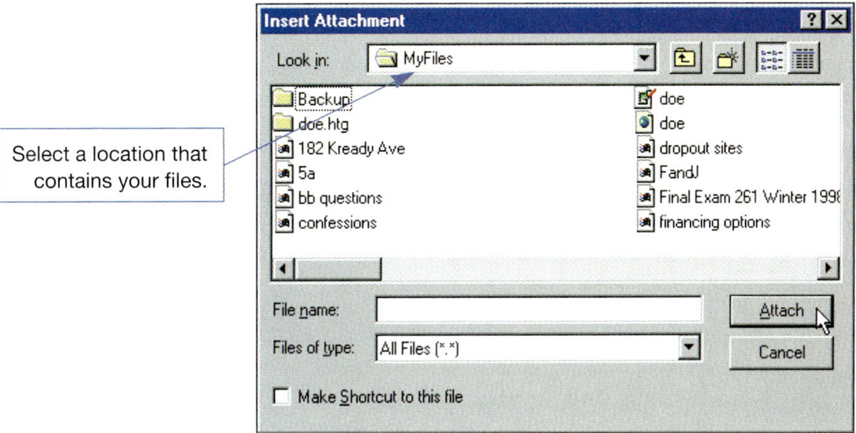

5. Select a word processing file or other file you have on disk to attach to a message and then click on the Attach button.
   The file now appears in the list of attachments (Image 6-15).

Image 6-15

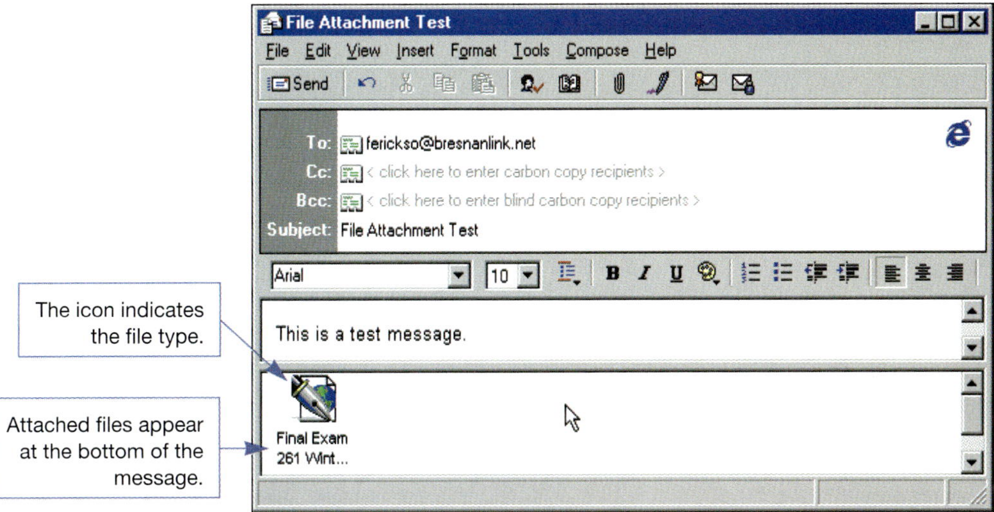

6. Click on the Send button to send yourself this message.
   Don't forget to click on the Send and Receive button in Outlook Express to send the message.
7. Wait a few minutes and then click on the Send and Receive button again.
   You should have received the test message with the attached file (Image 6-16).

Image 6-16

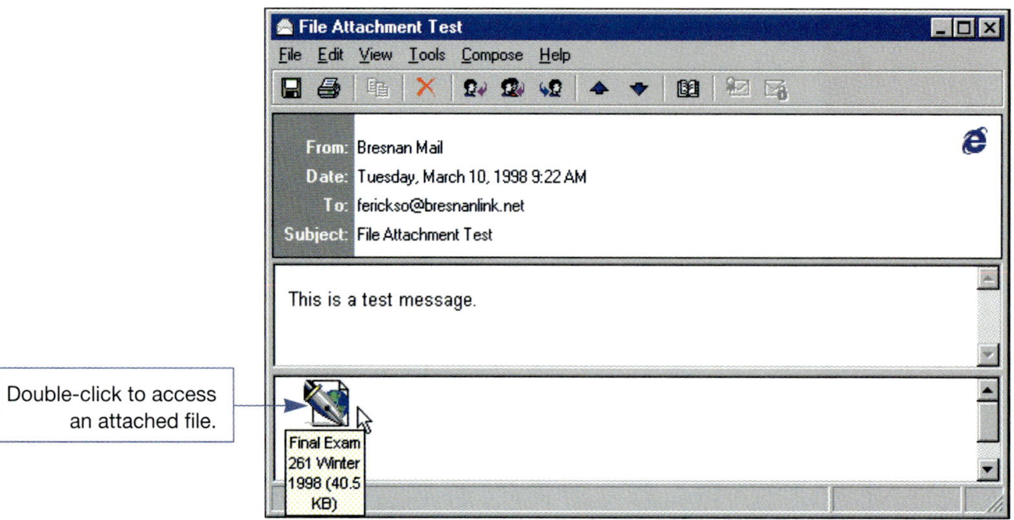

8. Double-click on the attached file link.
   Notice you have the option of opening or saving the attached file (Image 6-17).

Image 6-17

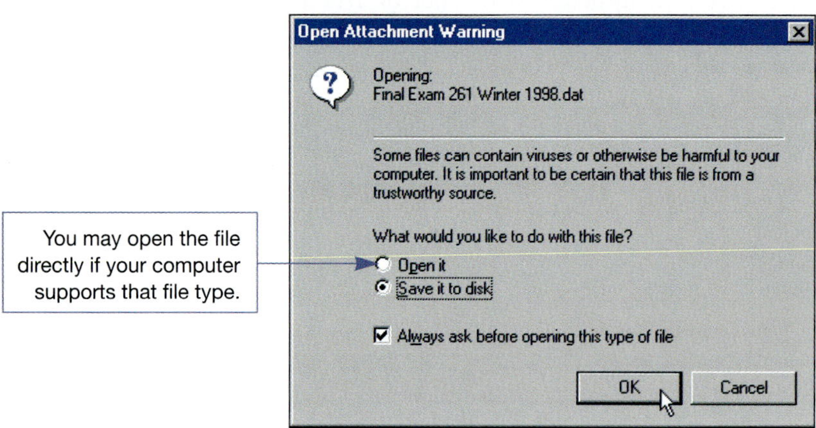

9. Save the file on a disk.

EXERCISE 6-2

It takes a bit of practice to send and receive attached files. Send one attached file to someone else with a message to return the file to you. When the file is returned, save it on a disk.

LOCATING ADDRESSES

The best way to get someone's address is to ask, just as you would ask someone for his or her postal address. However, what if you need someone's address and do not have the time or opportunity to ask directly? Fortunately, there are ways to find user addresses.

If someone sends you e-mail, it will include the sender's address. Therefore, it is a good idea, when you receive mail, to keep a log of addresses for those people who send you mail. Outlook Express gives you the option of creating an address book automatically. This feature is discussed in the next section. Even if you use the address book, it is a good idea to keep a written copy for your most important e-mail addresses.

In addition, various services can help you locate individual e-mail addresses. Whether you are able to locate the e-mail address of a long-lost friend or colleague depends on whether that person, or that person's organization (provider), wants to make the e-mail address public. Many people are very protective of their e-mail address.

One of the most popular tools for searching for e-mail addresses is the white pages. **White pages** are listings of e-mail addresses.

The *Learning Online* Web site includes several white pages for your use. One of the more popular services is called White NetPages; if you want to add your name and e-mail address to this database, anyone searching for you through this service will find the information you provide.

You can search for individuals on most white pages in much the same way. You enter the name of the individual, plus any additional supporting information (location, etc.), and then submit a search. All names matching the criteria you enter will be returned.

The **WHOIS** database was one of the first systems designed to keep a directory of user addresses. It was originally designed for system administrators but was expanded to include other Internet users. No single WHOIS database contains the names of all Internet users. Rather, hundreds of WHOIS databases have been developed by various systems to include directories of their users.

Tips, Tricks, and Ideas 6-12

Do You Really Want To?

Most white pages exist because users voluntarily submit their e-mail address. However, you need to ask yourself whether you want to make your address public. If you do, it is unlikely, but possible, that you could receive prank, threatening, and phony e-mail. If you post your e-mail account with a provider, be extra cautious when replying to e-mail.

Netiquette 6-5

Chain Letters

Do not use e-mail to send chain letters over the Internet. If you are caught sending chain letters, you may lose your Internet privileges.

> **Tips, Tricks, and Ideas 6-13**
>
> ***Find People***
>
> The Find People command in the Edit menu is a very useful tool for locating e-mail addresses. By selecting this command, you may enter a host of information about who you are looking for and specify the location for your search.

If you cannot locate someone by using white pages or through WHOIS, another method is to contact the administrator of a specific computer system. Because all system administrators are listed (or should be) in WHOIS, sending an e-mail message asking for an address might produce the information you want. Many system administrators will not directly provide the address of a user. However, most will forward your request to the user, who may then send you his or her address.

Another good source of addresses is the College Email Addresses listing in the group soc.college. You can get there with Usenet (discussed in Chapter 7).

If you still have trouble locating a specific address, there are some other techniques that may work. For example, if you know the host name, you might be able to guess the user name. Host names are often initials followed by the domain name. mtu.edu is the host name for Michigan Technological University. Many user names follow a convention in which the first initial and last name are used for the user name (up to eight characters). For example, ferickso stands for Fritz Erickson. Because erickson is more that eight characters, the user name is truncated to ferickso. Some systems just use the last name.

ACTIVITY

1. Activate Internet Explorer and go to *Learning Online.*
2. Select Web Search Tools. Then scroll down and select The White Pages link (Image 6-18).

Image 6-18

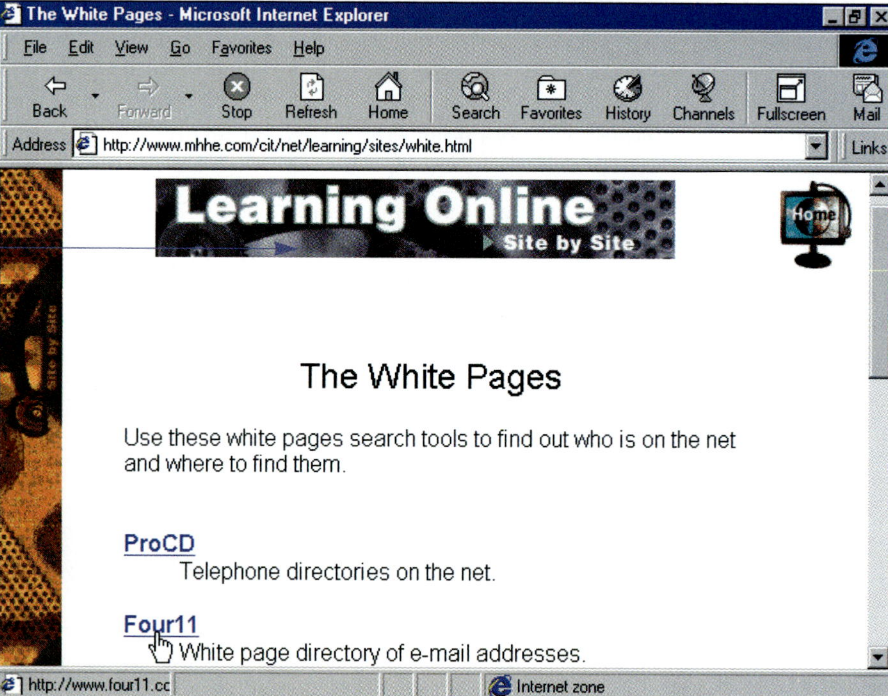

The White Pages helps you locate e-mail users.

3. Select Four11 (Image 6-19).
4. Type the last name of someone you want to search for next to Last Name (Image 6-19).

Image 6-19

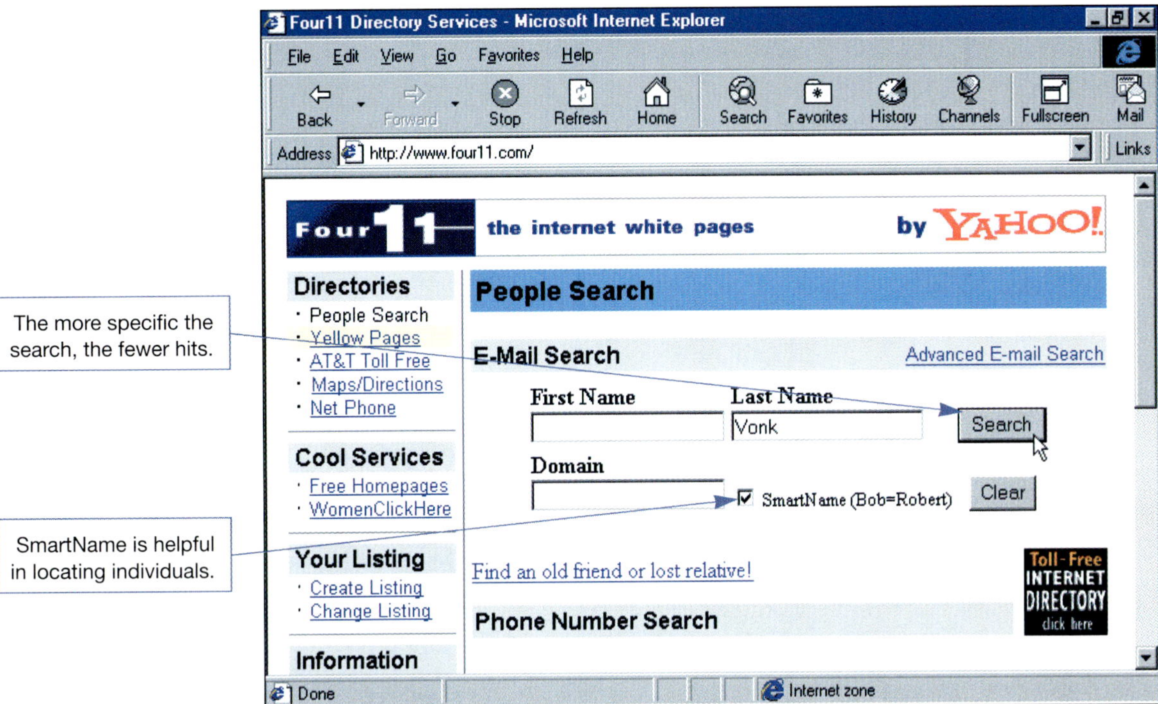

5. Click on Search.
   A list of individuals appears. If there are too many in the list, a sample will appear. In this case return and enter a first name and search again.
6. Take a few minutes and try some of the other white pages links.

EXERCISE 6-3

Locating e-mail addresses can take a bit of creativity. First try the white pages. If you do not succeed, try searching for white pages through any of the search tools such as YAHOO!, Excite, and the WebCrawler. As you locate various e-mail addresses, write them in a notebook. It is a good idea to keep a notebook of e-mail addresses much as you would keep a personal phone book.

ADDRESS BOOK

One of the most useful features of Outlook Express is the address book. With an **address book** you can create an electronic list of e-mail addresses much as you would a personal address book. One advantage of an address book is that it is much easier to remember a short name like Bob than a long e-mail address like bob.rakikfl@marckel.univwest.edu. Another reason for using an address book is speed. It is much faster to type "Bob" in the header than to type Bob's full address. Finally, the short-name method is more reliable and accurate.

> ### Tips, Tricks, and Ideas 6-14
> ***Public Address Books***
> If you are using a computer lab to access and use e-mail, it may be possible for you to create and use an address book. However, if you create an address book, depending on the software, your address book may be available for others to use. For example, Outlook Express stores the address book as a local file. Therefore, if you store names in an address book, it may remain on the hard disk of the computer you are using. You may not want to leave your personal address book in such a public place.

In Outlook Express the process of creating an address book starts when you click the Address Book button. The Address Book window is where you can add names to your address book by using the New Contact command from the File menu or toolbar. New Contact produces the Properties dialog box. In this dialog box you enter the name of the person, e-mail address, and nickname. You can also include other information about the individual by using the various tabs. Click on OK to add an individual to the address book.

Another way of adding individuals to your address book is to use the **Add to Address Book** command from the Tools menu. Add to Address Book appears in the Form window when you double-click on a message. Normally, you select Sender when choosing Add to Address Book. This option causes the Properties dialog box to appear with many of the information boxes filled. All you need do is verify and modify the information, provide a Nickname:, and then click on OK. The entry for Nickname: should not be used for any other individual within your address book.

ACTIVITY

1. Make sure that you are connected and that Internet Explorer is running.
2. Launch Outlook Express.
   If you have any new mail, take a few minutes to read it; then reply, forward, and/or delete the message.
3. Select the Address Book button.
   Notice the Address Book window (Image 6-20).

Image 6-20

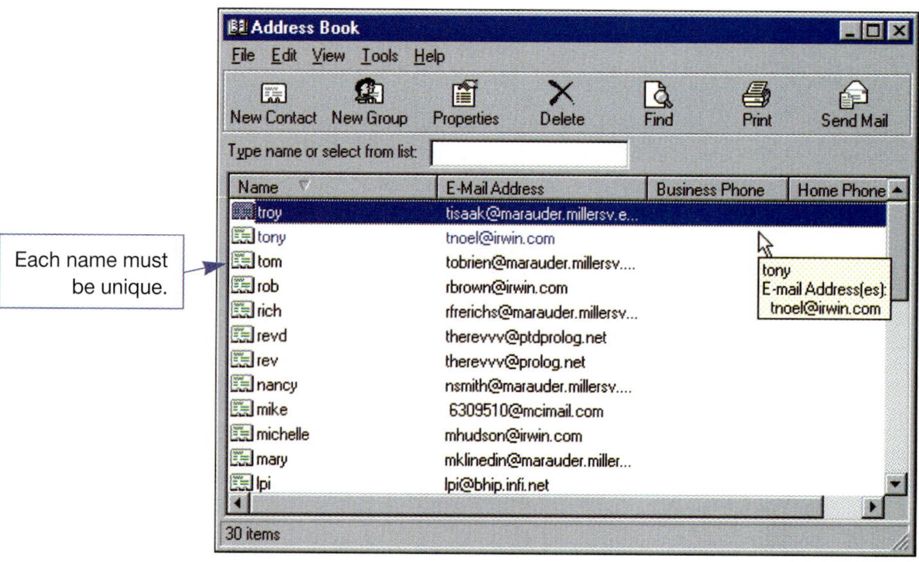

4. Select New Contact from the toolbar.
   The Properties dialog box appears (Image 6-21).
5. Fill in the information for any user you want (Image 6-21).

Image 6-21

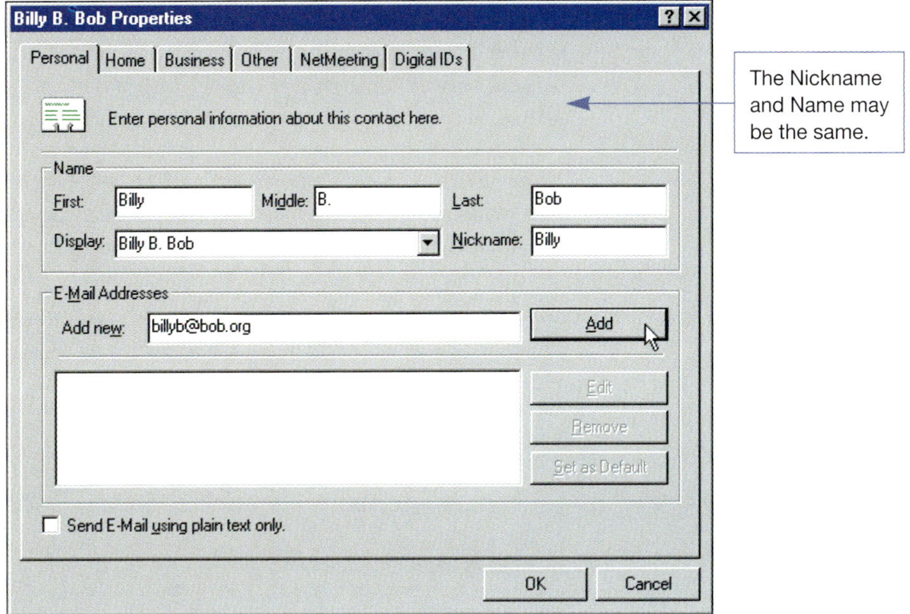

6. Click on OK.
   The name is added to your address book.
7. Repeat this process and add the names of any users you want to include in your address book.
8. Double-click to open any e-mail message.
9. Select the Add to Address Book command from the Tools menu and then select Sender.
   The Address Book dialog box appears.
10. Verify and modify any information and type in a Nickname:, then click on OK.
    Notice the new e-mail address in the address book.

EXERCISE 6-4

Keeping your address book in Outlook Express is very useful. However, there is a danger. If the file is lost or deleted, you can lose valuable information. Therefore, it is a good idea to keep a written address book as a backup. In addition, your personal address book is just that—personal. Make sure you keep your book secure.

MAILING LISTS

Mailing lists or groups provide a very easy method for sending messages to more than one Internet user. With mailing lists you can send messages to hundreds of users automatically by entering the mailing list name instead of the address of a single user. It is common to create several different mailing lists for various purposes. For example, you could create a mailing list of clients, another of friends, another of people interested in movies, another for family members, and so on. The exact ways in which you can use and create mailing lists or groups depend on your e-mail software.

In Outlook Express the process of creating a mailing list is very similar to adding any new user to the Address Book file. You begin by selecting the Address Book. When the Address Book window opens, select New Group from the File menu or toolbar. When the Properties dialog box opens, enter a group name. The next step is to add existing e-mail addresses in the address book to the group. Click on the Select Members button and then double-click on any name to add it to the Members: list. After all the names are added, click on OK to create the group. Any time you want to send the same e-mail to everyone on the mailing list, enter the group name next to To: in the header of a message.

ACTIVITY

1. Select Address Book from the toolbar.
2. Select New Group.
   The Properties dialog box opens (Image 6-22).
3. For Group Name:, type class (Image 6-22).

Image 6-22

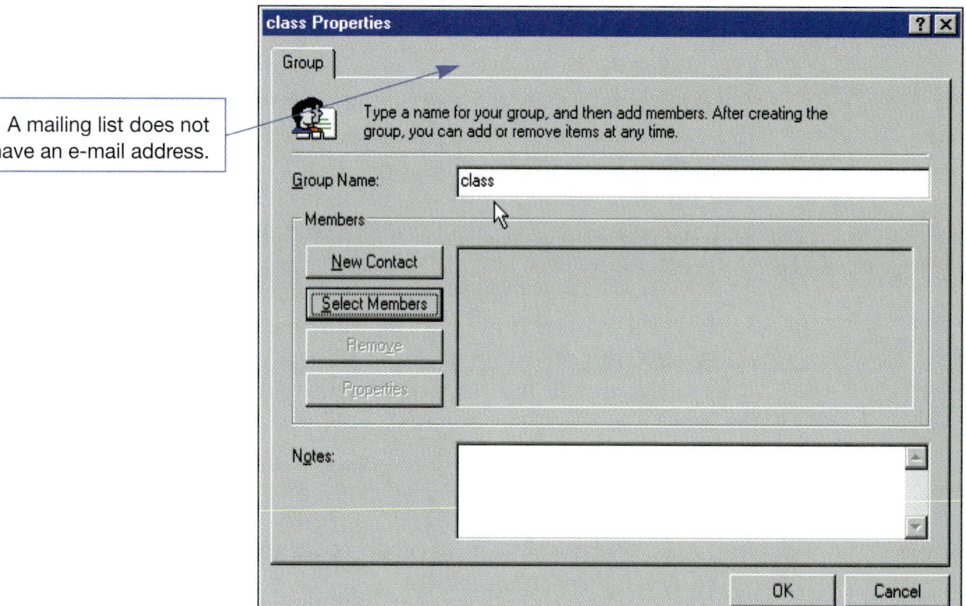

4. Click on Select Members.
   The Select Group Members dialog box opens (Image 6-23).
5. Double-click on any name.
   The name is added to Members (Image 6-23).

Image 6-23

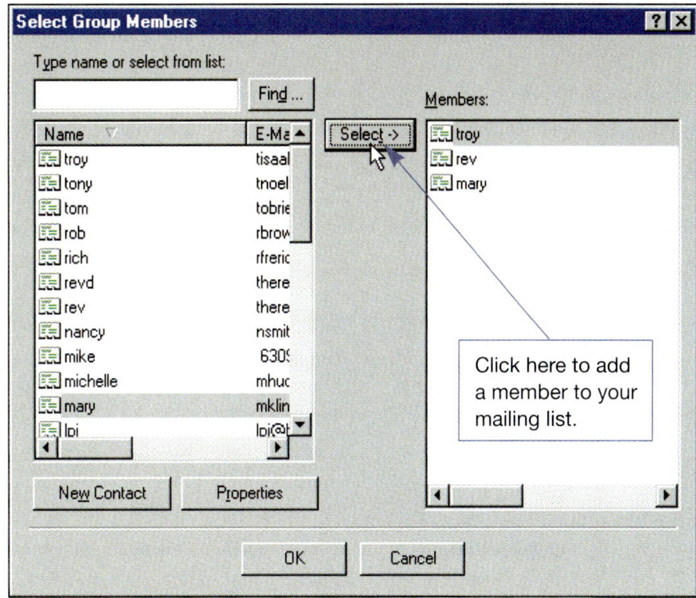

6. Continue this process to add as many names to the class folder as you desire.
7. Close the Address Book window.
8. Select Compose Message from Outlook Express.
9. Enter class for To:.
   The message will be sent to the mailing list or group.

EXERCISE 6-5

Mailing lists or groups can be one of the most effective tools in e-mail. Create three separate mailing lists—one for your friends, one for family members, and one of your choice. It is up to you to decide whom to include in your various mailing lists. It is also up to you to decide whether you want to send a message to everyone on your mailing list.

E-MAIL SECURITY

This message bears repeating: It is unlikely that your mail will be read by an unintended user; however, never assume that your mail is private. Delivery systems used to route your mail have human operators who have access to your mail. In most cases no one will ever care what you send, but your mail can be monitored. Be especially careful with company e-mail.

E-mail can also be forged. Because delivery systems are not designed to verify the contents of header lines, it is possible for someone to send mail to you using a false name. It is not all that difficult for a sophisticated user to use another person's address to send mail. Keep this point in mind, particularly if someone requests personal information. Children are especially vulnerable to forged, or inappropriate, mail and should be warned never to provide personal information such as a phone number, address, or age.

Tips, Tricks, and Ideas 6-15

A Little Common Sense

A little common sense when using e-mail can go a long way. People who never respond to unsolicited mail at home may put that common sense aside and respond to e-mail that solicits personal information. Remember the old adage, "If it sounds too good to be true . . ."

One of the problems that almost all regular e-mail users encounter is unwanted mail. This mail can range from junk mail, much like you may receive through the postal service, to harassing mail. The more your e-mail address is available, the more likely it is that you will receive unwanted mail. Before you give someone your e-mail address, make sure you want to receive mail from that source.

If you receive unwanted mail, you have several options. First, just delete the mail. This response is the easiest. If you continue to get unwanted mail from a particular source, send a reply asking to be removed from the mailing list. If this fails, send the system administrator a message indicating that you have asked not to receive any mail from a particular source. These tips may or may not work. Unwanted mail is a price that users pay for the freedom of open access to the Internet.

You also have the option of using the Inbox Assistant to route incoming messages to specific folders based on criteria you establish. For example, you can set a filter that routes, or delivers, messages from a specific e-mail account to a specific personal folder.

KEY POINTS

- E-mail was one of the first applications on the Internet, and remains one of the primary reasons that so many people use the Internet.
- E-mail systems consist of two programs: user agents and mail delivery systems. You interact with a user agent, also known as an e-mail client.
- The mail delivery system, or mail server, routes your mail to its intended destination.
- Outlook Express is the user agent for Internet Explorer.
- Before you can use Outlook Express, you must have a valid e-mail address. You must also have the e-mail address for those to whom you want to send messages. In addition, you must set up Outlook Express to access your e-mail account.
- Most Internet providers furnish you with the SMTP and POP servers' Internet addresses. Your provider should also tell you how to handle messages that have been read.
- E-mail has two very important components: header lines and mail body. Header lines tell the computer where to send the mail. The mail body is the message you create.
- The most important element of an e-mail message is the address. If you want to send e-mail to someone, you must know his or her unique Internet address. If you misspell someone's address by even one character, the mail will not be routed through the Internet.
- To launch Outlook Express, you have two choices. You can click on the Mail icon, or you can select the Mail command.
- The Mail command provides access to all of Outlook Express, whereas the Mail button al-lows you to go directly to a specific Mail function.
- Do not leave e-mail in your electronic mailbox.
- You can use the Print button to print a copy of your message.
- To delete an e-mail message, read the message and then click on the Delete button on the toolbar.
- The Folders window enables you to organize your e-mail messages into various folders.
- Receiving messages is only half the process of using e-mail. You also need to be able to create and send messages.
- Creating an e-mail message is much like using a word processor. You can insert and delete text, check spelling, modify the e-mail, and perform various e-mail creation tasks.
- One of the most useful features of e-mail is the ability to attach files to an e-mail message that you send.
- To attach a file you need to know the name of the file and where it is located on your computer.
- When you receive a message that contains an attached file, the file will appear as an icon at the bottom of the message as a link.

- The best way to get someone's address is to ask, just as you would ask someone for his or her postal address.
- It is a good idea, when you receive mail, to keep a log of return addresses.
- One of the most popular tools for searching for e-mail addresses is the white pages.
- The WHOIS database was one of the first systems designed to keep a directory of user addresses. It was originally designed for system administrators but was expanded to include other Internet users.
- If you cannot locate a user from the white pages or through WHOIS, another method is to contact the administrator of a specific computer system.
- One of the most useful features of Outlook Express is the address book. With an address book you can create an electronic list of e-mail addresses.
- Use the Address Book button to create an address book.
- Mailing lists or groups provide an easy method for sending messages to more than one Internet user. You can send messages to hundreds of users automatically by entering the mailing list name instead of the address of a single user.
- Never assume that your mail is private.
- It is not all that difficult for a sophisticated user to send mail in another person's address.

KEY TERMS AND COMMANDS

Add to Address Book
address book
Bcc:
Cc:
Delete
Deleted Items
delivery system
destination header lines
e-mail
e-mail client
Folders
Forward Message
header lines
host name
Internet Options
mail body
mail server
New Folder
Outlook Express
reply to address
Reply to Author
signature file
Simple Mail Transport Protocol (SMTP)
Subject:
To:
user agent
user name
white pages
WHOIS

STUDY QUESTIONS

1. What is included in a signature file?
2. Describe the procedure for deleting old e-mail with Outlook Express.
3. Why is it important to fill out the Subject: line in the header?
4. What is a WHOIS database?
5. What are the two elements of an e-mail delivery system?
6. Why should you be cautious about placing your name and address in the white pages?
7. Describe the procedure for creating an address book.
8. Describe the structure and process of using e-mail with Outlook Express.
9. How would you use a mailing list?
10. What problems are associated with e-mail security?

PRACTICE TEST

1. E-mail systems consist of which two programs?
   a. User agents and mail delivery systems.
   b. Simple mail and transport systems.
   c. Header lines and mail body.
   d. User agents and transport systems.
2. Within header lines, both To: and Cc: are called
   a. Receiver header lines
   b. Target header lines
   c. Source header lines
   d. Destination header lines
3. The e-mail message you create is called the
   a. Mail body c. Message body
   b. Body d. Content body
4. The most critical element of an e-mail message is the
   a. User name c. Subject line
   b. Host name d. Address
5. The unique name of the recipient's computer is called the
   a. Host name
   b. User name
   c. IP address
   d. Destination address
6. When you want to answer an e-mail message that you receive on Outlook Express, you can click on the
   a. Answer button
   b. Forward button
   c. Reply to Author button
   d. Return button
7. One of the most popular Web site tools for searching for e-mail addresses is the
   a. White pages c. Address book
   b. Yellow pages d. Mailing list
8. Which of the following was one of the first systems designed to keep a directory of user addresses?
   a. White Net pages
   b. Yellow Pages database
   c. Whodat database
   d. NetWhite pages
9. Which of the following can you use to send one e-mail message to multiple Internet users?
   a. Address book c. White pages
   b. Mailing list or group d. Yellow pages book
10. It is difficult for someone to send mail using a phony name.
    a. True b. False

FILL-INS

1. With e-mail, you interact with a user agent, which is also known as an ______________.
2. E-mail systems consist of two programs. These are ______________ and ______________.
3. E-mail is made up of two very important components. These are ______________ and ______________.
4. The ______________ is the message you create.
5. The easiest way to configure Outlook Express is to use the ______________ that appears the first time Outlook Express is loaded.
6. You can save e-mail messages by putting them into specific ______________.
7. In Outlook Express the process of creating an address book is accomplished by selecting the ______________ button.
8. One of the most popular tools for searching for e-mail addresses is the ______________.
9. The ______________ database was one of the first systems designed to keep a directory of user addresses.
10. ______________ provide a very easy method for sending messages to more than one Internet user.

PROJECTS

1. Enter your personal address book into Outlook Express or into some other e-mail system that allows you to store addresses. Remember, however, that an electronic address book can be lost (that is, the computer might fail) or opened by other people. (In fact, you may want to delete your entries after completing this exercise.) Therefore, it is a good idea to keep a paper copy of your address book, and it is a good idea to carefully consider what information you want to put in an address book that is public.
2. The best way to let someone know that you have access to e-mail is to send an e-mail message. If you are using this book in a course, send your instructor an e-mail message. Indicate that you are now available to receive e-mail messages. This message will help your instructor; instead of having to type e-mail addresses into an address book, your instructor can use a capture process directly from your mail.
3. Mailing lists or groups are very useful. The trick to developing a successful mailing list is to determine what makes all members of a mailing list similar. For example, your instructor may have a separate mailing list for each class where class membership is the unifying factor. What mailing lists would be useful to you? On what basis would you create a mailing list? On a sheet of paper, identify at least five different mailing lists you might find useful. If you have an electronic mail system that allows you to store your own personal mailing lists, create these mailing lists and try using them.
4. Be sure you go through your mailbox periodically. Save any e-mail addresses that are not included in your personal address book or saved on your system. It is also a good idea to delete old or unwanted e-mail messages from your folders. This practice helps you find old messages and keeps your system operator happy.
5. Practice using the powerful features of your e-mail system. Send a copy of a message to more than one person by using Cc: in the header line. Also, forward a copy of a message you received to a friend. It is usually a good idea to send the friend a message explaining the message you forwarded or the message you copied. Be sensitive to the concerns of others. Some people may not wish to receive e-mail.

INTERNET AT WORK

Like many employees of major corporations, the frustrations of your job can be overwhelming. One common practice is to vent your frustration on your spouse, dog, or friends. You have recently moved to a new city and your phone bill is already excessively high; send an e-mail message to one of your friends (or classmates) complaining about your new job, Mrs. Agee, or your lack of social life because you are spending all your time on the Internet. Remember, there is no guarantee that your e-mail will remain private. Therefore, use a bit of caution and common sense.

7 Usenet and Listserv

OUTCOMES

When you complete this chapter you will be able to . . .

Define Usenet.

Identify the Usenet structure.

Define newsgroup or discussion group.

Use Outlook Express as a newsreader.

Identify various Usenet features.

Define Listserv.

Locate Listserv lists.

Subscribe to a Listserv.

Unsubscribe to a Listserv.

WHAT IS USENET?

In the days before the World Wide Web, another system enabled users with similar interests to exchange messages. This system became known as Usenet. As with the Internet, different people define Usenet (user's network) differently. The reason is that Usenet is not owned by any entity and is not a distinct component of the Internet. **Usenet** describes a collection of electronic articles called **messages.** All messages are organized into topical areas called **newsgroups** or **discussion groups,** which provide a vehicle for reading and posting messages on the Internet. Users who share similar interests place (or post) messages in a newsgroup. For example, the Usenet newsgroup soc.culture.peru is a newsgroup about the people of Peru. If you want to read about Peruvian culture or send messages related to the culture and people of Peru, this group is a valuable resource.

To use Usenet, you must have software called a **newsreader.** With Internet Explorer, Outlook Express is used both for e-mail and as a newsreader. Outlook Express works much the same way with newsgroups as it does with e-mail. In fact, the major difference lies in where a message is sent. Messages created as e-mail are sent to individual e-mail boxes, whereas messages for newsgroups are sent to a place where everyone can read the message.

USENET STRUCTURE

Usenet organizes newsgroups into several thousand topics. It does so by using a prescribed naming scheme. A newsgroup name is always lowercase with each group name separated by a period (.). The name always reads from the general to the specific. For example, with soc.culture.peru, soc is the major group name for newsgroups related to social sciences and cultural issues, and culture refers to cultural issues. Finally, peru identifies the specifics of the group.

Usenet users can create newsgroups on almost any topic. However, because so many categories are available, most users are able to locate a group that fits their particular interest.

> **Tips, Tricks, and Ideas 7-1**
>
> *An Electronic BBS*
>
> Usenet is like a set of thousands of electronic bulletin boards. You send messages to the newsgroup. Any member of the newsgroup can then read your message and reply. Newsgroups act as an open forum for discussion.

Image 7-1

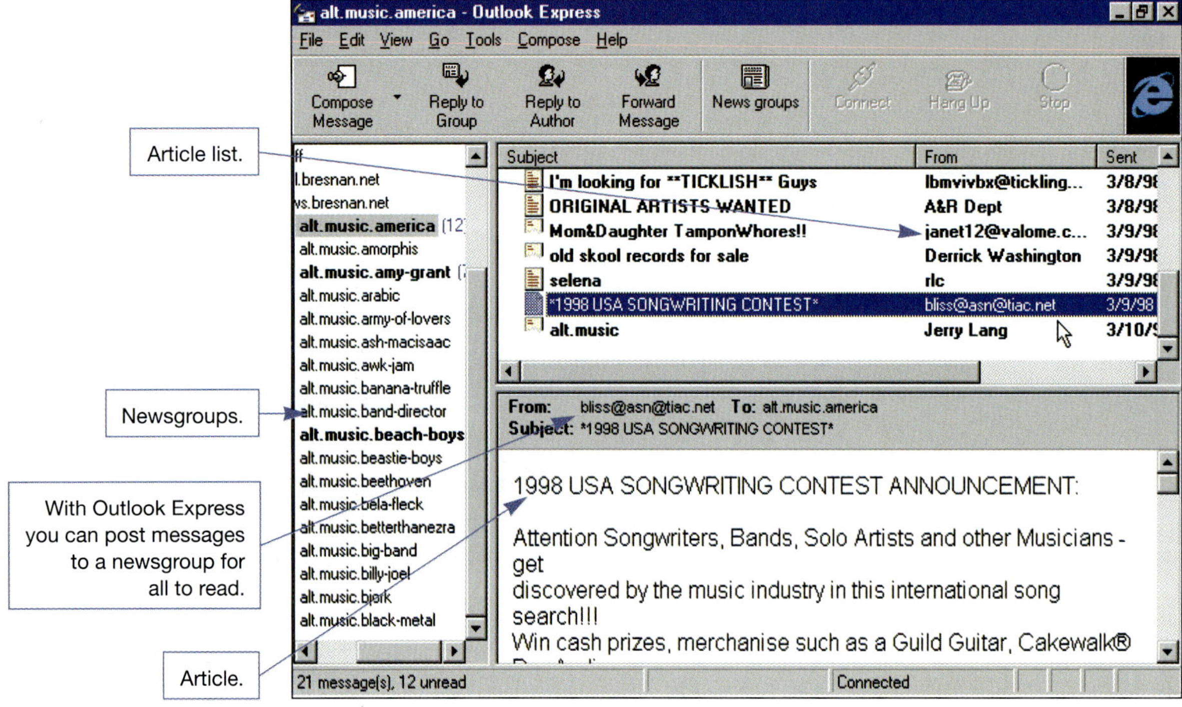

OUTLOOK EXPRESS

Before you can use Outlook Express as your newsreader, you must set up the name of the server that will provide you with access to newsgroups. The procedure is much the same as the procedure for identifying a mail server: Select the Internet Options command from the View menu of Outlook Express, click on the Programs tab, and set News: to Outlook Express.

After you have identified Outlook Express as the newsreader for Internet Explorer, you need to set up, or format, Outlook Express. The easiest way to configure Outlook Express is to use the Configuration Wizard that appears the first time Outlook Express is loaded. However, in some cases, especially in computer labs, you may need to set the configuration manually.

> **Tips, Tricks, and Ideas 7-2**
>
> *Joining a Newsgroup*
>
> The most difficult issue is deciding which newsgroups to join and then joining. There are well over 10,000 newsgroups. Narrowing down the list to something that is meaningful to you can be a bit daunting. At first, the best way to decide which newsgroups to join is to select from a list of all available newsgroups—not an easy task considering the number of choices you have.

To set the configuration, you must access the Accounts command from the Tools menu. From this dialog box you select the News tab and then select Properties. The Properties option allows you to identify the name of your news account, the server name, and your user name. This information is required; you will not be able to access Usenet without these settings. Your instructor should provide a valid group server. When you have successfully identified your news server, it will appear in the list of options for Outlook Express.

As with e-mail, when you are ready to use Outlook Express as your newsreader you must select the server name. The first time you select the server, you will be asked whether you want to see a list of all available newsgroups. If you click on Yes, a dialog box listing all newsgroups should appear. At this point you need to click on the Reset List to update the full list of newsgroups. You may have to wait several minutes for all the groups to appear. Displaying the names of all newsgroups can take a long time, especially if you have a slow connection. Be patient.

From the Newsgroups dialog box, you may subscribe to, or join, any newsgroup by simply clicking on the newsgroup name and then by clicking on the Subscribe button. To unsubscribe, click on the Unsubscribe button. When you have made your selections, click on OK to complete the subscription process. The list of your subscribed newsgroups will appear under the name of your Usenet server. You can subscribe or unsubscribe at any time by clicking on the Newsgroups button on the toolbar.

After you join a newsgroup, that newsgroup name appears in Outlook Express below the name of the group server. The procedure for viewing newsgroup messages is similar to the procedure for reading e-mail messages. You can list all available messages by clicking on the newsgroup name. You can use the same processes for reading, creating, and replying to group messages as you would for e-mail. The difference is that the messages sent to a group have a different address than an individual address. You also need to remember that messages sent to a group are available for public consumption.

You should read a few of the messages from the list of selected newsgroups to get an idea of the issues and topics discussed in that group. If the topic is interesting to you, you can keep it. If not, you may return to the Newsgroups dialog box, select the Subscribed tab, and Unsubscribe to the newsgroup.

In addition to their content, messages contain additional, useful information. Often at the top of the message is a listing of all newsgroups in which the message is posted. You can use this information to learn about related groups that you may wish to join.

> **Netiquette 7-1**
>
> *Use Both Upper- and Lowercase Characters*
>
> Do not use all uppercase letters when you are communicating with a newsgroup. Using all uppercase characters is viewed as shouting on Usenet.

Tips, Tricks, and Ideas 7-3

A Little Self-Control

The tendency for many new newsgroup users is to join many newsgroups. Unless you have a lot of time to spend reading messages, it is a good idea to join only groups with which you intend to actively participate. If not, you can easily get overwhelmed in a sea of meaningless messages.

Reading messages is only half the fun. Posting messages is the other half. If you intend to join a newsgroup, you should plan on being an active member and posting relevant and meaningful information or questions.

To post a message, first select the newsgroup. Once there, clicking on the Compose Message button on the toolbar will produce a screen similar to that used for e-mail. The active newsgroup address appears next to Newsgroups:. At this point you can include a subject and a message to post; then write your message. Click on the Send button to post your message.

There are a few guidelines that you should follow when posting messages to a newsgroup. First, you should post messages only that are related to the newsgroup topic. The idea of a newsgroup is to communicate with others interested in a common topic. Therefore, avoid general types of messages, unless that is the topic of the newsgroup. Second, you should not post threatening or insulting messages. Every message you post includes your e-mail address. If you post inappropriate messages, you can expect a barrage of e-mail reminding you of the need for common decency. Finally, you should post only messages that all readers will find interesting. If you want to send a message just to an individual who posted a particular message, you can do so by using the Reply button and then selecting Reply to Sender. If you select Reply to Group the message will be addressed to the newsgroup.

What happens if you locate a message that you would like to send to someone outside of the newsgroup? Outlook Express provides many of the same options for newsgroups that it does for e-mail. For example, you can use the **Forward Message** command or button to send a newsgroup message to a valid e-mail address.

Netiquette 7-2

Usenet Has Unwritten Laws

With most newsgroups, the only rule is the rule of common courtesy. There usually isn't a formal administrator to tell you how to behave. But this doesn't mean you can do anything you want to the group. The group can find ways to retaliate. One common form of retaliation is to flood an offender's mailbox with impolite and hostile messages. This tactic effectively interferes with an offender's use of e-mail.

Netiquette 7-3

Offensive Material

Don't be surprised if you find offensive material in a newsgroup. Members of newsgroups are very tolerant of others' ideas, but there are limits. If you are offended, unsubscribe.

ACTIVITY

1. Connect to the Internet and launch Internet Explorer.
2. Select Internet Options from the View menu and then click on the Programs tab.
   Make sure that the entry next to News: is Outlook Express (Image 7–2).

Image 7-2

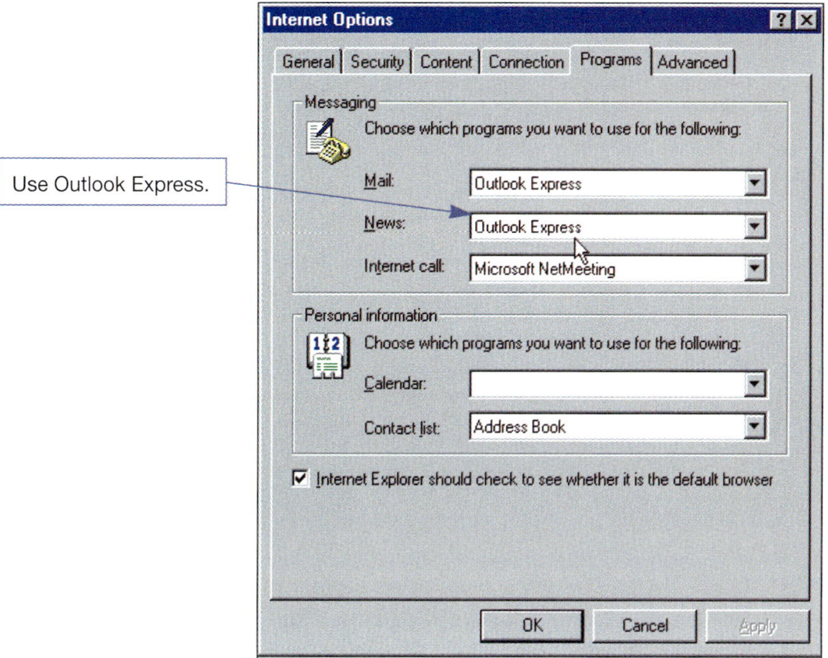

3. Close Internet Explorer and launch Outlook Express.
4. If the news server name does not appear, then select the Accounts command from the Tools menu.
5. Select the News tab and then enter the name of the news server provided by your instructor (Image 7–3).

Image 7-3

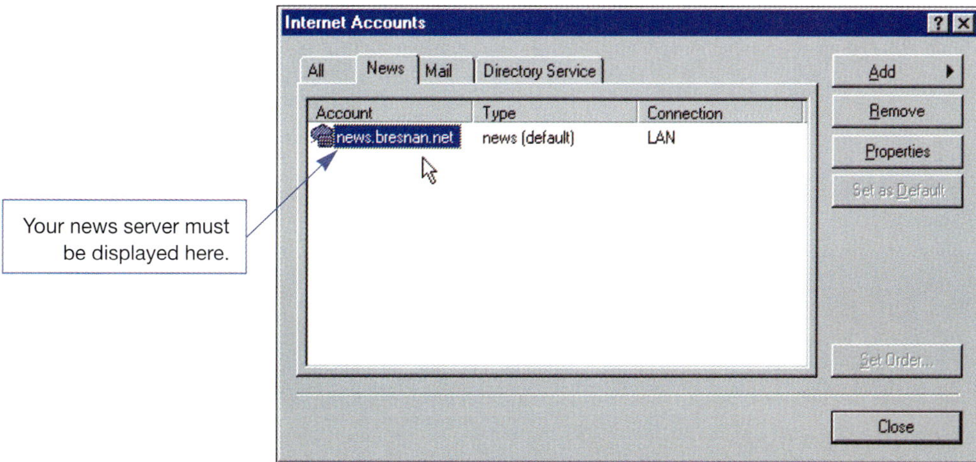

6. Click on Close and return to Outlook Express.
7. Select the newsgroup server name in Outlook Express (Image 7–4).

Image 7-4

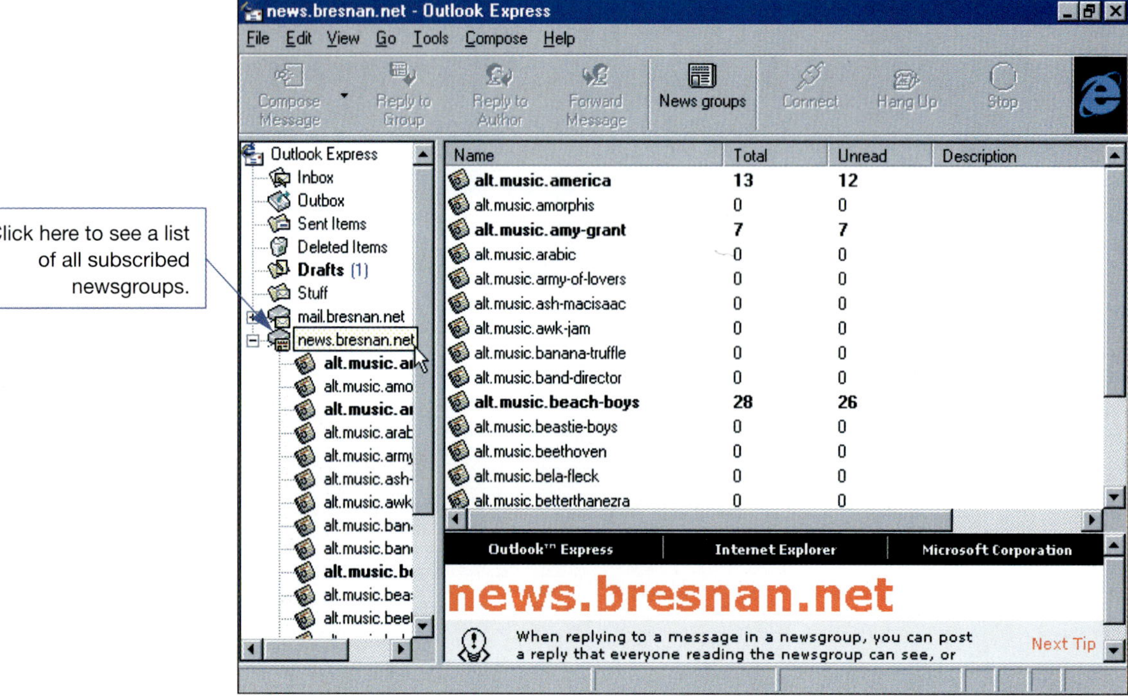

8. Click on the News groups button on the toolbar.
   Notice the Newsgroups dialog box (Image 7–5).
9. Click on Reset List.
   In a few moments an updated list of all available newsgroups appears; be patient (Image 7–5).

Image 7-5

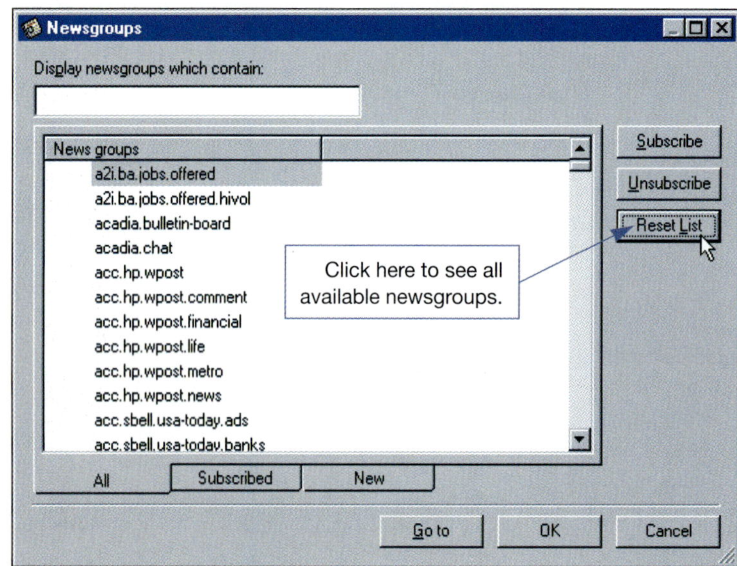

10. Scroll down the list of categories under Newsgroup name until you see soc.history.ancient; then click on the Subscribe button.
    The mark next to the newsgroup name indicates that you have subscribed to this newsgroup (Image 7–6).

Image 7-6

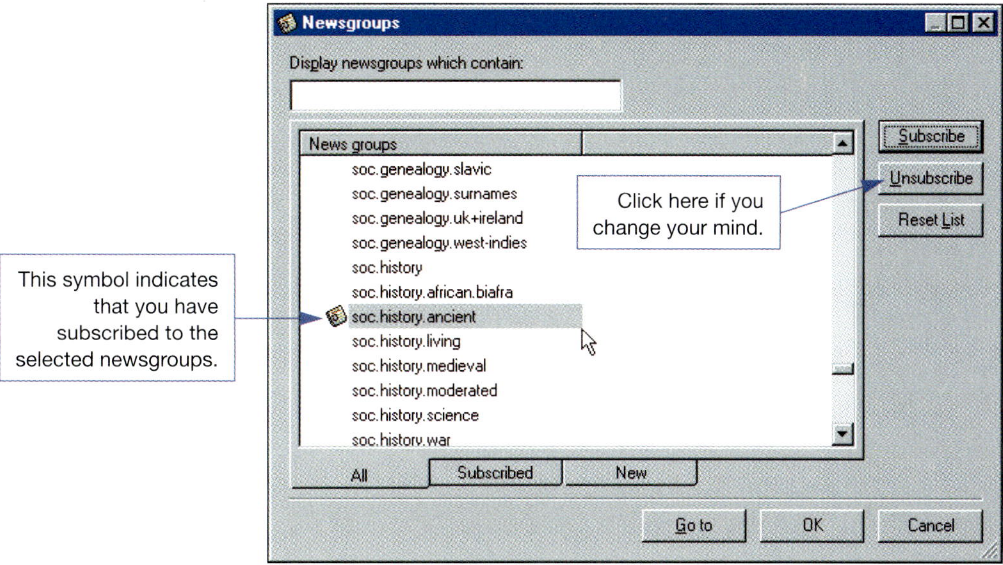

11. Click on the OK button to close this selection window.
12. In Outlook Express double-click on the news server name and notice that the newsgroup name appears.
13. Double-click on the newsgroup name.
    Notice a list of messages that is very similar to the e-mail messages.
14. Click once and pick any message you think looks interesting.
    Notice the message appears at the bottom of the newsreader (Image 7–7).

Image 7-7

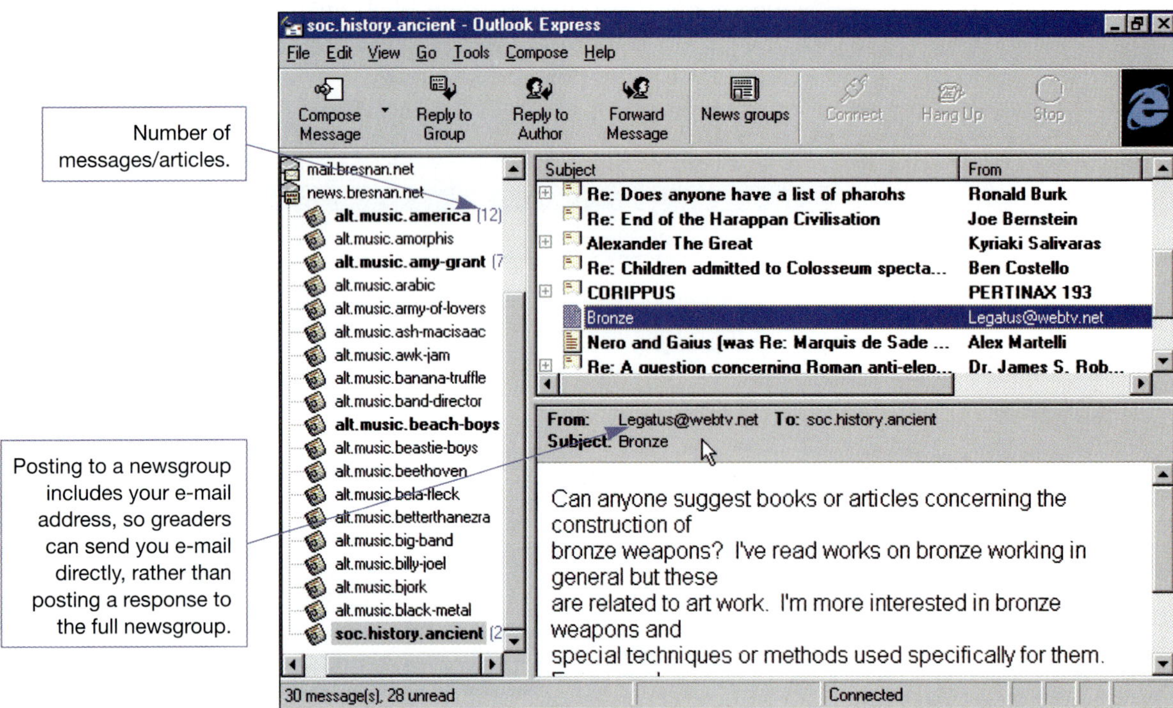

15. Take a few minutes to examine several messages in this newsgroup.
16. Subscribe to any other newsgroup you desire.
17. Open a newsgroup in Outlook Express.
18. Click on the Compose Message button on the toolbar.
    Notice a window appears similar to e-mail. Instead of To: the message is addressed to Newsgroups: (Image 7–8).

Image 7-8

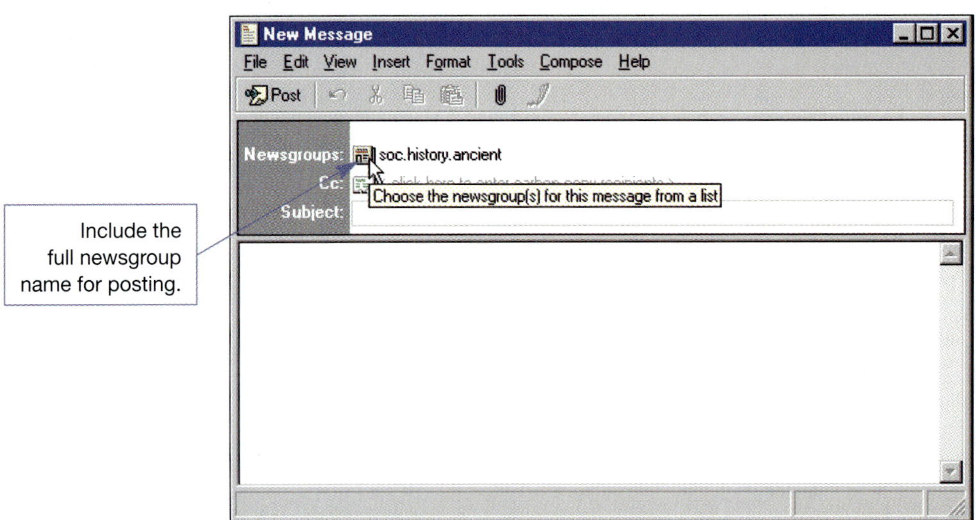

19. If you want to post a message, complete the message and then click on the Post button. If not, use the Close button.
20. From Outlook Express, select the Newsgroups button and then choose the Subscribed tab. At this point unsubscribe to any newsgroup you no longer want to view.

Netiquette 7-4

Avoid Flame Wars

Flame wars are extremely heated arguments between two or more people. Flames can become very intense because of the anonymity associated with the Web. Usually, no one wins a flame war. Many times the arguments center around political or religious beliefs or personal opinions. The best advice is to not get drawn into a flame war.

A Warning: Since Usenet is where the majority of "questionable" exchanges occur, you may need to exercise some caution. It is not uncommon to visit a newsgroup and see messages that contain strong sexual content and even graphic images. This can happen in any newsgroup, not only those that are clearly identified as such.

EXERCISE 7-1

Regardless of the newsreader, selecting a newsgroup to join can take a bit of effort. There are so many choices on so many topics that the sheer magnitude of Usenet can be overwhelming. To give you an idea of how to use newsgroups, join at least two newsgroups. These can be any newsgroups that you find interesting. Be sure to read several of the messages posted in the newsgroup before joining. On a sheet of paper, identify each newsgroup that you are joining both by name and location.

WHAT IS LISTSERV?

Listserv (List Server) is a system that allows you to exchange e-mail with thousands of users. As with Usenet, Listserv was designed as a system to facilitate communication between people with similar interests. However, unlike Usenet, Listserv is a system that works with your e-mail. Instead of posting public messages as you do with a newsgroup, Listserv allows you to route an e-mail message directly to the e-mail accounts of specific Listserv participants.

Listserv is software that is designed to route mail to all members on a particular list. The **list** is where Listserv routes mail. This distinction is important because the Listserv software and the list have separate and distinct e-mail addresses. When you want to join a list, you send your request to a Listserv. After you are on the list, you use the list address to send your messages or e-mail. For example, if you want to join the Forum for Discussion of Concerns of Drinking and Driving, send mail asking to join listserv@admin.humberc.on.ca. The list address you join is add-l@admin.humberc.on.ca.

Lists exist on thousands of topics. In fact, almost any topic of interest to you probably has a Listserv list. When you find a list that you want to participate in, you should join. Joining involves adding your e-mail address to the Listserv mailing list. However, not all Listserv lists are open to the public.

After you join, any e-mail that you send to the list address will be sent to all members of that specific list, and any mail sent to the list by other members will be sent to you. Usually, when you first join, you will receive

Tips, Tricks, and Ideas 7-4

List of Lists

The Listserv link on the *Learning Online* Web site provides access to lists of lists. If you are not sure which lists to join, you may want to take some time and explore this link.

e-mail that explains what the list is about, how to operate within the list, and how to terminate (unsubscribe) your membership. It is critical that you keep a record of this message (either a printout or save it in your e-mail system). You are also likely to receive some back mail to give you an idea of what members have been discussing.

Two major types of Listserv lists are available: moderated and unmoderated. **Moderated lists** have an individual (moderator) who monitors incoming and outgoing mail. The moderator's normal duties include making sure that the type of mail matches the topic of the list, weeding out inappropriate mail, and posting mail to keep a discussion moving. **Unmoderated lists** (which are very common) are free flowing. With unmoderated lists, you get every piece of mail, no matter how offensive or annoying.

One of the most annoying messages is a faulty message to unsubscribe. This happens when a user either forgets the unsubscribe procedures or loses the initial message detailing how to unsubscribe. If you want to make a group of people mad at you, post an unsubscribe message on a list that goes out to all members. It is a sign that you are incompetent and/or inconsiderate.

When you first join a list, spend some time reading messages before sending messages to the list. This way you will be informed about how the list operates, the manner in which users post messages, and the topics of interest to users. Also, some lists are high volume. You could be sending mail to thousands of users at one time. Make sure you proofread your messages before posting. You do not want to appear foolish and receive derogatory return mail.

You are free to join any public list. However, if you join a very active list, you can easily receive 50 mail messages a day. If you join a high-volume list and don't read your mail every day, your e-mail account can quickly fill up, leaving no room for other mail. Therefore, before you join a list, be sure you want to participate actively.

If you join a list that is not to your taste or interest, just unsubscribe. Again, be sure you follow the unsubscribe procedures detailed in one of the first messages you received from the list.

Tips, Tricks, and Ideas 7-5

How Many Messages?

One of the pitfalls of joining a Listserv list can be the volume of e-mail you receive. If you join multiple active Listserv lists, you could receive 10, 20, 50, or more messages a day. You may want to limit the number of Listserv lists you participate in to keep the amount of information manageable.

Netiquette 7-5

Keep the Directions

When you want to remove yourself from a Listserv list, you need to send the appropriate request to the appropriate e-mail address. This address is normally provided as the first message you receive from the Listserv. Print a copy of this message and save it; also save the message in your e-mail account. When you want to unsubscribe, you will then have the appropriate address and procedures.

VISITING LISTSERV

If you only want to join and not create or operate a list, then you will never need to know how to use Listserv software. This software is only for creating and moderating a list. Most users can use their e-mail software to join and participate in lists.

> **Tips, Tricks, and Ideas 7-6**
>
> *Vacation*
>
> If you are away from your e-mail for a while, you could come back to several hundred messages stacked in your e-mail. If you do not plan to access your e-mail for any length of time, you may wish to unsubscribe. You can always resubscribe when you are ready to receive messages again. In addition, many Listserv lists have a nonmail option to hold mail until you ask for it.

The critical element in joining a list is knowing the Listserv address. The Listserv link on the *Learning Online* Web site provides access to some of these lists. In addition, your host system may provide access to a variety of Listserv lists that you can join. Another way to find out about lists is through public announcements, books, and, of course, word of mouth.

Listserv lists are usually not permanent. They materialize to meet a particular need, operate for awhile, and then disappear as interest in the topic subsides. Even if you obtain an address to join a list, it may not be functioning. The only way to tell in many cases is to join and see what happens.

The process of joining a Listserv list is fairly standard. After you have the Listserv address, you send e-mail to that address with the following notice on the first line of your e-mail message:

SUBSCRIBE listname firstname lastname

In this message, listname is the specific name of the list; firstname and lastname are your first and last names. Here's how Fritz Erickson joined the Forum for Discussion of Concerns of Drinking and Driving:

To: listserv@admin.humberc.on.ca.
From: Fritz Erickson (fericks o@mtu.edu)
Subject: (leave blank)

SUBSCRIBE add-l Fritz Erickson

This one and only line is sent to the Listserv address. This line is known as the **subscribe line.** Do not send a formal letter. Do not try to be polite. (It is only a computer system.) Just create a single line e-mail message like the one above.

Unsubscribing is very important, and the procedure differs from list to list. However, most lists follow the same basic format. Just as with subscribe, send unsubscribe to the Listserv address. The mistake most new users make is sending an unsubscribe message to the list and not the Listserv. Remember the list and the Listserv are two different addresses. To unsubscribe to the Forum for Discussion of Concerns of Drinking and Driving your message should look something like this:

To: listserv@admin.humberc.on.ca.
From: Fritz Erickson (fericks o@mtu.edu)
Subject: Unsubscribe

UNSUBSCRIBE add-l Fritz Erickson

If the To: line in your message is add-l@admin.humberc.on.ca, then all members—but not the Listserv—will get your unsubscribe message. In this case you will still be a member, and you are likely to receive a great many messages informing you of your ignorance and your annoying behavior.

One final note about using and interacting with lists: Because the list is an e-mail address, you can use the standard e-mail commands, including forward and reply. Be careful with reply. You should reply to the sender only. Otherwise, you may end up sending your reply to every member. With the Forward command you can send a copy of mail you receive on your list to any other user or any other list. You also can use the Reply command to send a message back to the list and all users, which makes it easy for users to carry on a discussion over the list. However, just because it is easy to reply does not mean you should send ill-conceived messages. Create your replies with the same care and consideration you use for any other message you send to a list.

EXERCISE 7-2

Locating Listserv lists you want to join can be a bit time-consuming. Use the Listserv link on the *Learning Online* Web site to begin your search. Another method is to use any of the search tools available through *Learning Online* to search for Listserv. This search will produce a list of Web sites that refer to specific lists. Perform several searches for Listserv lists with each of the search tools found on the *Learning Online* Web site. It is up to you which lists to join.

KEY POINTS

- Usenet is a system that enables users who share interests to exchange messages.
- Usenet (user's network) describes a collection of electronic messages. Usenet organizes newsgroups into several thousand topics. It does so by using a prescribed naming scheme.
- Newsreader software is required to access Usenet, and Outlook Express is a popular newsreader for Internet Explorer.
- The first step for using Usenet is to decide which newsgroup(s) to join. This is not an easy task because there are thousands of available newsgroups.
- To read a message from a newsgroup, click on the desired message and the message will appear.
- When you read a message, you frequently have the option of posting a response or follow-up message.
- Listserv (List Server) is a system that allows you to exchange e-mail with thousands of users.
- To join a list, send your request to the Listserv. After you are on the list, you send your messages or mail to the list address.
- Listserv is software that is designed to route mail to all members on a particular list.
- Two major types of Listserv lists are available: moderated and unmoderated.
- The critical element in joining a list is knowing the Listserv address. The Listserv link on *Learning Online* provides access to some of these lists.
- Because a list is an e-mail address, you can use standard e-mail commands.

KEY TERMS AND COMMANDS

discussion groups	**message**	**subscribe line**
Forward Message	**moderated lists**	**unmoderated lists**
list	**newsgroups**	**Usenet**
Listserv	**newsreader**	

STUDY QUESTIONS

1. What is Usenet?
2. Describe the structure of Usenet.
3. How does Usenet structure the addresses for newsgroups?
4. Describe the process for establishing Outlook Express as your newsreader.
5. Describe the procedure for identifying and joining a newsgroup.
6. Why is it important to use both upper- and lowercase letters when communicating with a newsgroup?
7. What is Listserv?
8. Explain the difference between Usenet and Listserv.
9. Describe the two types of Listserv lists.
10. Discuss the guidelines that you should follow when posting messages to a newsgroup.

PRACTICE TEST

1. A newsgroup name is always presented with each group name separated by a period (.) in which of the following formats?
   a. Lowercase.
   b. Uppercase.
   c. Mixed upper- and lowercase.
   d. Doesn't make any difference.
2. The term used to describe a collection of electronic messages is
   a. Newsreader c. Usenet
   b. Listserv d. Internet
3. The newsgroup name always works from the general to the specific.
   a. True b. False
4. Outlook Express is used both for e-mail and as a newsreader.
   a. True b. False
5. With which type of lists do you get every piece of mail, no matter how offensive or annoying?
   a. Free lists
   b. Unmoderated lists
   c. Moderated lists
   d. Monitored lists
6. One of the major drawbacks to Usenet is that you cannot send a message to someone outside of the newsgroup.
   a. True b. False
7. One major drawback of Outlook Express is that only a limited number of newsgroups are available.
   a. True b. False
8. The first step for Outlook Express is to
   a. Show all newsgroups.
   b. Decide which newsgroups to join.
   c. Select Show subscribed newsgroups.
   d. Read a message.
9. To read a message from a newsgroup, all that is required is to
   a. Select the Reply button.
   b. Select I.
   c. Click on the message.
   d. Click on follow-up.
10. Which system allows you to route an e-mail message directly to the e-mail accounts of participants?
    a. Listserv b. Usenet

FILL-INS

1. A newsgroup name is always ________ case with each group name separated by a period (.).
2. The newsgroup name always works from the ________ to the ________.
3. To join and use a newsgroup you need ________ ________ software.
4. ________ describes a collection of electronic messages.
5. ________ is software that routes mail to all members on a particular list.
6. The two major types of Listserv lists are ________ and ________.
7. ________ allows you to send a reply only to the sender and not the full newsgroup.
8. Use the ________ command or button to send a Listserv message to any valid e-mail address.
9. To join a newsgroup, highlight or select the desired newsgroup; then use the ________ command.
10. When you read a message, you frequently have the option of posting a response or follow-up message. You use the ________ command for this feature.

PROJECTS

1. The computer newsgroup is an excellent source of information about computing and computers. Connect to a newsgroup in this category by using Outlook Express. On a sheet of paper, identify three messages that you have read from this group. Be sure to locate this newsgroup through the *Learning Online* Web site.
2. If you like going to movies or visiting your local video store, you know that picking a good movie can be a bit difficult. See if you can find a recreation, arts, or movie review newsgroup. It is a great way to find opinions about what movies to watch. On a sheet of paper, write down which movie reviews are currently available on a newsgroup.
3. Use the Internet to learn about the Internet. Access a newsgroup in the News category to learn even more about newsgroups. Write down two interesting points you learned about newsgroups that you did not know before.
4. Usenet provides a great deal of opinion and information on current news. Locate a Usenet that deals with news headlines or a current and controversial news event. Write down the date and the headline messages that are available on this newsgroup or describe some of the controversial opinions expressed in this newsgroup.
5. Joining a Listserv is a very personal decision because it directly links your e-mail account to others. Compared to other Internet resources, it is much more difficult to examine Listserv lists anonymously. If you decide to join any lists, it is a good idea to keep a log of which lists you belong to; be sure to keep the instructions for unsubscribing to each list. Select one or two Listserv lists to join and write down the procedure for unsubscribing.
6. Some Listservs are called "bounce back," which means that you will receive mail only when you send a request. Try to locate a bounce-back Listserv to get an idea of how this type of Listserv works. Make a list of two or three different bounce-back Listservs.
7. If you are going to become an active Usenet user, then you should understand the basic rules and procedures for Usenet contributions. Write down and discuss several guidelines you should follow when joining Usenet or Listserv.

INTERNET AT WORK

Almost everyone at the Agee Candy Company knows that you would like to join a Usenet or a Listserv list that will help you deal with a boss who wears her hair in a tight bun, is usually cranky, makes unreasonable demands on your time, and likes to take credit for your work. However, you do not want to join this type of list on the company computer. Instead, find a Usenet or a Listserv list that deals with some of your leisure time interests. These might be hobbies that include collecting objects (such as coins, stamps, or figurines) or making objects (such as arts and crafts, models or prototypes of trains, cars, or planes) or physical skill activities (such as juggling, football, or in-line skating). Be sure to keep a record of activities that you can show to the CEO, but try not to inform Edith of your activities.

8

Multimedia, DirectX, Java, NetMeeting, and Other Cool Tools

OUTCOMES

When you complete this chapter you will be able to . . .

- Use audio capabilities found on the World Wide Web.
- Use video capabilities.
- Use graphics capabilities.
- Use animation with VRML.
- Talk to other Web users with Microsoft NetMeeting.
- Use the Chat tool in Microsoft NetMeeting.
- Use the Whiteboard tool in Microsoft NetMeeting.
- Identify the purpose of Java and JavaScript.
- Access and use a global chat room.
- Use Microsoft Chat.

OVERVIEW

The flexibility of Internet Explorer that results from the use of add-ons and plug-ins seems almost endless. In Chapter 5 you learned how to install plug-ins and add-ons to extend, or expand, the capabilities of Internet Explorer. One important reason for using plug-ins and add-ons is the access they provide to multimedia tools on the World Wide Web. Multimedia is a multisensory approach to the delivery of information. Not everyone agrees with this definition, but **multimedia** generally refers to incorporating audio, graphics, video, animation, and other multisensory tools into a Web site. Multimedia enables users to experience a wider range of information over the World Wide Web.

In Chapter 4 we described the process for downloading and installing add-ons and plug-ins. However, simply adding capabilities to Internet Explorer is not enough. You should also know how to take advantage of these additional capabilities. One goal of this chapter is to introduce you to some of the more powerful add-ons and plug-ins that make using the World Wide Web more interesting, exciting, and useful.

In addition to multimedia add-ons and plug-ins, various other tools help bring a Web site to life. One of these tools is Java. **Java** is a programming language, but it is also a technology that Web developers use to create programs that run on Web pages. Specialized programs created in Java are referred to as **Java applets.** Java applets can add new dimensions to a Web page. For example, a Java applet can cause text to appear as a marquee across a Web site. Java may be used to produce animated cartoon characters, crossword puzzles, or interactive educational games; to provide access to stock market quotes; or to run thousands of programs written in Java directly on the World Wide Web.

Another tool for developing multimedia applications on the Web is Macromedia. **Shockwave** is a viewer that supports documents created by Macromedia Director. Macromedia Director allows Web developers to create presentations, video segments, and audio and video combinations on Web pages.

No one knows the future of the Web, but one thing is certain—the Web is in a constant state of change. New applications and new uses of the World Wide Web are appearing almost daily. For example, NetMeeting now allows you to talk live with other NetMeeting users across the country without having to pay long-distance phone charges. VRML is the beginning of virtual reality on the Web. These and other Web features are covered in this chapter. You will begin to use these features to make the Web even more interesting and exciting.

Finally, this chapter examines Microsoft NetMeeting as a tool for communicating with other Microsoft NetMeeting users. With NetMeeting you can have real-time discussions by using a microphone and speakers. You can also text-chat, browse files with any other user, work together on graphics images, and use other features that make the Internet a collaborative environment. This chapter concludes with a discussion of the various options for real-time chatting. The section discusses Microsoft Chat as well as chat rooms available through other Web sources.

THE INTERNET EXPLORER COMPONENT PAGE

One of the best ways to expand Internet Explorer is to use the Internet Explorer Component Download page provided by Microsoft. With this page you are able to add a variety of features to Internet Explorer in a quick and convenient fashion. In fact, it is the one site you must visit if you want to take full advantage of the Web with Internet Explorer.

Once you access the Component Download page, you can enable the Active Setup option, which displays a status indicator for each component currently installed with Internet Explorer. From this list you may also select which components to download and install. Throughout this chapter you will be directed to download and install various components. You may choose to use the Component Download page in lieu of other Web sites (Image 8-1).

Image 8-1

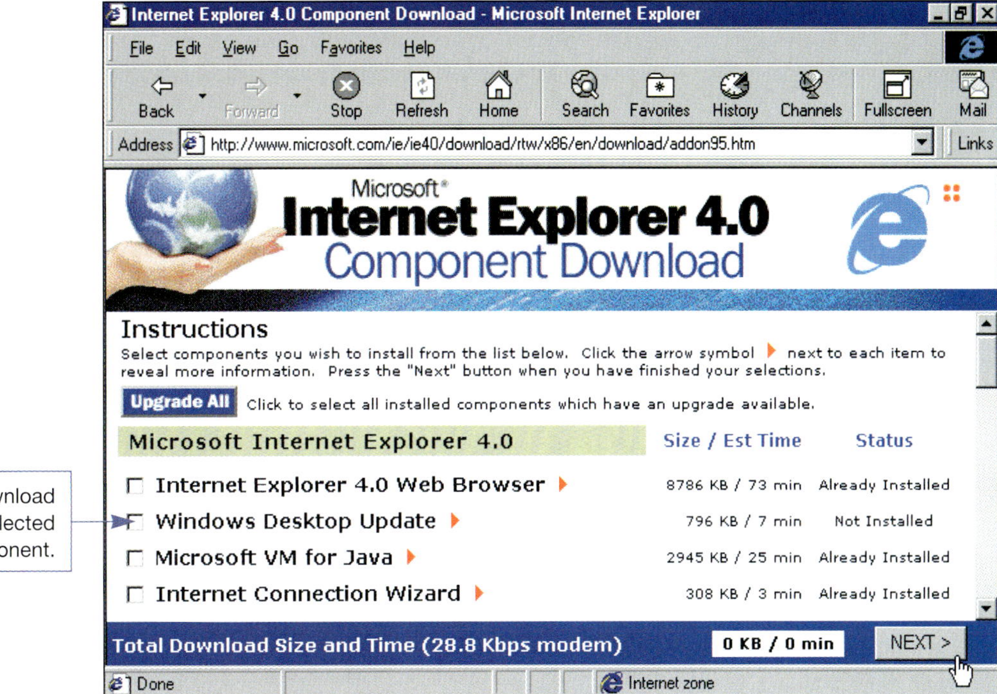

GREAT AUDIO

Audio is an indispensable component of multimedia. The addition of sound files to a Web page brings exciting dimensions to Internet Explorer. A number of significant sound file formats are supported directly by Internet Explorer. Several additional formats are supported by plug-ins and add-ons. Files supported directly by Internet Explorer include .au, .wav, and .aif (.aiff, .aifc) files. Although these sound file formats are important and many Web sites use audio files created in one or more of these formats, a number of other important sound formats also add great sound features to Internet Explorer and the World Wide Web.

One important audio file format is RealPlayer (formerly Real Audio), also referred to as .ra. RealPlayer has become very popular because it is quick and allows users to **stream** audio and video. In other words, with RealPlayer you can get a continuous stream of audio such as live news broadcasts, large streams of lectures, and other audio files. Today, RealPlayer allows you to access thousands of live broadcasts transmitted in a remarkably high quality.

Tips, Tricks, and Ideas 8-1

New Versions

One of the most exciting features of the World Wide Web is the ability software developers have to distribute new versions of plug-ins, add-ons, and other software. You may find new versions of audio plug-ins as well as new versions and new software for other multimedia applications. Keep your add-ons up-to-date by downloading and installing the most recent versions. This way you will continue to be able to receive the latest the World Wide Web has to offer.

ACTIVITY

1. If you have not installed RealPlayer, return to Chapter 4 and follow the installation instructions (Image 8-2).

Image 8-2

2. From the *Learning Online* Web site, select the Audio site. Notice the variety of audio links available from this site (Image 8-3).

Image 8-3

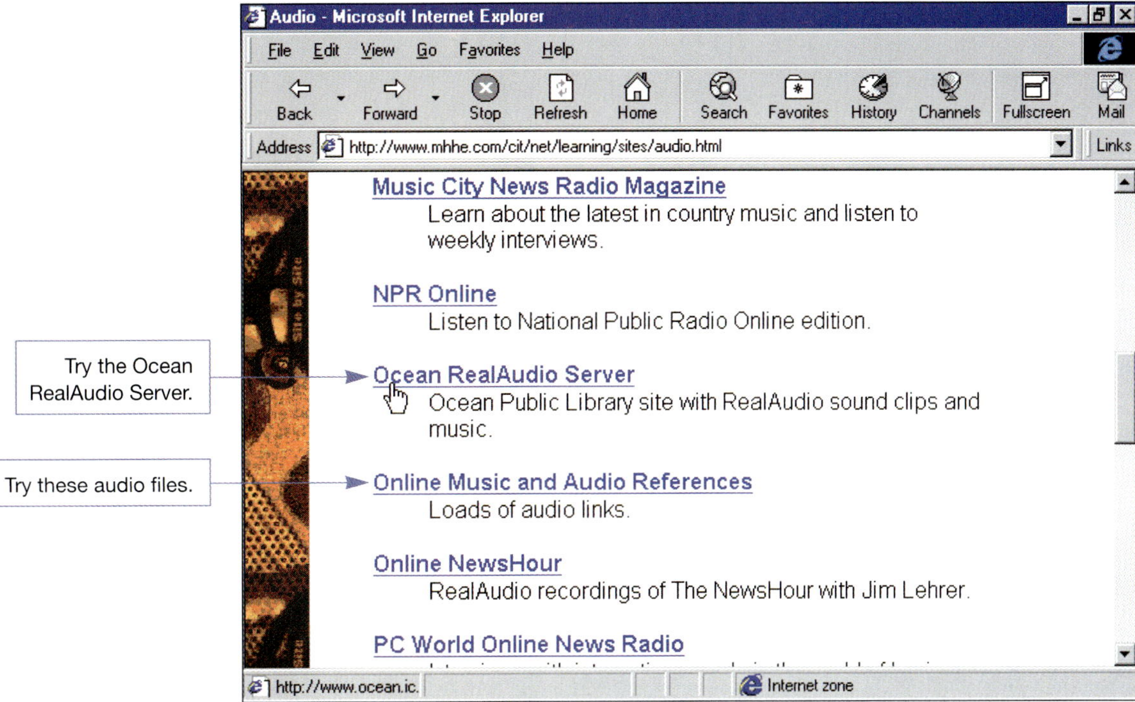

3. Select Ocean RealAudio Server.
   Notice the various audio links on this site (Image 8-4).

Image 8-4

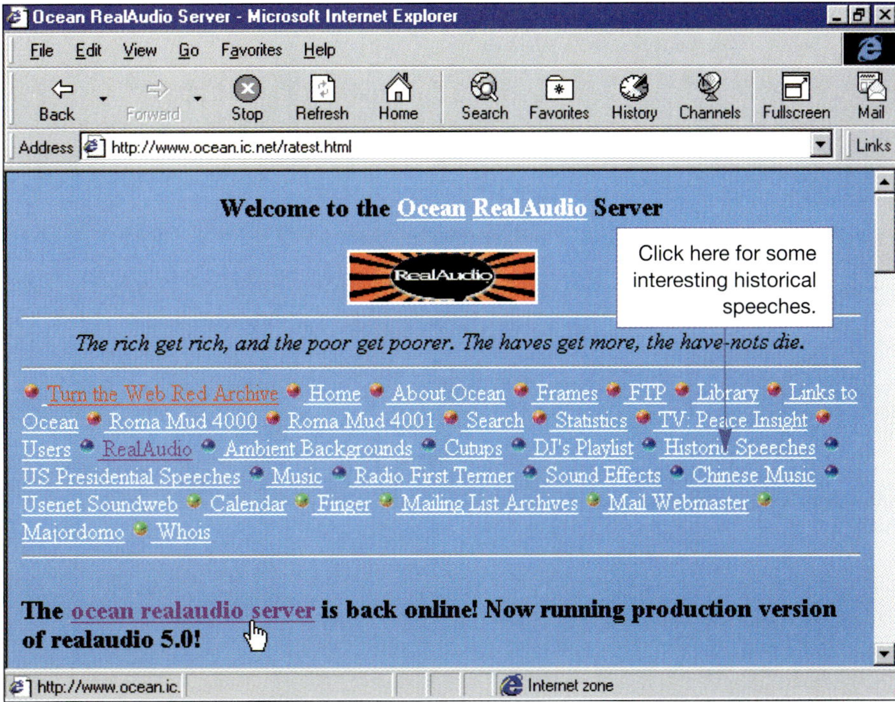

Henry Edward Hardy, hhardy@ocean.ic.net, http://www.ocean.ic.net/.

4. From Ocean browse through and explore the audio links.
5. Return to the Audio site of *Learning Online* and select MP Music Previews.
   Notice that this site lists audio links to several musicians, listed by category (Image 8-5).

Image 8-5

6. Select any category; then select any musician or group. A listing of audio link samples will appear.
7. Take a few minutes to explore various musical samples.

EXERCISE 8-1

Return to the Audio links of *Learning Online* and take some time to explore each of the available audio links. As you find new and interesting sites, send e-mail to your friends and your instructor letting them know what you have found.

EXERCISE 8-2

Pick any audio link available through *Learning Online* and write a one-paragraph evaluation of that link. Send your evaluation to your instructor via e-mail.

COOL VIDEO

As the World Wide Web expands and as users develop quicker access to the Web, one of the applications that is growing in popularity is video. Although Web video is not yet ready to replace television, or video rental stores, it does offer a great deal of promise.

Video is made up of two parts: moving pictures and audio. This combination of multimedia elements requires a fast computer with a great deal of RAM and a fast connection to the Internet. A short video segment can easily take several megabytes of memory. You need RAM to process the video and hard disk space to store the video. Be careful not to fill your hard disk with too many video files.

Internet Explorer needs an add-on to display video. Just as audio is available in a variety of formats, so is video. For each video format you use, you will need an add-on that supports that format. Some of the more popular video formats include .avi (Microsoft video), .qt/.mov (Apple QuickTime video), and .mpg/.mpeg/.mpe (Moving Picture Experts Group video).

Moving Picture Experts Group (MPEG) video is one of the most popular video file formats because it uses a compression technique that makes the video file smaller than many other types of video files. Because MPEG video is compressed, it requires a video viewer, or MPEG add-on, to decode the compression and play the video. MPEG plug-ins are available from many software developers.

Tips, Tricks, and Ideas 8-2

Purge Video Files

Unless you really need to store your video files, it is a good idea to delete unnecessary video files from your hard disk. Otherwise, you can quickly fill a hard disk and make it impossible to work on all the other applications you may need.

Tips, Tricks, and Ideas 8-3

DirectX/DirectShow

You can add DirectX and DirectShow to Internet Explorer easily by accessing the Internet Explorer Component Download page or by using other Internet software resources such as TUCOWS. By downloading and installing DirectShow, you can view most of the popular video files that are available on the Web.

Tips, Tricks, and Ideas 8-4

View Offline

Many users prefer to use video off line. In other words, they prefer to download the video file and then use a viewer to look at the video. The advantages to off-line viewing are speed and convenience. By downloading and saving the video file, you can view it over and over. Otherwise, you will need to go through the lengthy downloading process each time you want to view the video.

DirectShow

DirectShow is a video viewer for Internet Explorer. Actually, it is a video viewer based on the DirectX technology. **DirectX** is an interactive multimedia technology from Microsoft. In some ways it is similar to ActiveX. DirectX incorporates sound, graphics, and interactive capabilities to allow a new set of multimedia applications. DirectX is not an application. Rather, it is a set of standards, or protocols, that developers can use to create applications. DirectShow is one of the most popular DirectX applications.

ACTIVITY

1. From the Internet Software page on *Learning Online,* select the Microsoft Internet Explorer Component page (Image 8-6).

"Not Determined" will appear if you fail to let the Component Download page analyze your installation.

Image 8-6

2. Click on Yes to allow the Component Download page to determine what components are installed in your version of Internet Explorer (Image 8-7).

Image 8-7

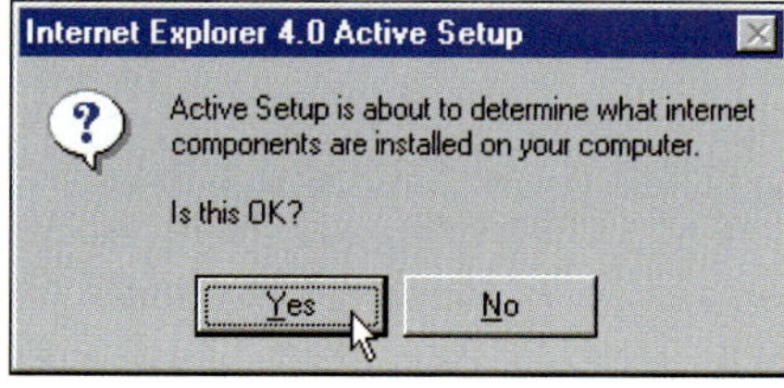

3. If DirectShow is not installed, check with you instructor to get permission to install DirectShow. If this poses a problem, do not continue with this activity.
4. Click on Next.
   Notice DirectShow is downloaded and installed.
5. Go back to *Learning Online;* then select the Video site.
   Notice the number of available video sites listed.
6. Select MPEG Monster List or any other link you desire (Image 8-8).

Image 8-8

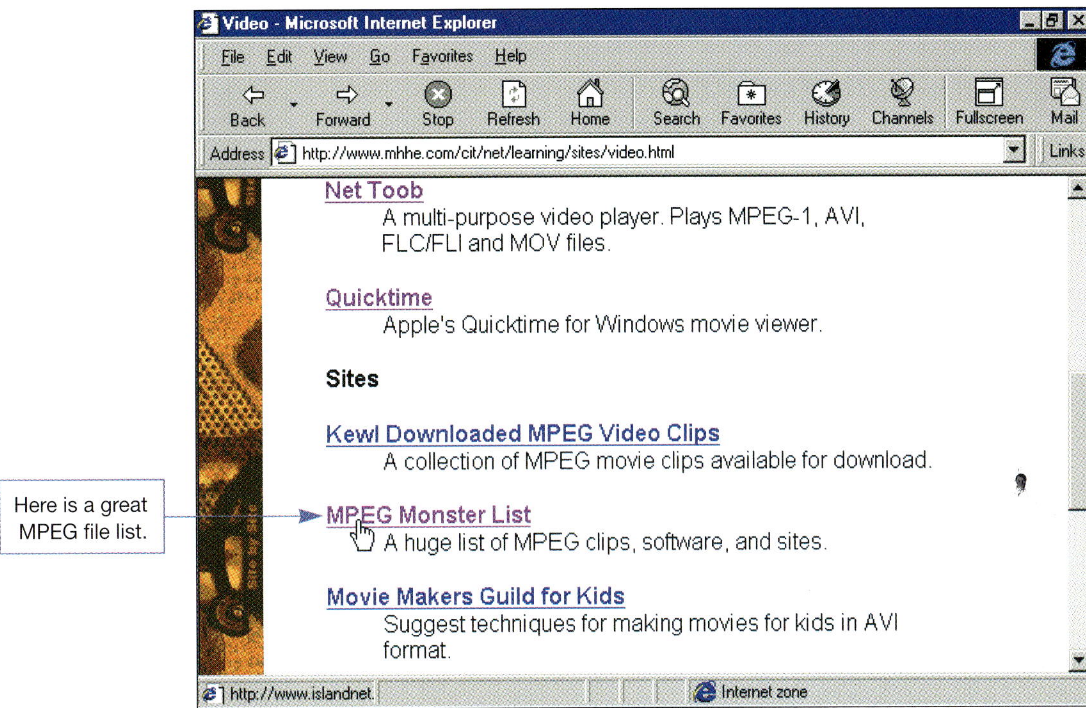

7. Take a few minutes to explore this site. Remember, downloading video files can take a long time so be patient (Image 8-9).

Image 8-9

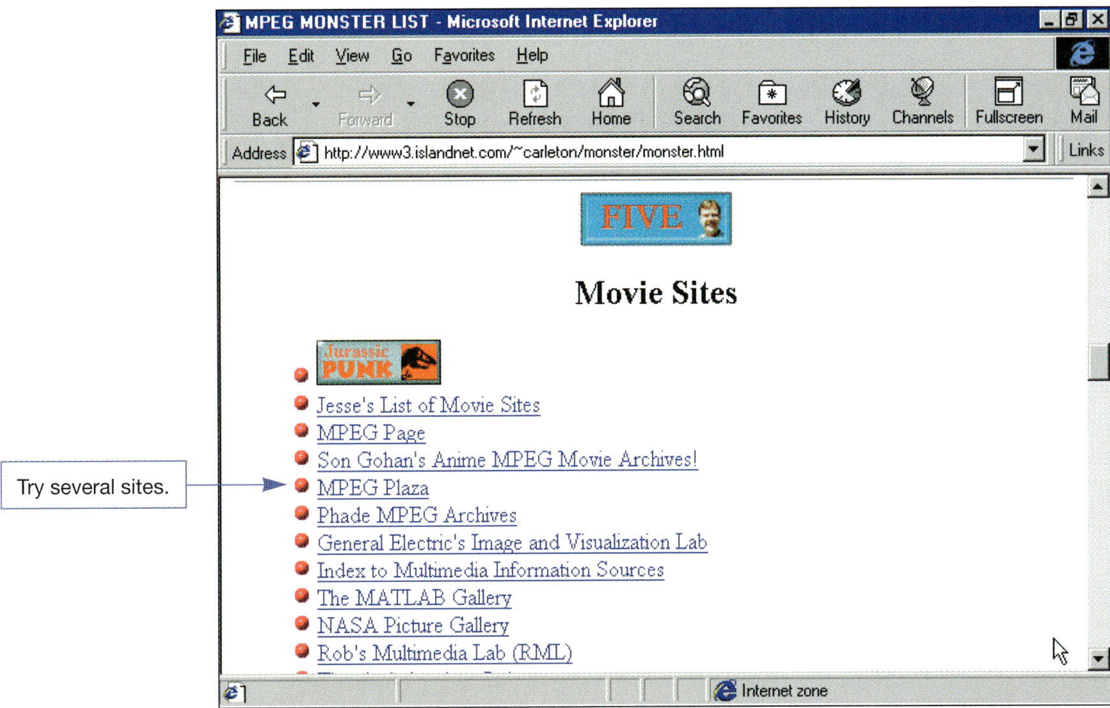

8. Return to MP Music Previews in the Audio site of *Learning Online*. Locate a favorite musician or group and see whether an MPEG music video is available.

9. Select an MPEG video.
   Notice that you can open or save the file (Image 8-10).

Image 8-10

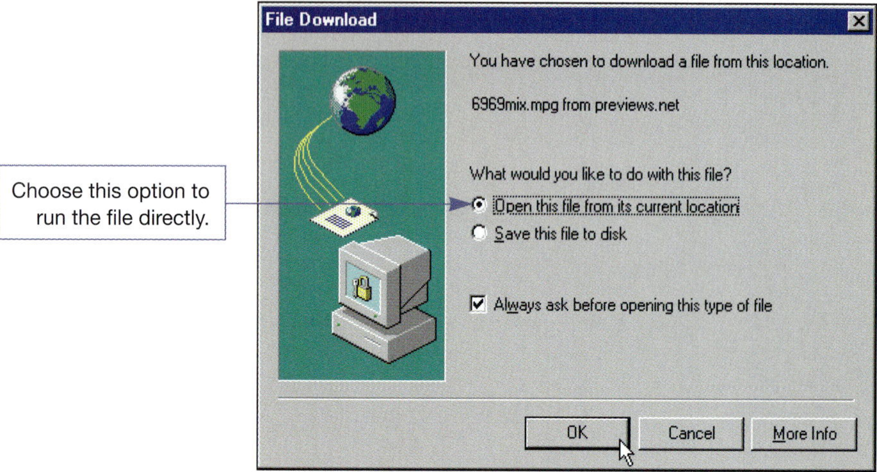

10. Try several music videos and make sure you use each of the major video file formats.

EXERCISE 8-3

Now that you have had an opportunity to examine video files in each of the three major formats, which do you like best? Is there a quality difference? Is there a speed difference? Send your instructor an e-mail with your opinions.

NEAT GRAPHICS

Graphics are the multimedia backbone of the World Wide Web, and Internet Explorer is able to use these graphics inline. **Inline** means that the graphics appear as part of a Web page just as text is a part of a Web page.

Two of the most popular inline graphics supported by Internet Explorer include .gif (called gif) and .jpg (pronounced "jay peg"). You do not need to do anything to view .gif or .jpg graphics in Internet Explorer. However, to save and manipulate a graphics file you locate over the Web, you will need an image viewer. Various image viewers are available. Some produce higher quality graphics; others save and use graphics in a smaller file size. Some do both. The trick is to determine which graphics file you will need and then locate and download the viewers that best fit your needs.

If you are using Microsoft Office, you automatically have a great plug-in for graphics files other than .gifs and .jpgs. This program is called Microsoft Imager. Microsoft Imager supports .bmp, .dib, .pcd, and .pcx graphics as well as .gif and .jpg. In most cases there is no need to use Microsoft Imager for .gif and .jpg, as they are already supported within Internet Explorer.

ACTIVITY

1. You have already used the graphics capabilities for .gif and .jpg files. Most of the graphics you encounter on the Web use this format.
2. Select the Internet Software site from *Learning Online.*
3. Select TUCOWS.
4. Select the location nearest you.
   Notice that this site contains some of the most popular and useful add-ons and plug-ins available (Image 8-11).

Image 8-11

Choose locations nearest to your location.

5. Select Windows 95/98.
   Scroll down and notice the menu of applications (Image 8-12).

Image 8-12

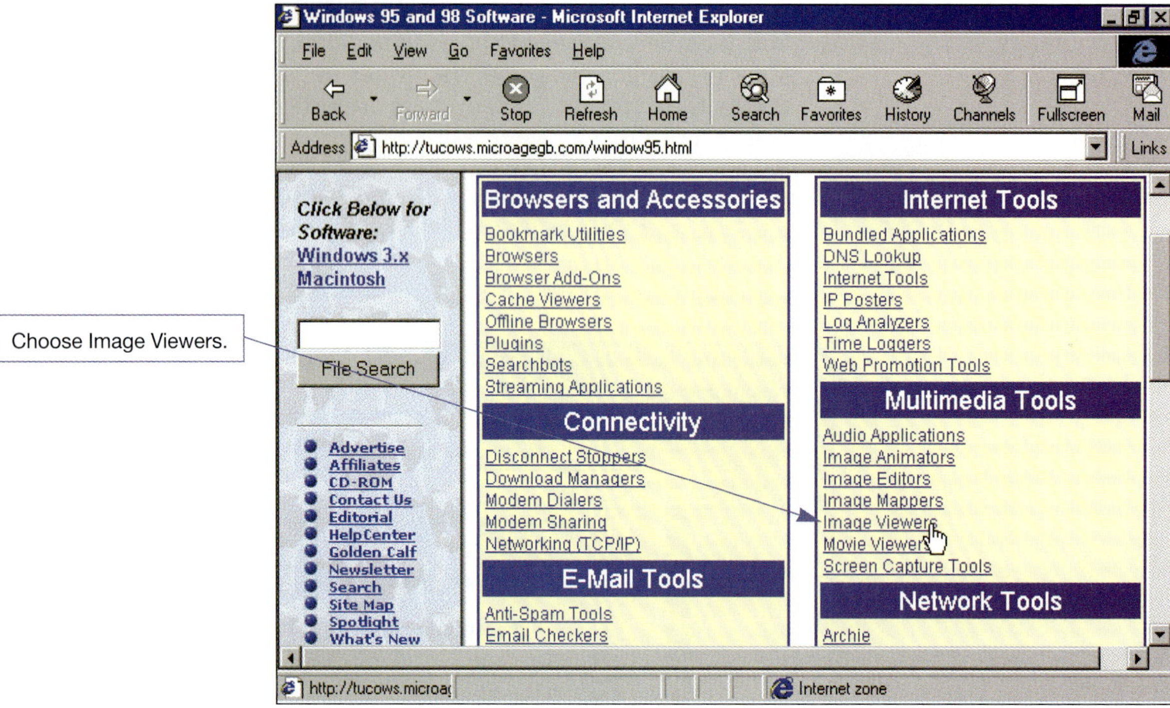

6. Select Image Viewers.
   Notice the long list of graphics image viewers available (Image 8-13).

Image 8-13

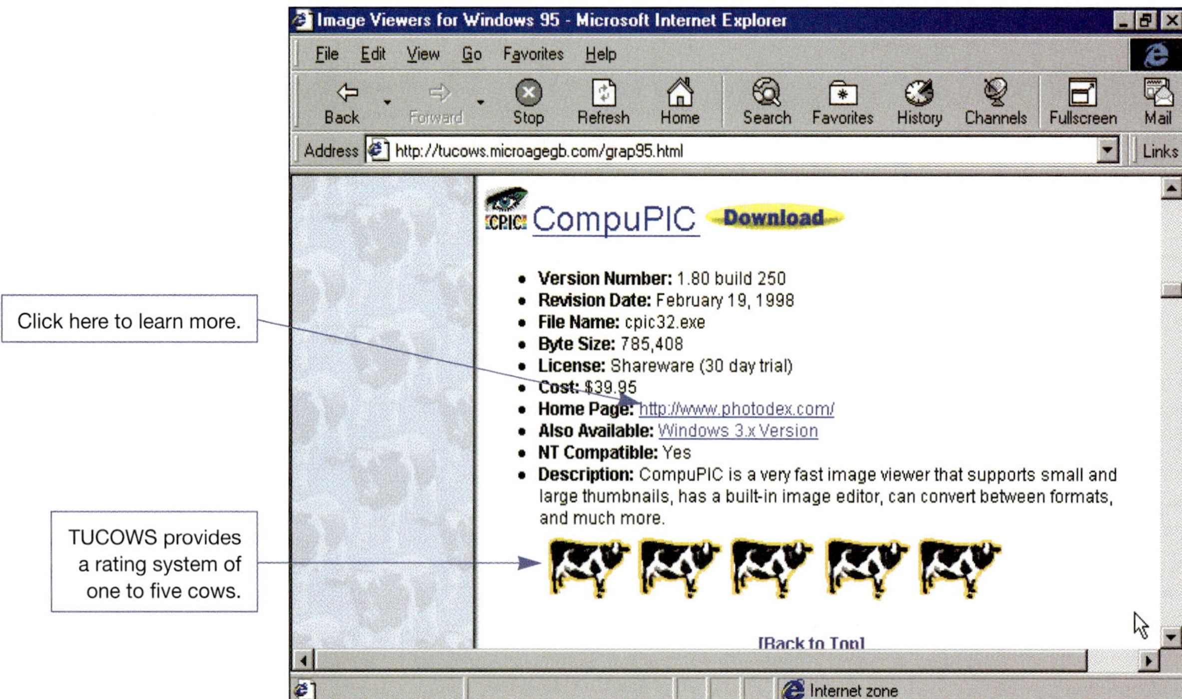

7. Select a graphics image viewer of your choice and download the software. Once it is downloaded, leave Internet Explorer and install the software.

EXERCISE 8-4

Almost any Web page contains a graphic. Point at a graphic and click the right mouse button; then select Save Picture As to save the graphics image. Use the image viewer downloaded in the previous activity to view the image. Take a few minutes to explore the options of your viewer. On a sheet of paper, create a list of 10 features of your viewer.

USING ANIMATION WITH VRML

Virtual Reality Modeling Language (VRML) is, in many ways, like HTML. VRML is a programming language that produces Web documents that a browser (with a plug-in) can interpret and display. Web developers using VRML, instead of HTML, can add many features to their Web pages that are not available to Web developers using HTML.

From a user's point of view, VRML is the 3-D world of the Web. In VRML a scene is developed. You can interact with that screen by moving around within it, using a series of tools provided with the VRML plug-in. For example, a VRML scene may consist of a museum. With the tools provided on the toolbar, you can walk through that scene and view different areas of the museum. VRML supports many exciting features. Some are listed in Table 8-1 above. By incorporating all of these multidimensional features, VRML is a one-stop location for multimedia. The interaction of a virtual reality scene is what makes VRML an exciting world on the Web (Table 8-2).

Table 8-1
Common VRML Features

Common VRML Features
Background graphics images
Texture animation
Texture mapping
3-D text
Morphing
Gravity
Viewpoints
RealPlayer

Tips, Tricks, and Ideas 8-5

It Is Just the Beginning

VRML is in its infancy. By many standards it is slow and a bit awkward to move about a virtual scene. VRML holds a great deal of promise, but you have to be a bit patient with this emerging technology.

One of the most popular VRML tools for Internet Explorer is Microsoft's VRML 2.0 Viewer. In fact, a VRML 2.0 viewer is a "must have" for Internet Explorer, as the viewer will provide you with access to VRML 2.0 Web pages. The major feature that you will notice when you connect to a VRML Web site is the

Table 8-2
Typical VRML Toolbars

Walk	Moves forward, backward, left, or right (drag with the mouse to move around)
Pan	Allows you to slide from left or right
Turn	Allows you to swing to the left or to the right
Roll	Allows you to rotate
Goto	Allows you to click on the VRML image and move toward the item
Study	Allows you to rotate an object in any direction
Zoom out	Allows you to see the entire VRML world
Straightenup	Returns you to an even upright position
View	Allows you to shift perspectives
Restore	Allows you to return to where you started

VRML toolbar. This toolbar enables you to interact with the Web page and control movement of 3-D objects. For example, with the toolbar you can move to new locations on a 3-D scene.

Tips, Tricks, and Ideas 8-6

VRML Toolbars

When VRML was introduced, there was no standard for VRML 1.0 toolbars; however, a standard is emerging with VRML 2.0 browsers. Although all VRML 1.0 toolbars perform the same tasks, the actual tools may differ. This variation is not a problem as most tools on a toolbar are self-explanatory. All that is required of you is to spend a few minutes of practice with the tools specific to the VRML plug-in you select.

ACTIVITY

1. Select the Virtual Reality Modeling Language link from *Learning Online* and then scroll down and select the VRML Models link (Image 8-14).

Image 8-14

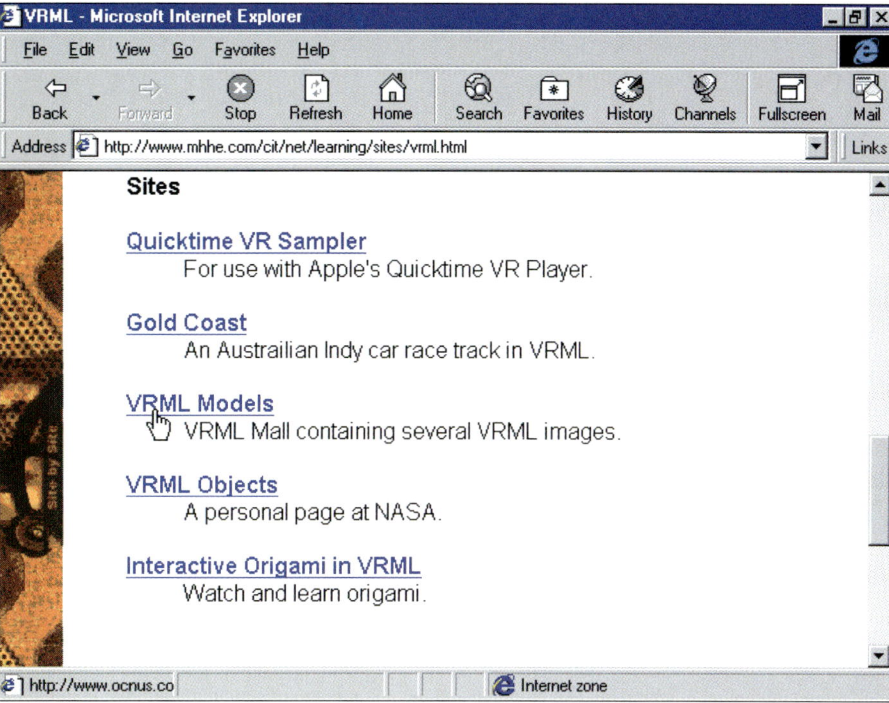

2. Scroll down and select Animals in the Categories table. Notice that several VRML animal models appear.
3. Select the shark (Image 8-15).

Image 8-15

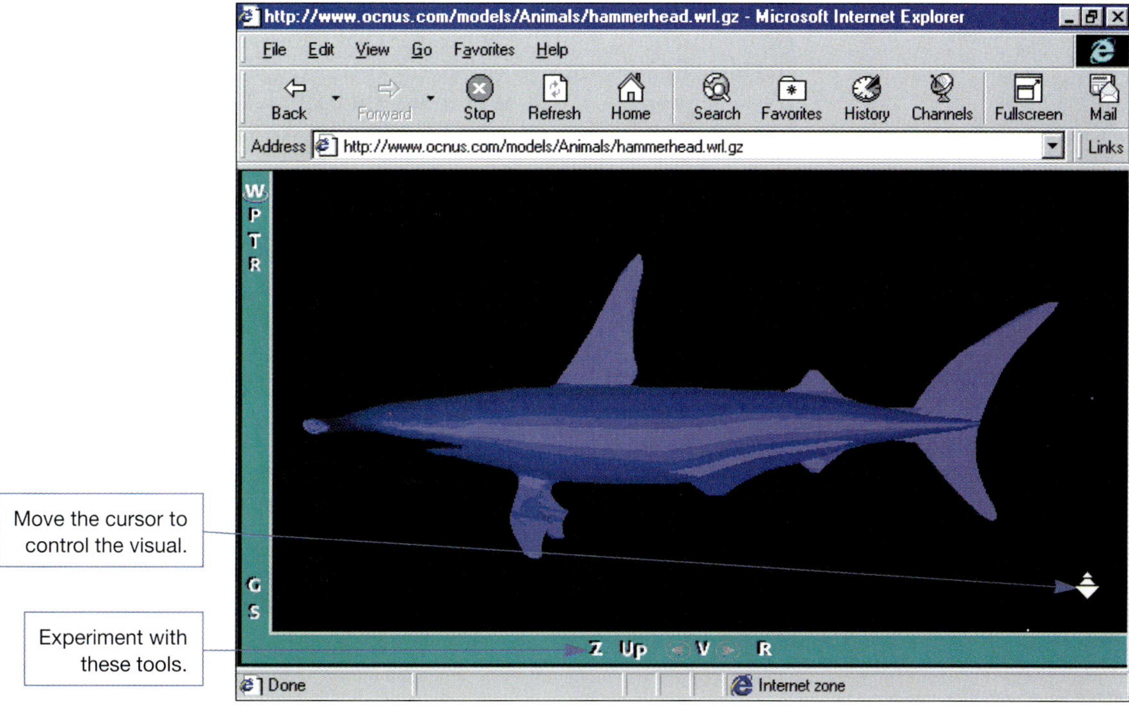

Move the cursor to control the visual.

Experiment with these tools.

4. Experiment with each tool on the VRML toolbar. Notice how you can change your view of the shark.

5. Click on the Back button and select a different animal.
   Take a few minutes to practice using the various VRML tools.
6. Return to the Categories table and explore some of the VRML 3-D scenes that are available.
7. Return to the VRML site and explore some of the other VRML links that are available.

EXERCISE 8-5

Use YAHOO! or any other search tool to look for VRML sites. Send your instructor an e-mail identifying three interesting VRML sites. Be sure to include the URL and a brief description of each site. We encourage you to send us any recommendations of the best sites by sending e-mail to WebDude at *Learning Online.*

ADOBE ACROBAT READER

Another must-have is the Adobe Acrobat Reader. This add-on allows you to view files that were produced in Adobe Acrobat format (.pdf). Typically, these files appear as typeset quality text and graphics and were produced with programs such as PageMaker. For example, newsletters displayed on the Web will often use Adobe Acrobat format files. With Adobe Acrobat you can view the newsletter in its original format and print the document in typeset quality (Image 8-16).

Downloading and installing Adobe Acrobat Reader is similar to downloading and installing other add-ons. In fact, when you locate various .pdf documents on the Web, there typically is a link to download and install Adobe Acrobat. After you install this add-on, you can view .pdf files from the Web. Loading an Acrobat file into Internet Explorer causes Acrobat Reader to open a blank window. This window transfers the capabilities of Acrobat Reader into Internet Explorer. Once this window is open, do not close it; doing so will terminate the capabilities of Acrobat Reader, and Internet Explorer will no longer be able to display a .pdf document.

Image 8-16

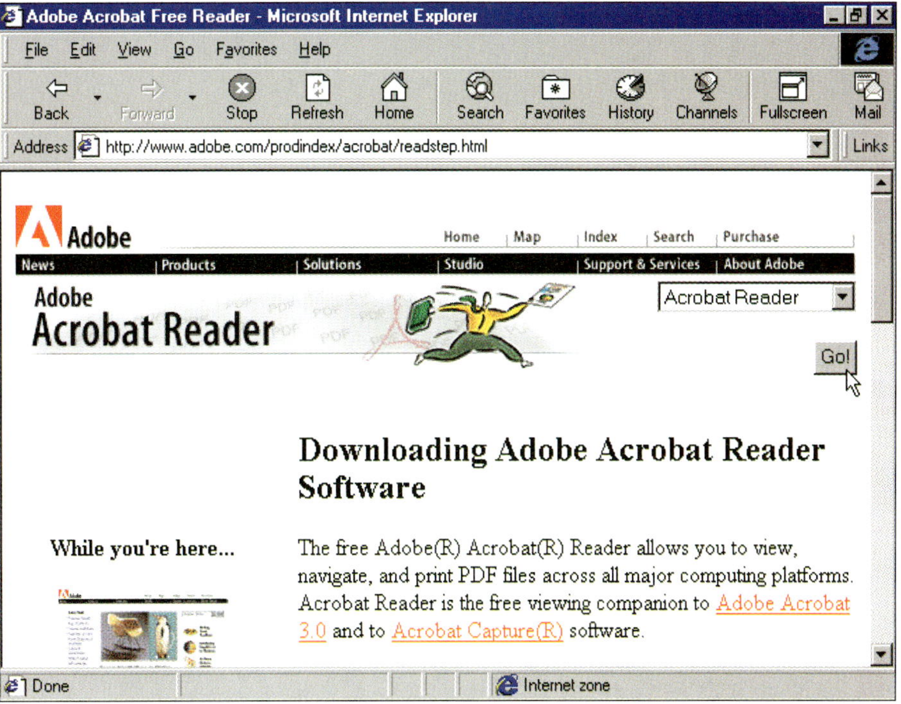

EXERCISE 8-6

Visit the Adobe Acrobat samples page from *Learning Online*. Make sure that Adobe Acrobat Reader is installed; then download and print a .pdf document.

COMMUNICATING WITH MICROSOFT NETMEETING

One of the most interesting features of the World Wide Web is the ability to communicate in real time with other World Wide Web users. To support real-time voice and video communication, Internet Explorer has **Microsoft NetMeeting.**

With Microsoft NetMeeting, a sound card, speakers, and a microphone, you can talk to any other Web user who has the same configuration. With Microsoft NetMeeting you can use the Web to talk long distance with other users without having to pay long-distance phone charges. Although the quality of Internet phone is still somewhat undeveloped, the promise of using the Web for live conversation is very exciting.

To use NetMeeting, you must first install the software. The first time you run NetMeeting, select Internet Phone from the Go menu or select NetMeeting from the Start menu. The Microsoft NetMeeting Setup Wizard takes you step-by-step through the full installation process. Subsequently, whenever you launch NetMeeting, the Microsoft NetMeeting window appears.

NetMeeting works by displaying a list of all users connected to a particular server. Therefore, when you want to speak with someone, you must know on which server the person resides. There are a number of different Internet phone servers, so knowing the correct server is critical.

After you identify the server, the NetMeeting Directory displays all the people who are currently logged on to the selected server. From this list you may double-click on a name to initiate a call (meeting). At this point NetMeeting will attempt to connect you and the individual you selected. If the person you select accepts your invitation, the Current Call window will appear. In this window you have the option of communicating via audio, the Chat window, the Whiteboard, and with video, assuming your computer has a video camera installed.

Talking through a microphone with NetMeeting, or other Internet phone programs, is somewhat different from using a telephone. Depending on the type of sound card installed in your computer and the remote computer, talking through a microphone is like using a walkie-talkie. One person talks while the other listens. This system takes a bit of getting used to, but it works fine. Some sound cards support full duplex, which allows a more natural conversation.

Tips, Tricks, and Ideas 8-7

Adjust Your Volumes

If you are planning to make an audio call, be certain your microphone volume and speaker volume are set correctly. If not, you may not hear or transmit the audio.

Talking with someone you don't know has its risks. Although most people are kind and considerate, there are those who prey on others. Be careful. Don't reveal personal information about yourself to total strangers.

Of course, not everyone has or uses Microsoft NetMeeting. To locate NetMeeting users, use the Web Directory from the Go menu.

If you want to receive NetMeeting calls, you must have NetMeeting running. You can set the AutoAnswer command from the Call menu to automatically answer any incoming calls or to prompt you whenever someone tries to contact you.

ACTIVITY

1. From the Go menu, select Internet Call.
   If this is the first time that NetMeeting is being used, the Microsoft NetMeeting Setup Wizard will appear (Image 8-17). Follow the steps until you complete the installation process.

Image 8-17

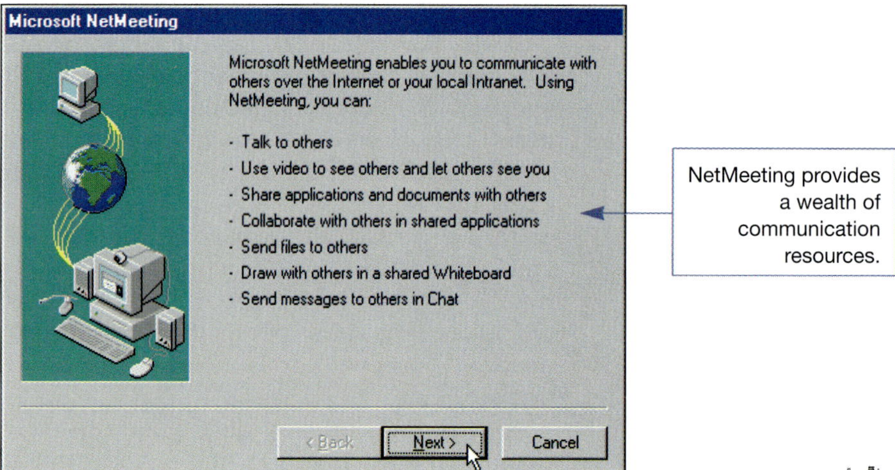

2. Make sure the Microsoft NetMeeting window appears (Image 8-18).
3. Select a server.
   Notice that the Directory contains a list of phone addresses for some NetMeeting users (Image 8-18).

Image 8-18

Be selective in choosing a conversation. Some people prefer "questionable" topics.

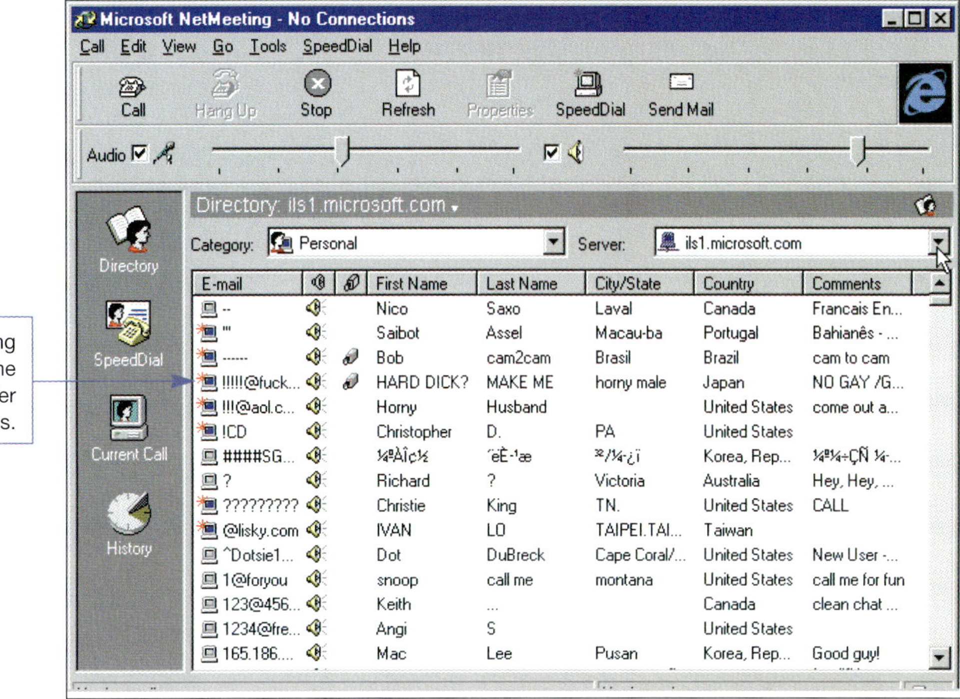

4. If you see someone you want to call, select the person's name and a call will be initiated.
5. Try several connections. If you do connect to someone, be polite and courteous and explain that you are just learning to use NetMeeting. Quite often people you connect to will be happy to provide you with some advice on making NetMeeting a functional tool.

EXERCISE 8-7

If you are a regular Web user and have friends and family members in other states who are also Web users, NetMeeting offers you the opportunity to stay in touch without expensive long-distance charges. Contact friends and family that you think might be interested in using NetMeeting and establish a connection with them. Be prepared to share your experiences with the rest of the class.

CHAT, WHITEBOARD, AND FILE EXCHANGE NETMEETING FEATURES

You are not required to have speakers and a microphone to use Microsoft NetMeeting. Once you establish a call you can use the **Current Call** window to invoke text-based chatting by clicking on the Chat button. This will launch the Chat window where you can communicate with other

> ### Tips, Tricks, and Ideas 8-8
>
> ***Fewer Resources***
>
> Transmitting and receiving audio takes a great deal of system resources. The Chat tool does not. Many users prefer to use the Chat tool rather than an Internet phone because it is often much faster and the Chat tool users are able to use their computer and connection for other resources.

NetMeeting users by typing in the message area. You must be connected to a call before you can use the Chat tool to send messages.

Another popular resource is the **Whiteboard** tool. This tool allows you to share image files and to edit them interactively. In other words, the Whiteboard is a simple drawing area that anyone in the call can modify. To access the Whiteboard, click on the Whiteboard button on the toolbar. The Whiteboard window is very similar to many draw and paint programs.

Another useful feature of NetMeeting is **Share,** which allows you to share an application with another user. In other words, if you want to work on Microsoft Excel with another person, you start the application you want to share and then click on the Share button in NetMeeting. This feature can be very useful if you are having an audio conversation and want to work together on the same application.

The last tool for Microsoft NetMeeting is **File Transfer.** Selecting File Transfer from the Tools menu allows you to send files to and receive files from a user during a connected call. In other words, you can send a file to a user while you are having an audio or text conversation.

ACTIVITY

1. Make a connection through NetMeeting with another user.
2. Select Chat from the Tools menu.
   Notice the NetMeeting Chat window (Image 8-19).

Image 8-19

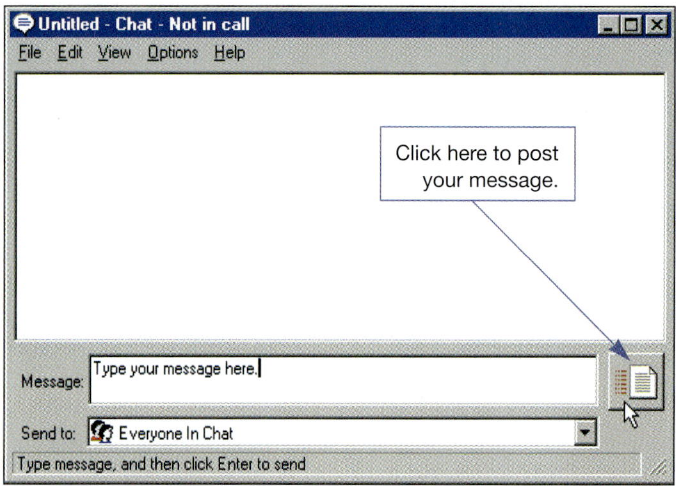

3. Type your message in the Message: field.
4. Click on the Send button to send your message.
5. Close the NetMeeting Text Chat window and select the Whiteboard from the Tools menu.
   The NetMeeting Whiteboard window appears (Image 8-20).

Image 8-20

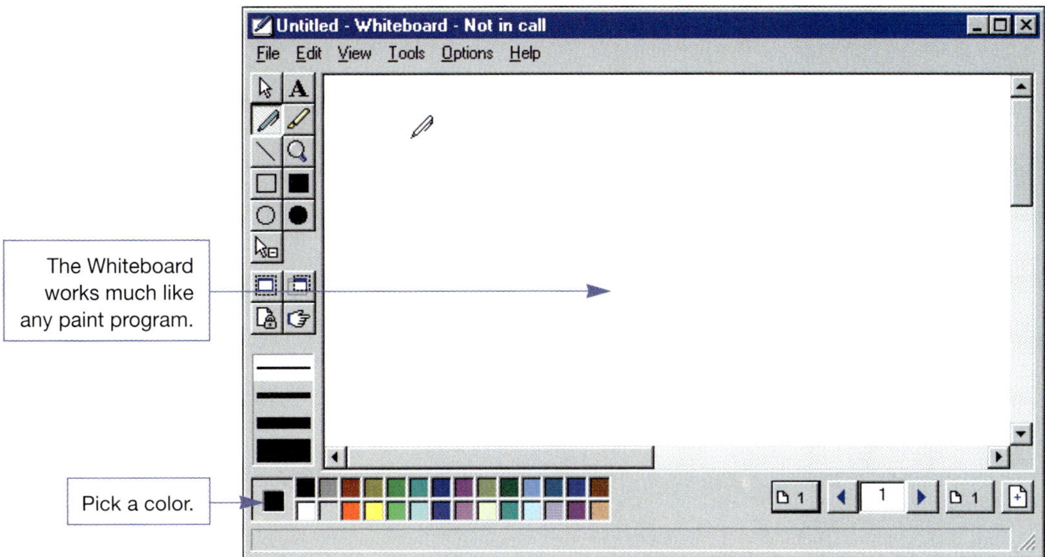

> **Tips, Tricks, and Ideas 8-9**
>
> *Just the Beginning*
>
> This section briefly introduced some of the possibilities of using NetMeeting. By launching NetMeeting and then experimenting with the various NetMeeting features, you should be able to quickly become adept at using NetMeeting.

6. Take a few minutes to experiment with several of the Whiteboard tools. Click on each tool and then use that tool in the drawing area.
7. Close the NetMeeting Whiteboard window.
8. Select the File Transfer command from the Tools menu.

   If you have a call in progress, you may select Send File.
9. Close the File Transfer window and close Microsoft NetMeeting.

JAVA AND JAVASCRIPT

In 1995, Sun Microsystems introduced Java as a new programming language designed to support animation, games, browsers, and interactive televisions. Java enables Web developers to create interactive Web sites and to produce small programs that can be run from within a Java-supported Web browser such as Internet Explorer. These small programs are called *applets*. Applets can be very simple animations, complex interactive games, fill-in forms, or chat sites, to name just a few types of applications. One of the most exciting features of Java is that it frees Web developers to produce very interesting effects within a Web page.

Because Internet Explorer supports Java, when a Java applet on a Web site is encountered, Internet Explorer has the ability to run the applet. Not all Web browsers have this capability. For the user, applets appear as an integral part of a page. For example, you may see text that appears as a marquee across a page. In all likelihood this feature is the result of Internet Explorer running a Java applet. You may find the equivalent of a chat host on a Web page running without Internet Explorer Chat. This feature is also a Java applet.

> **Tips, Tricks, and Ideas 8-10**
>
> *Is It Java? Is It JavaScript?*
>
> Java and JavaScript both allow Web developers to add interactive features to a Web page. If you become interested in Web page development, it is worth learning Java and particularly JavaScript to make your Web pages more interesting, exciting, and interactive.

JavaScript differs from Java in that the former

provides a full set of commands and functions that are built into HTML documents. HTML is a static language. After a Web page is developed in HTML, you cannot interact with the page. JavaScript offers several interactive extensions that add interactive capabilities to an HTML document. As with Java, users find that JavaScript is, for the most part, transparent. You may not always be aware that JavaScript is used within a document unless you are aware of the interactive features that a Web page may offer.

ACTIVITY

1. Activate the *Learning Online* Web site.
2. Click on the Java site.
   Notice the available Web sites that contain Java applets (Image 8-21).

Image 8-21

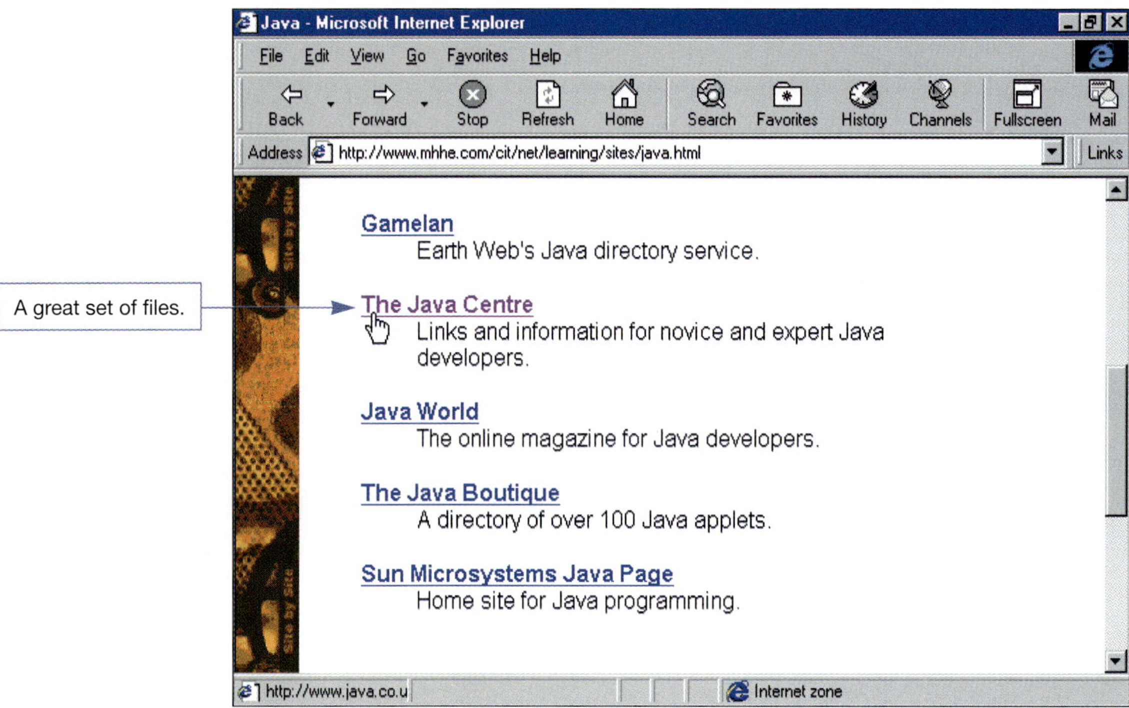

3. Select The Java Centre.
   This site provides access to several Java applets (Image 8-22).

Image 8-22

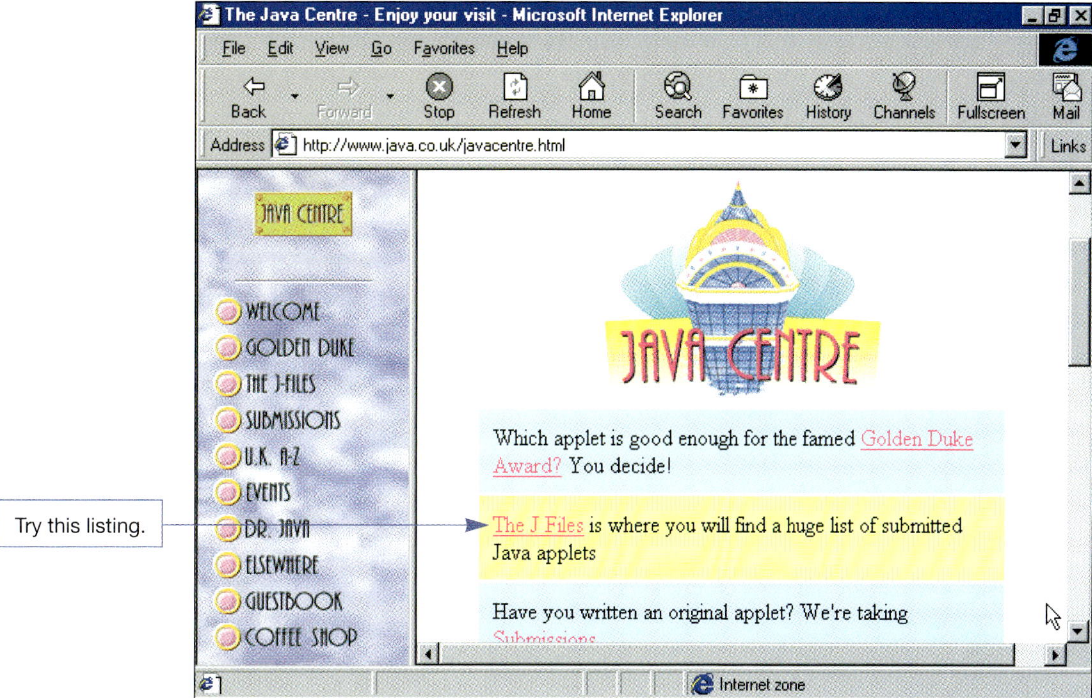

4. Select The J Files.
   Here you will find several Java applets (Image 8-23).

Image 8-23

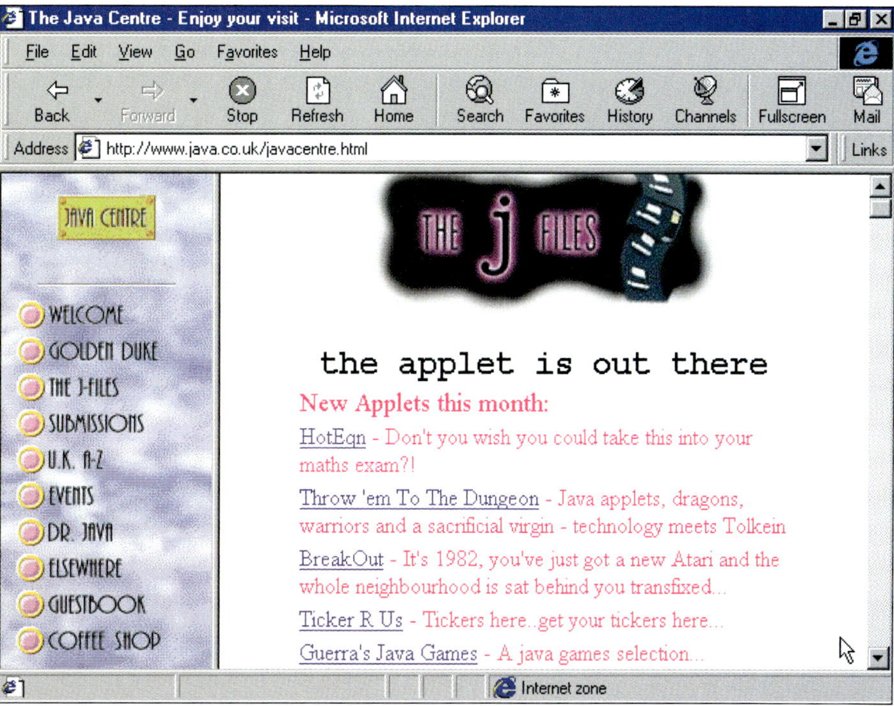

5. Take a few minutes and explore these Java applets.

EXERCISE 8-8

The Java link from *Learning Online* contains access to several interesting Java applets. Locate and run three Java applets. Be prepared to share these with the rest of the class.

CHAT ROOMS

One popular use of the Web is commonly called *chatting*, and it occurs in a Java chat room. To enter a chat room, you need to go to a specific interactive URL. A JavaScript typically allows you to sign in to the chat room with a nickname. After you sign in, you can "chat," that is, write a comment for all other participants in the chat room to view.

Some chat rooms require you to have an account and password before you can enter. In most cases, however, all you need to do is provide an identification or nickname. No password is required.

When you enter a chat room, there is a specific code of etiquette that you need to follow. The first rule is stick to the topic. If the chat is about politics, then discuss politics. Other chat room participants will become agitated if you deviate from the host topic. Also, be polite and avoid derogatory or profane language. Remember, you are "talking" with others, so be courteous. Finally, never send personal information. You never really know with whom you are chatting, so a bit of caution is in order.

Tips, Tricks, and Ideas 8-11

Search Chat

If you are looking for chat rooms for specific subject areas, do a Web search with YAHOO! or any other search tool and search for chat, followed by the topic. For example, if you search for chat political, you will find some political chat rooms to enter.

Tips, Tricks, and Ideas 8-12

Some Common Sense

Chatting with others over the Web can be a lot of fun. However, the "few bad apples" adage does apply. You never know for sure to whom you are "talking." You should never reveal too much personal information. Anything you say in a chat room can be read by anyone in the chat room. Be careful and use some common sense.

Netiquette 8-1

Listen First

It is usually a good idea to listen in on the discussion before joining in. You should become acquainted with the culture of the group before jumping in to participate.

Netiquette 8-2

Respect Anonymity

If a user is using a nickname, recognize that this person desires anonymity. Even if you know that person quite well, use his or her nickname. Don't reveal a person's identity if that person wishes to remain anonymous.

Netiquette 8-3

Don't Ask

Just as you shouldn't reveal too much information, don't "badger" others in the chat room. It is inappropriate to ask for personal information such as their sex, age, or location.

MICROSOFT CHAT

Microsoft Chat provides another option for communicating in real time with others on the Internet. The big difference between Microsoft Chat and other chat options is that Microsoft Chat uses a cartoon and a comic strip format to add visual appeal to the traditional text-only chat room. Messages from each participant appear as words from comic strip characters. When you launch Microsoft Chat, you are assigned a character. You have the option of selecting a character expression. When you chat, your character appears in the comic strip.

To choose your character, select the Options command from the View menu and then click on the Character tab. You also have the option of determining how your message will appear in the comic strip. The **Say** option places your text within a word balloon over your character. **Think** displays your text as a thought balloon. **Whisper** allows you to send your message only to those characters you select rather than to all chat room participants. Finally, **Action** places your text in the upper-left corner of the comic strip.

Microsoft Chat allows you to connect to various chat servers. To connect to a different chat server, select the New Connection command from the File menu; then select Show all available chat rooms. You will see a complete room list.

ACTIVITY

1. Go to the YAHOO! site and select Chat.
   Notice YAHOO! Chat (Image 8-24).

Image 8-24

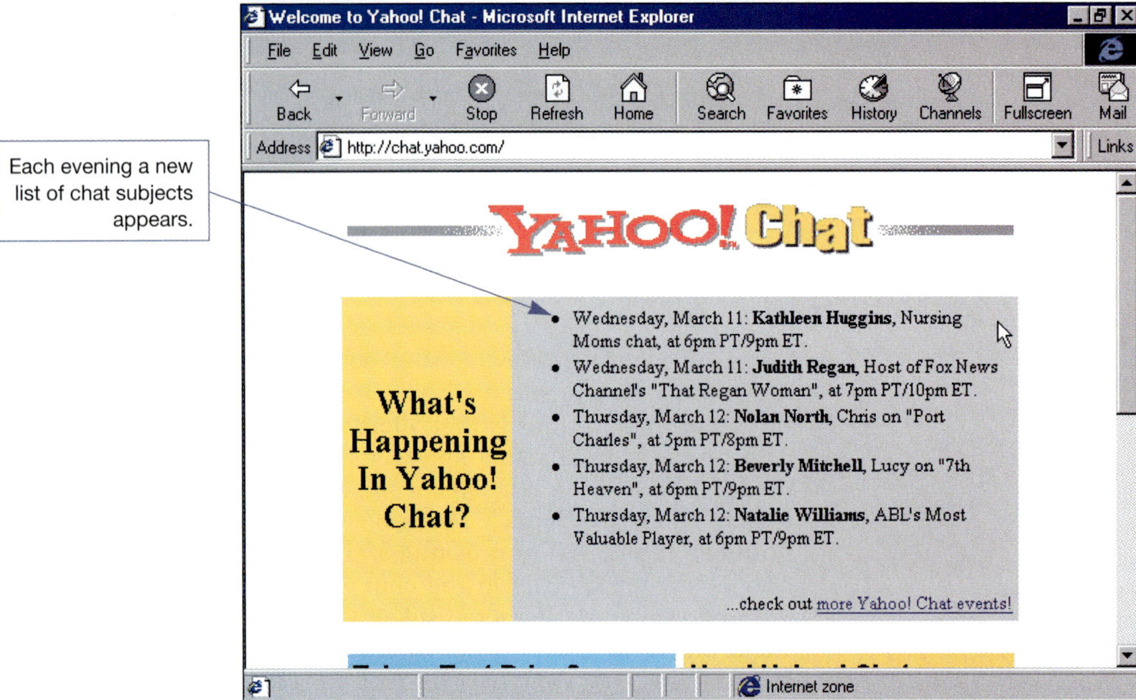

2. Click on Get Registered.
3. Provide the information requested (Image 8-25).

Image 8-25

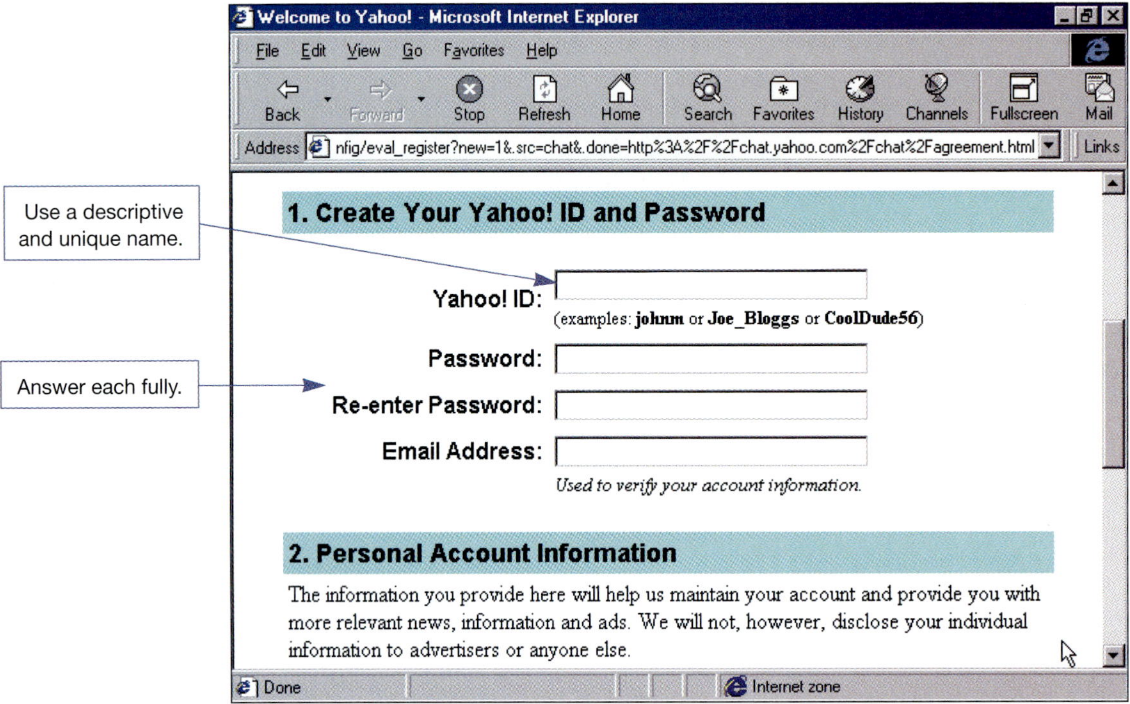

4. Be sure to read the Chat Agreement; then, if you agree, click on the I Accept button.

   Notice the YAHOO! Chat menu (Image 8-26).

Image 8-26

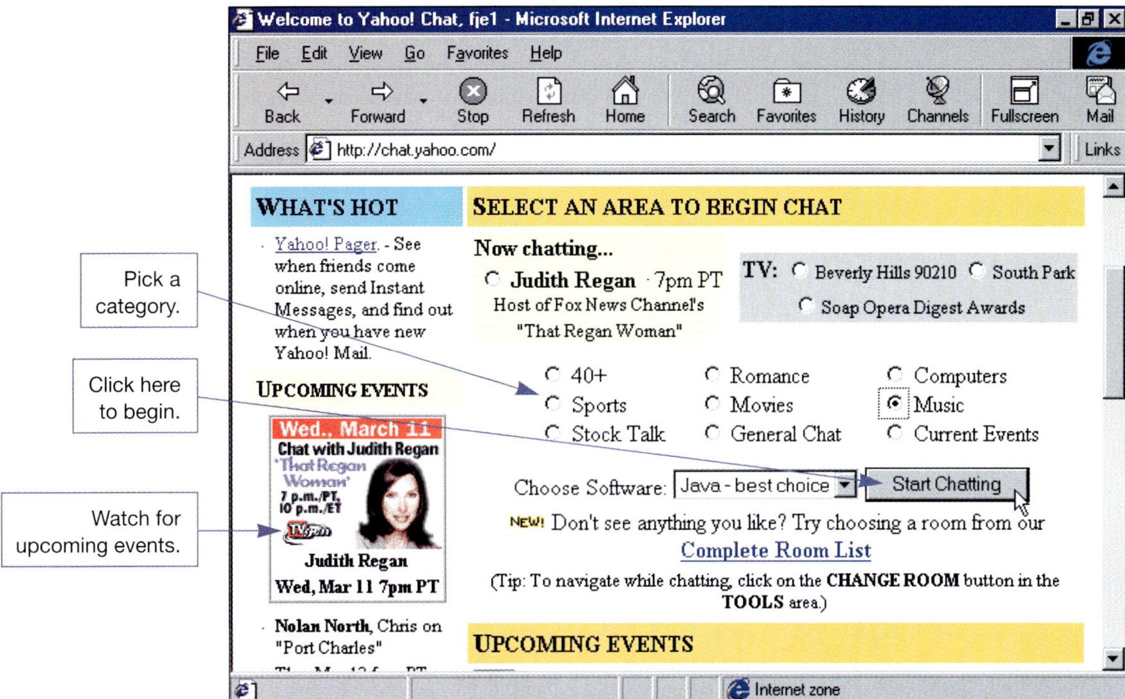

5. Under Select an Area to Begin Chat, select Music; then click on Start Chatting.
   Notice the Chat screen (Image 8-27).

Image 8-27

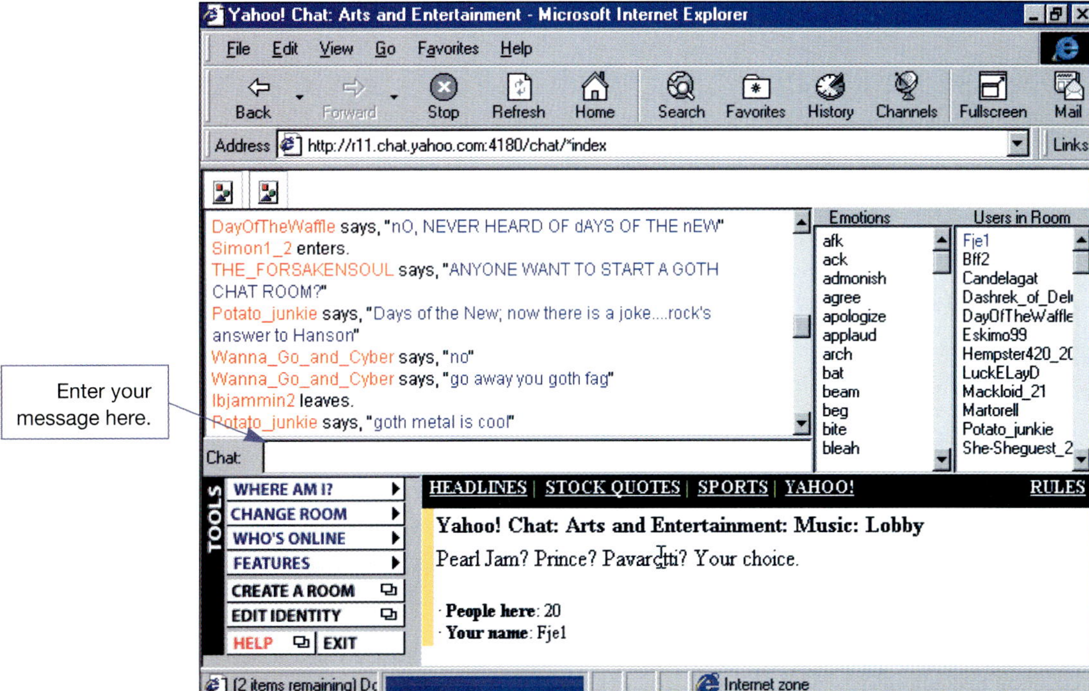

6. It is up to you to decide whether you want to participate in the chat.
7. If you have not already done so, download and install Microsoft Chat.
8. Launch Microsoft Chat.
9. In the Connect dialog box, select any server and then click on OK. Notice the comic strip format of Microsoft Chat (Image 8-28).

Image 8-28

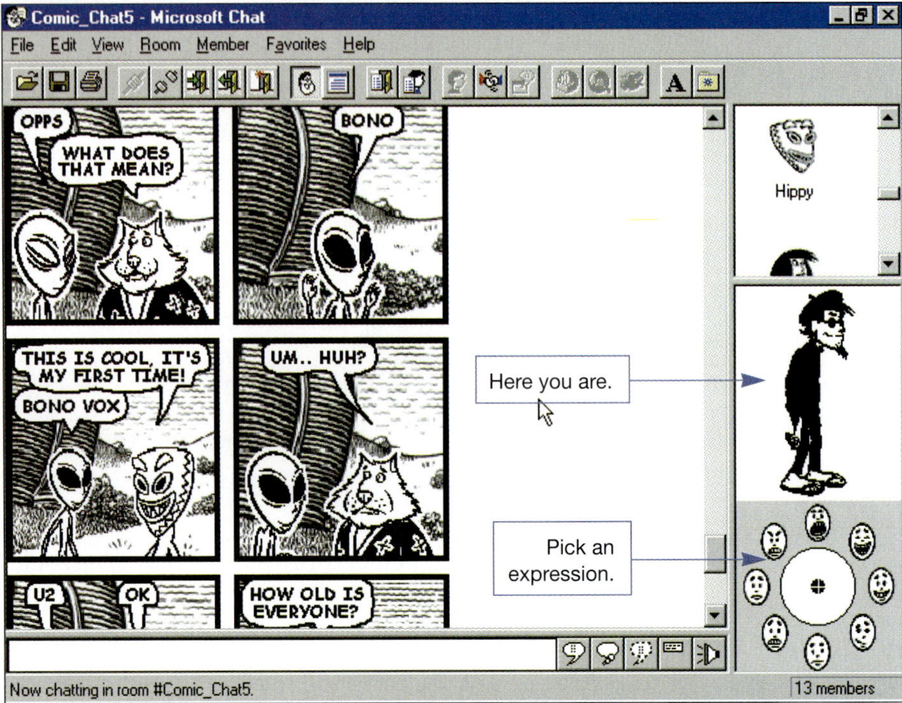

10. It is up to you to decide whether to participate in the chat.

> **Tips, Tricks, and Ideas 8-13**
>
> *Watch Your Language*
>
> For some reason, far too many people who use chat rooms think that because they are not talking face to face, they can use offensive language. Don't follow their example.

EXERCISE 8-9

Go chatting. Find at least three chat rooms to join. Chat with others in the room. If you are new to chatting, say so and you will likely receive lots of helpful advice on how to use not only the current chat room, but other chat rooms in general. Visit at least three chat rooms and then add them to your Chat address book.

KEY POINTS

- Add-ons and plug-ins add almost endless flexibility to Internet Explorer. One important reason for using plug-ins and add-ons is to get access to multimedia tools.
- Multimedia is a multisensory approach to the delivery of information.
- In addition to multimedia plug-ins and add-ons, various other tools help bring a Web site to life. One of these tools is Java. Programs created by Java are referred to as Java applets.
- One way to expand Internet Explorer is to use the Internet Explorer Component Download page provided by Microsoft.
- Audio is an integral component of multimedia.
- RealPlayer has become very popular because it is quick and allows users to stream audio. With

RealPlayer you can get a continuous stream of audio such as live news broadcasts, large streams of lectures, and other audio files.

- One of the applications that is growing in popularity is video. However, a short video segment may easily take several megabytes of memory.
- MPEG video is one of the most popular video file formats because it uses a compression technique that makes the video file smaller than many other video files.
- DirectShow is a video viewer for Internet Explorer. Actually, it is a video viewer based on the DirectX technology. DirectX is an interactive multimedia technology from Microsoft.
- Graphics are the multimedia backbone of the World Wide Web, and Internet Explorer is able to use these graphics inline. That is, graphics appear as part of a Web page, just as text is a part of a Web page.
- VRML is a programming language that produces Web documents; a browser can interpret and display these documents.
- Web developers using VRML are able to develop Web sites that include 3-D images, interactive simulations, multiuser interfaces, and a host of other features that are not available to Web developers using HTML. To use VRML, you need a VRML plug-in.
- To support real-time communication, Internet Explorer has Microsoft NetMeeting.
- With Microsoft NetMeeting you can use the Web to talk long distance with other users without having to pay long-distance phone charges.
- You are not required to have speakers and a microphone to use Microsoft NetMeeting. Once you establish a call, you can use the Current Call window to invoke text-based chatting.
- The Whiteboard tool allows you to share image files and to edit these files interactively.
- The Share feature of NetMeeting allows you to share an application with another user.
- The File Transfer tool allows you to send files to and receive files from a user during a connected call. In other words, you can send a file to a user while you are engaged in an audio or text conversation.
- In 1995, Sun Microsystems introduced Java as a new programming language designed to support animation, games, browsers, and interactive television.
- Chatting occurs when users go to a Web location and have an open discussion on a specific topic.
- When you enter a chat room, you are expected to follow a specific code of netiquette: stick to the topic, be polite, avoid derogatory or profane language, and never send personal information.

KEY TERMS AND COMMANDS

Action
Current Call
DirectX
File Transfer
inline
Java
Java applets
JavaScript
Microsoft Chat
Microsoft NetMeeting
Moving Picture Experts Group (MPEG)
multimedia
Say
Share
Shockwave
stream
Think
Virtual Reality Modeling Language (VRML)
Whisper
Whiteboard

STUDY QUESTIONS

1. Describe the components of multimedia and indicate why this technology is becoming popular on the World Wide Web.
2. Distinguish between Java and a Java applet.
3. Discuss the importance of audio formats on the World Wide Web.
4. Describe what it means to stream audio.
5. Explain why it is important to have a very fast computer with a great deal of RAM and large hard disk space when using video off the Internet.
6. Describe what it means to display graphics inline.
7. Discuss why and when you would use VRML. What are the advantages of VRML?
8. Explain why you would use software such as NetMeeting. What are the difficulties and advantages of this activity on the World Wide Web?
9. What are the advantages of using VRML rather than using HTML?
10. Why is the application Share such a useful feature?

PRACTICE TEST

1. Everyone agrees that multimedia refers to the incorporation of audio, graphics, video, animation, and other multisensory tools into a Web site.
   a. True b. False
2. To cause text to appear as a marquee across a Web site, you need to use a programming language such as
   a. HTML c. VTML
   b. HTM d. Java
3. To control another computer over the Internet, you need to use which of the following programs?
   a. NetMeeting c. ControlPC
   b. NetCopy d. Internet Control
4. Which of the following has become very popular because it is quick and allows users to stream audio?
   a. RealPlayer c. NetMeeting radio
   b. SoundStream d. AudioGif
5. Streaming audio delivers a continuous stream of audio, such as live news broadcasts.
   a. True b. False
6. Which of the following is a popular video file format because it uses a compression technique to reduce the size of the video file?
   a. JPEG c. BPEG
   b. MPEG d. VideoShrink
7. One of the disadvantages of chatting on the World Wide Web is that it only operates like a walkie-talkie.
   a. True b. False
8. To send a message to selected characters only, rather than to everyone participating in a chat room, which of the following commands should you use?
   a. Secret c. Whisper
   b. Quiet d. Select
9. Which of the following programming languages would you use to create 3-D images?
   a. HTML c. JPEG
   b. VRML d. HTTP
10. For users, the distinction between Java and JavaScript is not very important.
    a. True b. False

FILL-INS

1. ______________________ may be used to provide access to stock market quotes or to run thousands of Web programs.
2. ______________________ has become very popular because it is quick and allows users to stream audio.
3. ______________________ describes graphics that appear as part of a Web page, just as text is a part of a Web page.
4. ______________________ is an interactive multimedia technology from Microsoft that is similar to ActiveX.
5. From a user's point of view, ______________ is the 3-D world of the Web.
6. Selecting ______________________ from the Tools menu allows you to send files to, and receive files from, a user during a call.
7. ______________________ allows you to share image files and edit these files interactively.
8. ______________________ displays your text as a thought balloon.
9. The ______________________ option places your text within a word balloon over your character.
10. ______________________ differs from Java in that the former provides a full set of commands and functions that are built into HTML documents.

PROJECTS

1. Locate several audio links that you think are impressive. Be sure to include .au, .wav, .ra, and .aif files. Also be sure to include at least one example of a stream of audio. Send an e-mail to the CEO of this class and include direct links in your e-mail message.
2. Be certain you have a video add-on or plug-in for each of the major video formats. Locate a video link that you would like to show to a friend. Write an e-mail message to this friend describing the video format for the video link and telling your friend which add-on or plug-in to use to view this site. Make it easy for your friend to see this video. In your e-mail message, include a link to an add-on viewer as well as a link to the site.

INTERNET AT WORK

Edith would really like to become an expert at using Internet Explorer. Your task, should you decide to accept it, is to teach her how to use the powerful features in Internet Explorer. She probably knows enough about e-mail to send and receive simple messages. You can begin to teach her about Internet Explorer by showing her how to include audio and video links in her e-mail messages. Write an explanation of this process, and in your message include the appropriate links (send this message to the CEO of your class). You can also begin to teach her how to download and install add-ons and plug-ins. Include a description of this activity in your e-mail to the CEO. Be sure to include any other activities that you think Edith should learn on her way to becoming an expert Internet Explorer user.

Creating Web Pages with FrontPage Express

OUTCOMES

When you complete this chapter you will be able to . . .

- Create Web pages with Microsoft's FrontPage Express.
- Set text attributes.
- Set text alignment.
- Include graphics.
- Establish links.
- Use paragraph styles.
- Use background colors and graphics.

OVERVIEW

For the unacquainted, the prospect of generating a Web page may seem a bit daunting. Many people view the creation of Web pages as a highly complex undertaking that requires an extensive programming background. Many people also assume that developing a Web page requires a complete knowledge of how information is generated, routed, and displayed via the Web. This perception may have been partially true a few years ago. Today, however, with Microsoft's FrontPage Express it is easy for you to generate your own Web page.

FrontPage Express is a HyperText Markup Language (HTML) authoring tool. As mentioned in Chapter 1, HTML is a formatting language that is used to create Web documents. Remember that a Web page is an HTML document. In the past, to be able to generate a Web page, you had to know HTML formatting. Today, FrontPage Express does much of this formatting for you. All you have to do is use the proper tool to design a page, identify links, insert graphics, and set the appearance of text. In many ways using FrontPage Express to generate HTML documents is much like using a word processor. Simply enter the information you want; then assign the font, size, and style you desire.

> **Tips, Tricks, and Ideas 9-1**
>
> *HTML*
>
> Although Microsoft's FrontPage Express makes it easy to create HTML documents, knowing a bit about HTML can be a big help. As you progress through this chapter, periodically take a look at the HTML code. It will help you get a better understanding of what is going on and how FrontPage Express is generating that HTML document for you.

Before you begin creating HTML documents with FrontPage Express, you must have a place to store the documents you create. In other words, to create and edit an HTML document, you must first have a location on the Web where you can place your document. That is, you must have a URL. Be sure to check with your instructor to see if you have a location (URL) where your HTML documents can be placed. In addition to a location, it is very likely that you will need to have an account and password. You will need to have access to your document to update it. No one else should have access to your documents until you are ready, regardless of where your HTML document or Web site resides. Security is a fundamental issue with the creation of Web pages.

GENERATING PUBLISHABLE PAGES

To start FrontPage Express, open the Start menu and select Program; then select FrontPage Express. If FrontPage Express is not available, you will need to download and install it from Microsoft. When you launch FrontPage Express, a new window that looks like a word processor will appear. FrontPage Express is very similar to a word processor in that it uses a what-you-see-is-what-you-get (or WYSIWYG) orientation. With FrontPage Express you use a set of tools very similar to those of a word processor to create your HTML document (Image 9-1).

Image 9-1

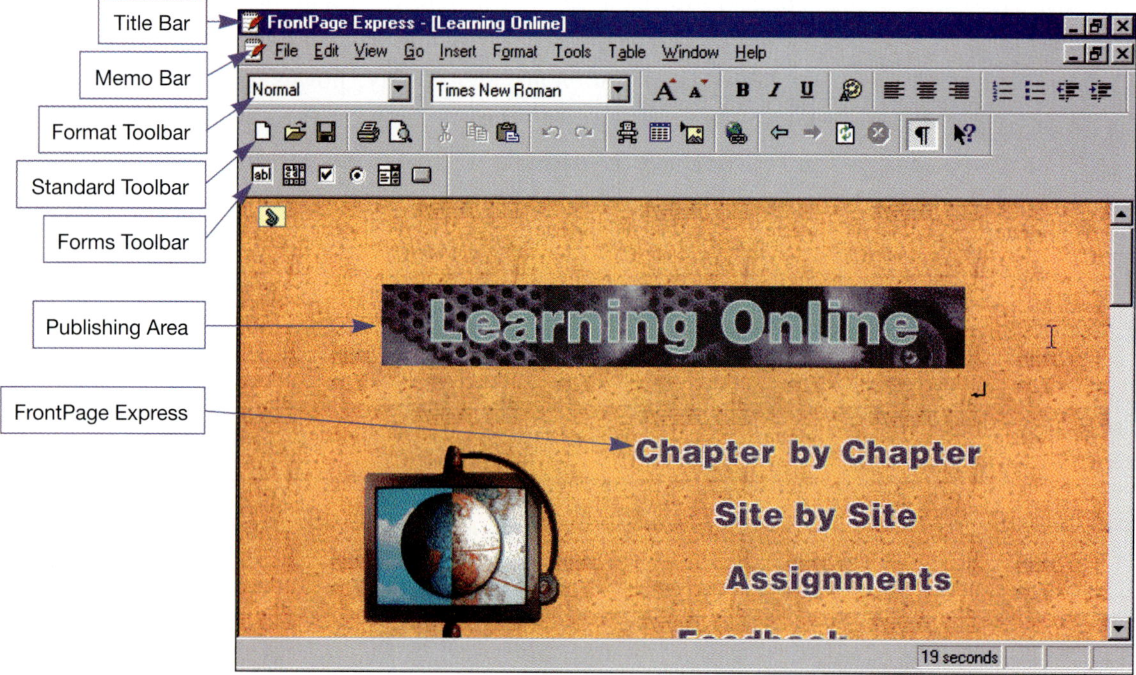

Several components make up the FrontPage Express window, including the Format, Standard, and Forms toolbars and the page composition area. The **page composition area** is where you generate your pages. The **Format toolbar** provides access to the various tools for setting the look of your Web page. The Standard toolbar provides access to basic commands such as New, Open, Save, and Print. The Forms toolbar provides access to a variety of tools used to create forms, insert text and check boxes, and include buttons on your Web page.

As with most word processors, Microsoft FrontPage Express gives you several ways to generate a new document. You have the option of creating a new Web page completely from scratch, or you can modify an existing page from a template. You can even have FrontPage Express help you create a Web page with a Page Wizard. The advantages and disadvantages of each method are covered later in the chapter. To understand how to use FrontPage Express, it is best to create a Web page from scratch.

PLANNING A WEB PAGE

There is no substitute for planning. Before you begin any Web page, it is very important to take time to plan what information to include on that page. You should also include in your plan the way you want your Web page to look.

One of the most critical elements of planning is to identify the number of Web pages desired. In most cases you will create several Web documents, each linked to a central home page. In this way you can add as many Web pages as you desire to your design. For example, if you are creating your own personal Web page, you might want a page that contains a set of links pointing to your areas of interest. You might want a music link on your home page that links to a separate Web page with links to all of your favorite music sites. You might have another link on your home page that links to a Web page for favorite recreational activities. In fact, most people create several HTML documents that support one Web site. The more you plan for these in advance, the easier it will be to create the pages you need.

Part of planning also includes the look of your Web pages. What size text should you use? Where will text be placed on a page? Where will the links to other Web pages appear? Will there be graphics? What about the use of color? Will there be background images? There are a number of questions that you should ask, and have answers to, before you launch FrontPage Express.

Although planning is vital, you need to have some idea of what you can include in a plan. For this reason, the Web site you initially create in this chapter omits the planning stage. You should try out as many features of FrontPage Express as possible. This exercise will give you a wealth of ideas for planning your next set of Web pages.

ENTERING AND FORMATTING TEXT ATTRIBUTES

As we mentioned earlier, entering text in FrontPage Express is very similar to entering text into a word processor. You insert text at the location of the insertion point. After text is entered, you have several tools available for setting the appearance of text. The four primary text attribute tools that you need to consider are Font, Size, Style, and Color.

> **Tips, Tricks, and Ideas 9-2**
>
> *Text First*
>
> The best approach is usually to enter all the text you want on a page first and then adjust the formatting. In other words, get all your information in place and then make it look like you want it to look.

Font, sometimes called typeface, refers to the overall appearance of text. Two major font types are available: serif and sans serif. **Serif** typefaces have a small extension, or serif, on each letter and number. **Sans serif** (without serif) typefaces look more like block letters. Depending on the capabilities of your computer, you will have a wide range of fonts to choose from. **Style** refers to the appearance of text within a font, which includes bold, italic, and underline. **Size** refers to the size of text. Size is measured in points. (One point is equal to 1⁄72 of an inch.) **Color** enables you to select from a wide spectrum of colors to assign to text.

You set any of the text attributes with FrontPage Express by selecting the appropriate tool from the Format toolbar or by choosing the corresponding command in the Format menu. When you want to set a text attribute, highlight the text you want to change; then choose the setting you want from the Format toolbar or use the Format menu.

ACTIVITY

1. Launch FrontPage Express.
   Notice that FrontPage Express looks very much like a word processor (Image 9-2).

Image 9-2

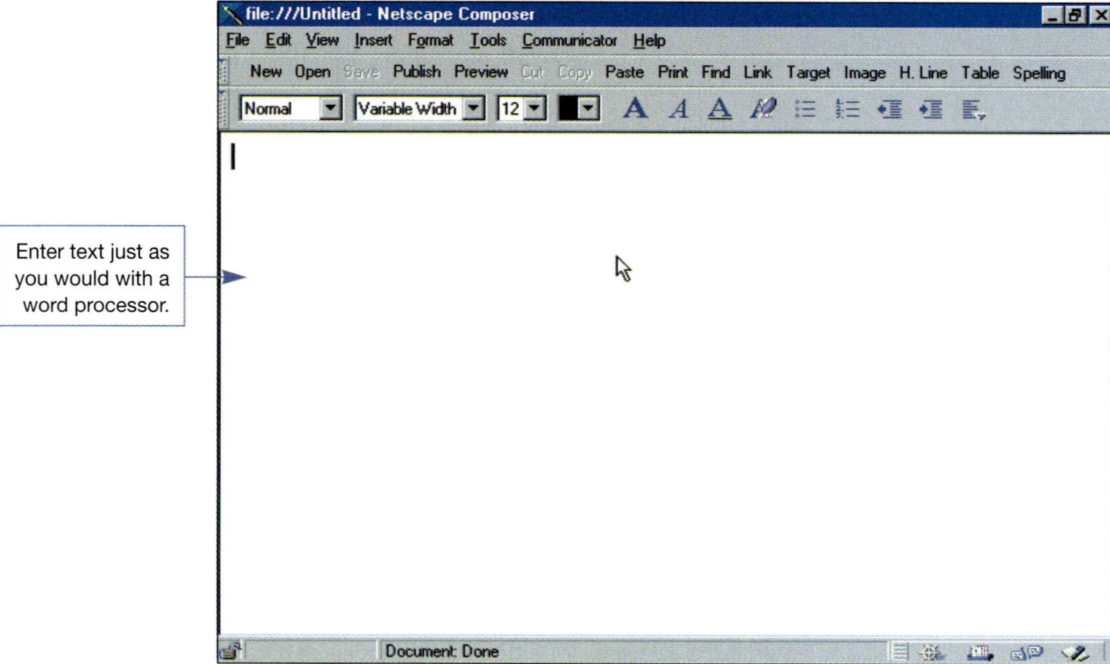

2. At the top of the page composition area, type The Agee Candy Company (Image 9-3).

3. Add the following text (Image 9-3):
   Welcome to the Agee Candy Company. Here you will find the latest product information, access to corporate information, and even a list of some of our favorite links.
   Company Profile
   Our Favorite Sites
   Other Candy Companies
4. Highlight The Agee Candy Company and set the Font to Arial, Size to 24, Color to Red, and Style to Bold.
5. Select the full list and leave the font set on the default font. Set Size to 14, Color to Blue, and Style to Italic.

Image 9-3

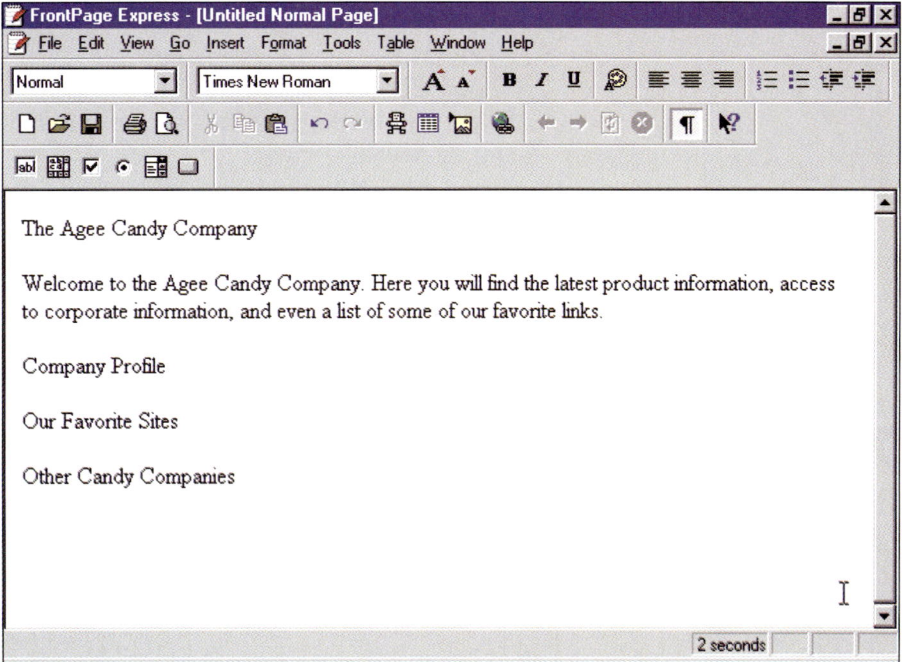

EXERCISE 9-1

You should be very comfortable with setting text attributes before you continue with the rest of this chapter. Take some time to experiment with several attributes. However, when you are done, be sure to return your document to the attributes described in the previous activity.

TEXT ALIGNMENT

Aligning text in an HTML document is very important, and FrontPage Express provides several **text alignment** tools. The three primary text alignment options are left, center, and right. These are established by first selecting the text you want to align and then selecting the option from the Alignment tool on the Format toolbar.

In addition to the primary alignment tools, you can use the Increase Indent and Decrease Indent tools to align text. These tools allow you to select a paragraph and then indent it. Each click adds or subtracts from the indenting.

The Numbered List and Bulleted List tools also align text within a paragraph. These two tools are very useful for creating lists such as a list of links or other text. These tools work as toggles. In other words, if you select a paragraph and click on the Numbered List icon, you enable the tool. Clicking on the tool again turns off the Numbered List option for the selected text.

ACTIVITY

1. Select the paragraph The Agee Candy Company.
2. Click on the Align Center button.
   Notice that this and only this paragraph is centered (Image 9-4).
3. Select the next paragraph (description) and set the alignment to left (Image 9-4).
4. Select the remaining text and select the Bulleted List tool from the Format toolbar.
   Examine the formatted document (Image 9-4).

Image 9-4

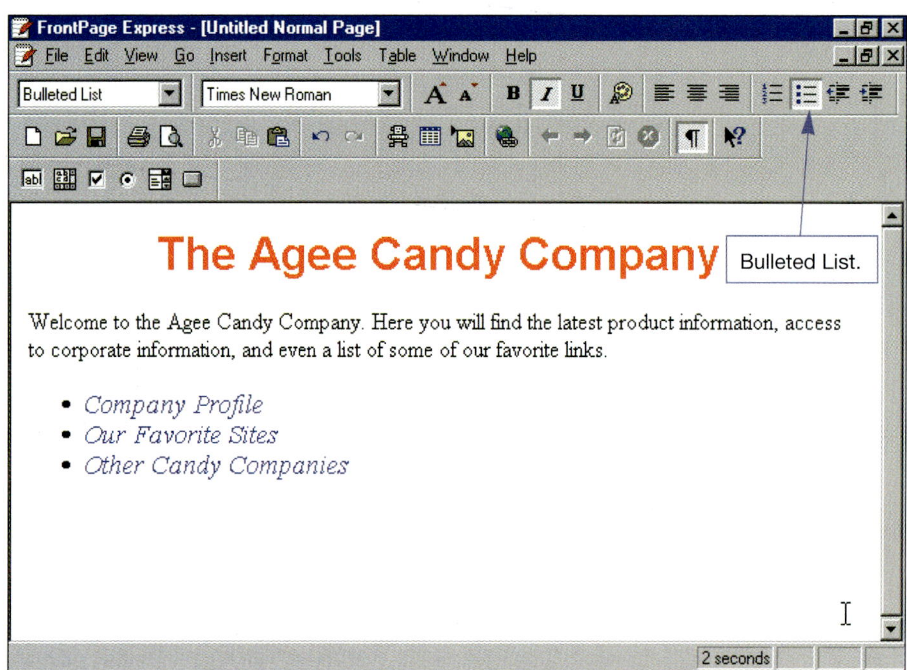

5. Take a few minutes to try each tool; then return the HTML document to the way it looks in Image 9-4.

SAVING AND PREVIEWING AN HTML DOCUMENT

After you begin creating a Web page, you will want to preview your work to see whether the page you are creating is in fact what you intended. Before you can preview your work, you must save it on a disk. You save your work on a disk by selecting the Save button or by selecting Save As from the File menu. Either way, the Save As dialog box appears.

FrontPage gives you the option of saving this file as an HTML document directly on a Web server. This way you can create and test your document in the location where it will be used. The other option is to save your HTML document as a file on your disk. This method is often preferred when you do not want to make your Web page available until it is complete. For this lesson, you should save your file to a floppy disk. However, your instructor may provide you with server space to save directly on a Web server. In this case, save to the location specified by your instructor.

Saving your HTML document to a file requires you to click on the As File button in the Save As dialog box. This action opens the Save As File dialog box. There are always two issues to consider when saving any type of file: location and name. If you are going to save the file on a floppy disk, you need to select 3½ Floppy (A:) next to Save in. If you are using a folder on the hard disk, you need to select the proper folder. The next step is to set the file name. You must enter the name of the document you want to save, and HTML Files must be selected next to Save file as type. After you set the name and location, click on Save to save your document.

> **Tips, Tricks, and Ideas 9-3**
>
> *HTM and HTML*
>
> The file extension is very important, as it is used to identify an HTML document. One would think that .html would be the most logical extension. It is. However, MS-DOS-based computers do not allow four-character extensions. Therefore, .htm is used as the preferred extension.

After you save a document, it is a good idea to view it with Internet Explorer. To see or preview a document that resides on your disk, include the full path for the file next to Address in Internet Explorer. You may also click on the selection arrow to choose a disk drive and then select from the list of available files. It is customary for the document displayed in Internet Explorer to appear exactly as it does in FrontPage Express. It is easy to get the two confused. Be sure to check the title bar and notice which program is displaying your document. After you preview the document in Internet Explorer, you may close Internet Explorer.

ACTIVITY

1. Select the Save As command from the File menu.
   The Save As dialog box allows you to save your document as a file or to publish it to a Web server (Image 9-5).

Image 9-5

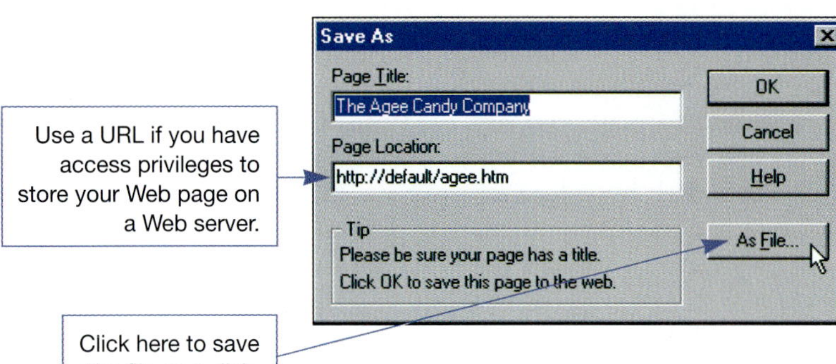

2. Click on As File.
   Notice the Save As File dialog box (Image 9-6).
3. Make sure you have a blank, formatted disk to insert into drive A: and select 3½ Floppy (A:) (Image 9-6).
4. Next to File name: enter AGEE (Image 9-6).

Image 9-6

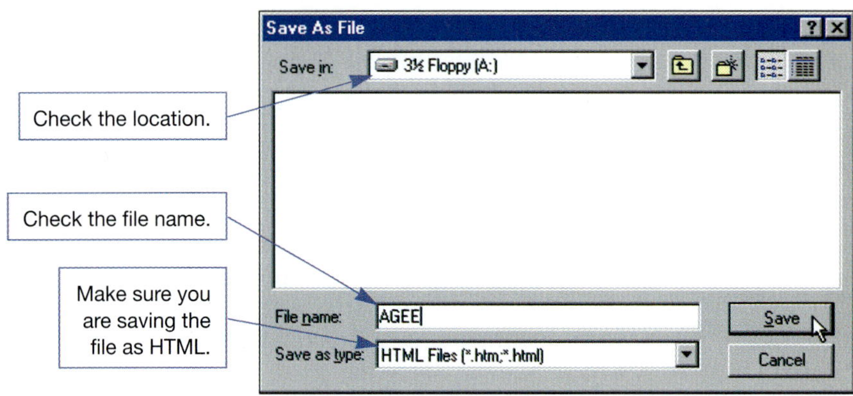

5. Click on Save.
   Notice that the file name now appears in the title bar for FrontPage Express.
6. Launch Internet Explorer.
7. Next to Address, enter A:\ (Image 9-7).
   Notice the list of files that are contained on the disk. Also notice the icon for HTML files (Image 9-7).

Image 9-7

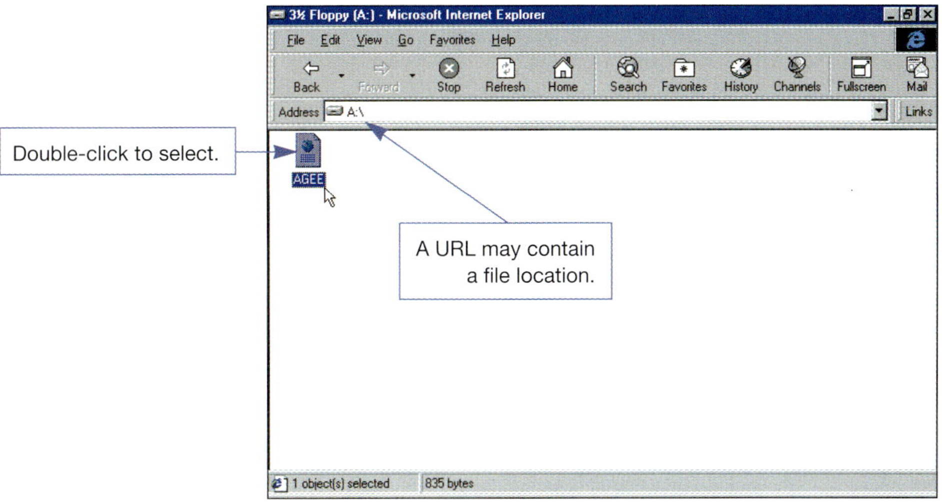

8. Click on AGEE.
   Notice that your HTML document now appears in Internet Explorer (Image 9-8).

Image 9-8

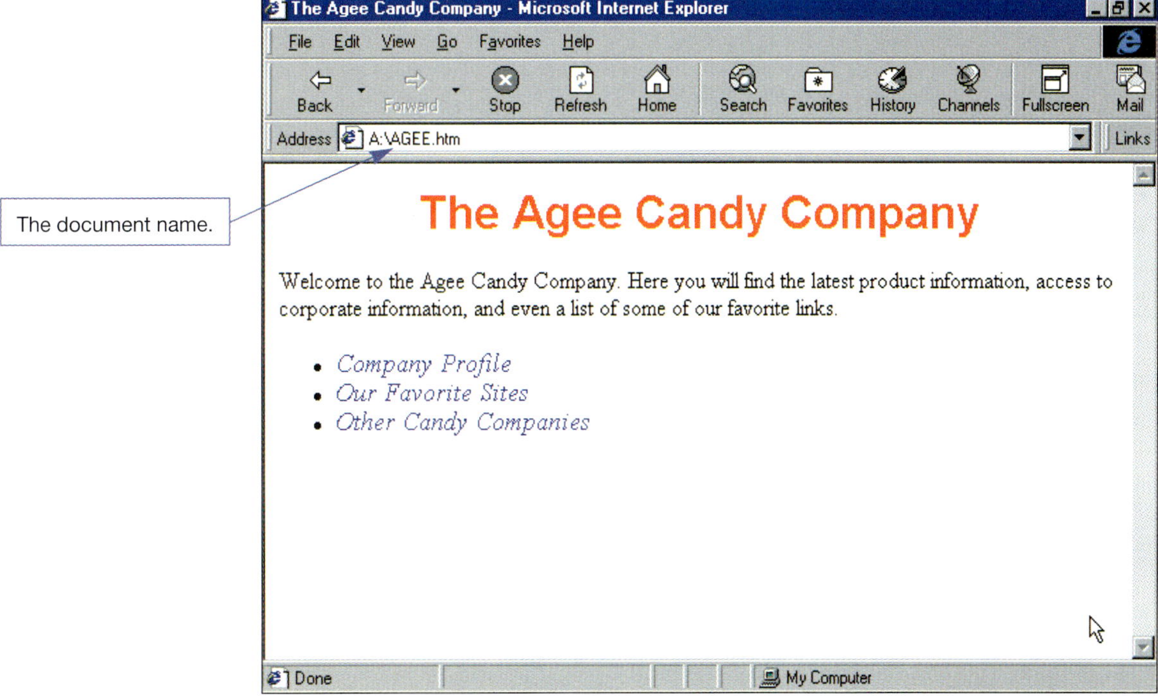

9. Close Internet Explorer.

EXERCISE 9-2

Now that you have created the basic framework for one Web page, it is time to create another. Create a new Web page called Other Candy Companies. It should include the title Other Candy Companies at the top of the page and then a list of candy companies. Search the Web for the URLs of as many candy companies as you can find. Write down the URL and include the company name in your new Web document. Be sure to save this HTML document as COMP.HTM on your disk. This step is important because you will use your new Web site in the next section.

CREATING HYPERLINKS

Although a text-only Web page has some value, most pages include links to other Web pages. These links can be to Web pages you create or to any page found on the Web. Links make a Web page dynamic.

The process of creating links to other Web pages or HTML documents is straightforward. Each link consists of two components: the name of the link and the link location, or URL. To set a link, first select the text that you want to use to attach the link. Typically, when you design a Web page, you include the link text as part of the design; then you establish the link to that text. However, you have the option of creating the link text when you create the link itself.

If you have already created text that you want to make into a link, simply select, or highlight, that text; then click on the Create or Edit Hyperlink button or select Hyperlink from the Insert menu. This step causes the Create Hyperlink dialog box to appear with the World Wide Web tab selected. At this point you need to enter the URL for the link or for an HTML document that resides on a local disk such as your hard disk drive. After you establish the location, click on OK to establish the link. In the page composition area of FrontPage Express, the link will appear as colored (often blue) underlined text.

Tips, Tricks, and Ideas 9-4

Viewing HTML Source Code

To get an idea of what your document looks like in HTML, try clicking on the HTML command from the View menu. Look carefully at the code to get a pretty good idea of how it generates Web documents.

Tips, Tricks, and Ideas 9-5

Test Frequently

Because the Web is in a constant state of flux, it is common for links that work one day to not work another. When you create and publish a Web page, you need to keep it updated by removing any dead links and inserting new links. Never leave dead links on your Web page.

ACTIVITY

1. Open the COMP.HTM document that you created in Exercise 9-2 (Image 9-9).

Image 9-9

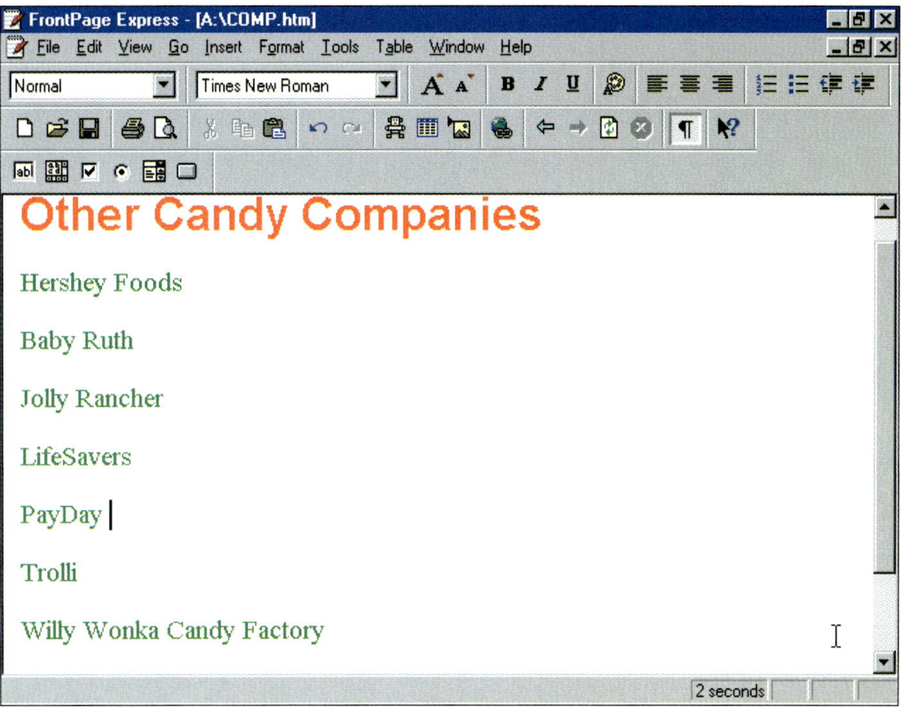

2. Select Hershey Foods and then click on the Create or Edit Hyperlink button in the Format toolbar.
   Notice that when the Create Hyperlink dialog box opens, the World Wide Web tab is active (Image 9-10).
3. Enter the URL for Hershey Foods (Image 9-10).

Image 9-10

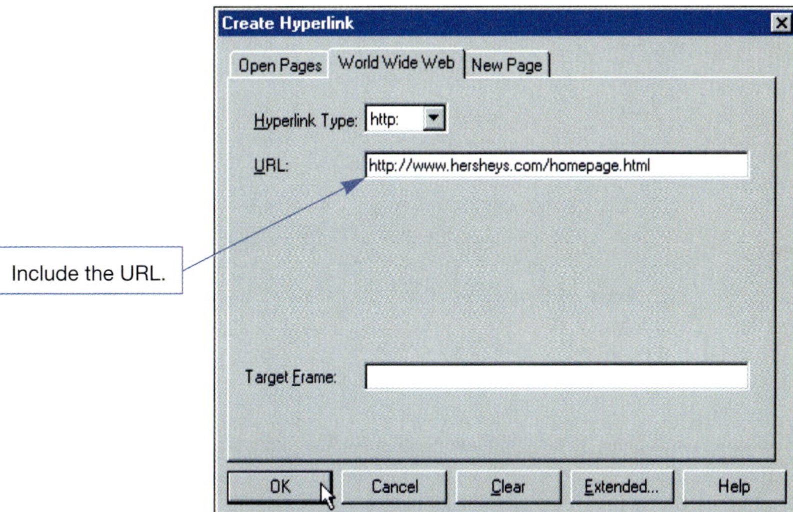

4. Click on OK.
   Notice that the text in your Other Candy Companies Web page is now a different color and underlined, indicating that text is now a link (Image 9-11).

Image 9-11

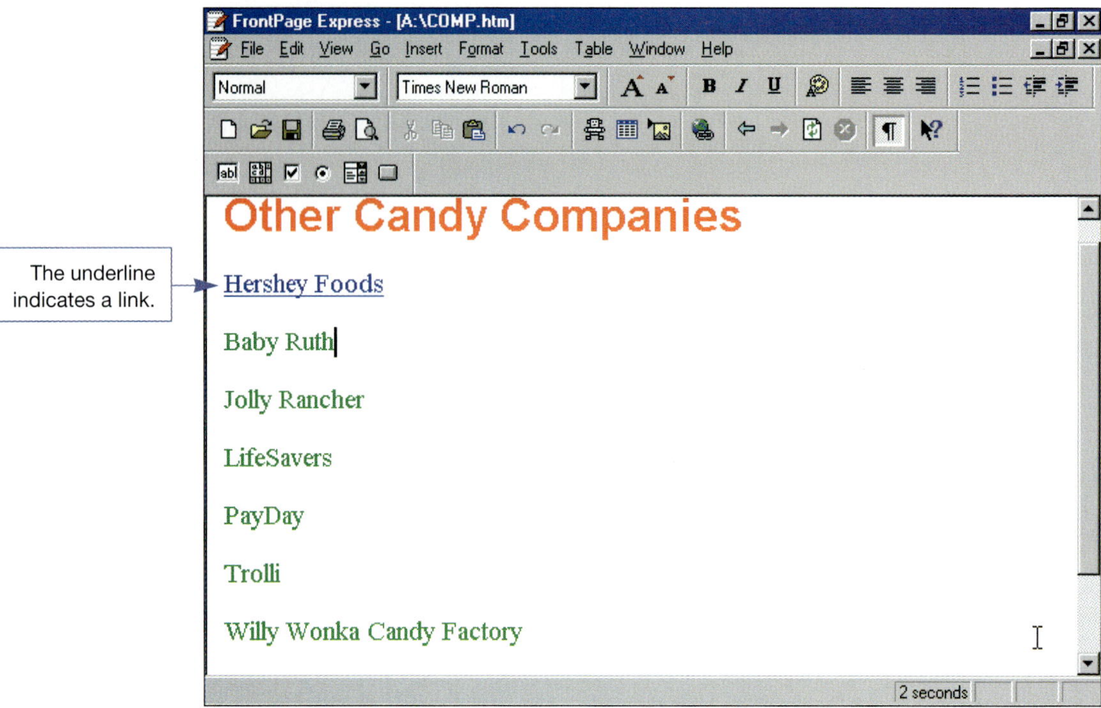

5. Save your Web page.
6. Use Internet Explorer to preview your adjusted HTML document.
7. Click on the Hershey Foods link.
   Selecting this link takes you to Hershey Foods Corporation. (Image 9-12).

Image 9-12

8. Close Internet Explorer.
9. Finish establishing all the links for your Other Candy Companies Web page. Be sure to save COMP.HTM; then test each link by using the Preview button.

EXERCISE 9-3

You now have a new document (COMP.HTM) that is referred to, and linked, in your AGEE.HTM document. In your AGEE.HTM document, create a link to COMP.HTM. This is a local file, so you must create the link as such. After you complete this link, you need to create the initial design for the other pages, including Company Profile and Our Favorite Sites. Make sure you have links to both of these Web pages in AGEE.HTM.

Tips, Tricks, and Ideas 9-6

Printing Pages

FrontPage Express gives you the option of printing your page by using the Print command from the File menu or by clicking on the Print command from the Composition toolbar. However, it is a good idea to use Print Preview before you print a document to make sure that you print what you want. This practice saves paper and saves you valuable time.

Tips, Tricks, and Ideas 9-7

Downloading and Using Images

Many users download an image from one Web site and then use that image in their own Web site. It is very easy to download an image by using the Save Image As command and then right clicking on any image. It is equally as easy to use the Insert Image command to apply that image to your Web page. However, you must be careful not to violate copyright laws. As a rule of thumb, never use graphics without first getting permission.

IMAGES

Graphics add life to an otherwise dull and drab Web page. There are several ways for you to add graphics to your Web pages. One of the easiest is by using horizontal lines. To insert a **horizontal line** at any point in your Web page, place the insertion point at the location where you want the line and then select the Horizontal Line command from the Insert menu. At that point a line will appear across your entire Web page. If the insertion point was in the middle of text, the horizontal line will split the text.

With FrontPage Express you also have the option of inserting almost any graphics image you desire. The image can be a drawing, picture, clip art, or virtually any graphic. There are two key concerns you should keep in mind when inserting images into a document. First, to be of any value, an image must enhance the content of the document. Graphics for graphics' sake only detract from your document. Graphics images should enhance the content and feel of the Web page. The second problem is speed and size. Graphics files tend to be large and, consequently, can take a bit of time to display over the Web—especially for people using slower connections. A good Web design always considers the speed and size of graphics.

To insert a graphics image, you will need to identify its file type. Most Web pages use either .gif or .jpg image formats. To insert a graphics file, begin by making sure the insertion point is at the location where you want the file to appear; then click on the **Insert Image** button. The Insert Image button produces the Image dialog box. In this box click on From File, click on Browse, and then locate the file you want to insert.

After you insert an image, you can drag the image to various locations within your document. You can also return to the Image Properties dialog box by **right clicking** on the image and then selecting the Image Properties command.

As with text, a graphics image may also be a link. For example, you may insert clip art in the form of a large back arrow. Then you can make that clip art image work as a link back to your home page. To make an image operate as a link, click the right mouse button on the image and then select the Image Properties command. When the Image Properties dialog box opens, select the General tab; then enter the URL or local file name of a Web document next to Location: under Default Hyperlink.

ACTIVITY

1. Launch Internet Explorer.
2. Search for a graphic that represents candy. You may want to search the Image site on *Learning Online* for some ideas. Once you find a graphic, right click on that graphic.
   Notice the pop-up menu (Image 9-13).

Image 9-13

Explore this URL.

3. Select the Save Picture As option and save the image on your disk.
4. Launch FrontPage Express and open your AGEE.HTM document.
5. Place the insertion point at the very beginning of your document and then click on the Insert Image button.
   The Image dialog box opens (Image 9-14).
6. Click on From File, click on Browse, and then locate the file you just downloaded from the Web (Image 9-14).

Image 9-14

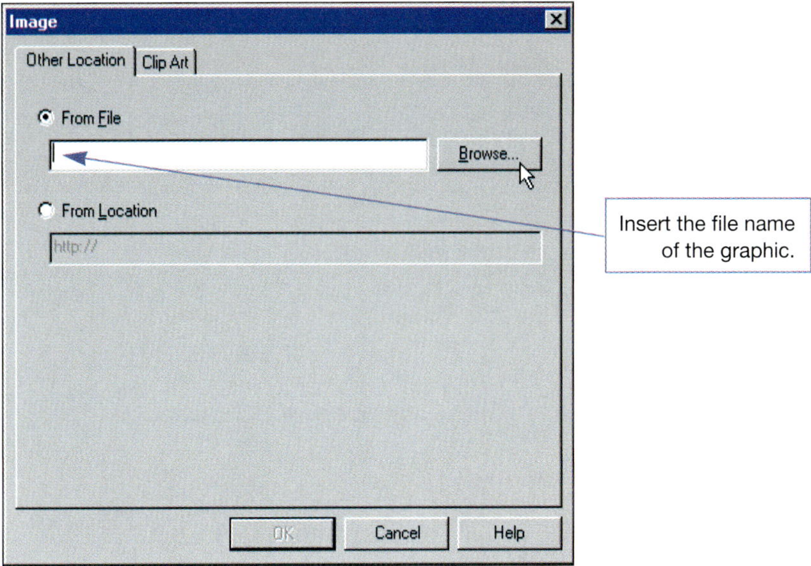

7. Click on OK.
   Notice that the graphic now appears in your Web document (Image 9-15).
8. Click and drag on any corner to resize your graphic until it fits appropriately within your Web page (Image 9-15).

Image 9-15

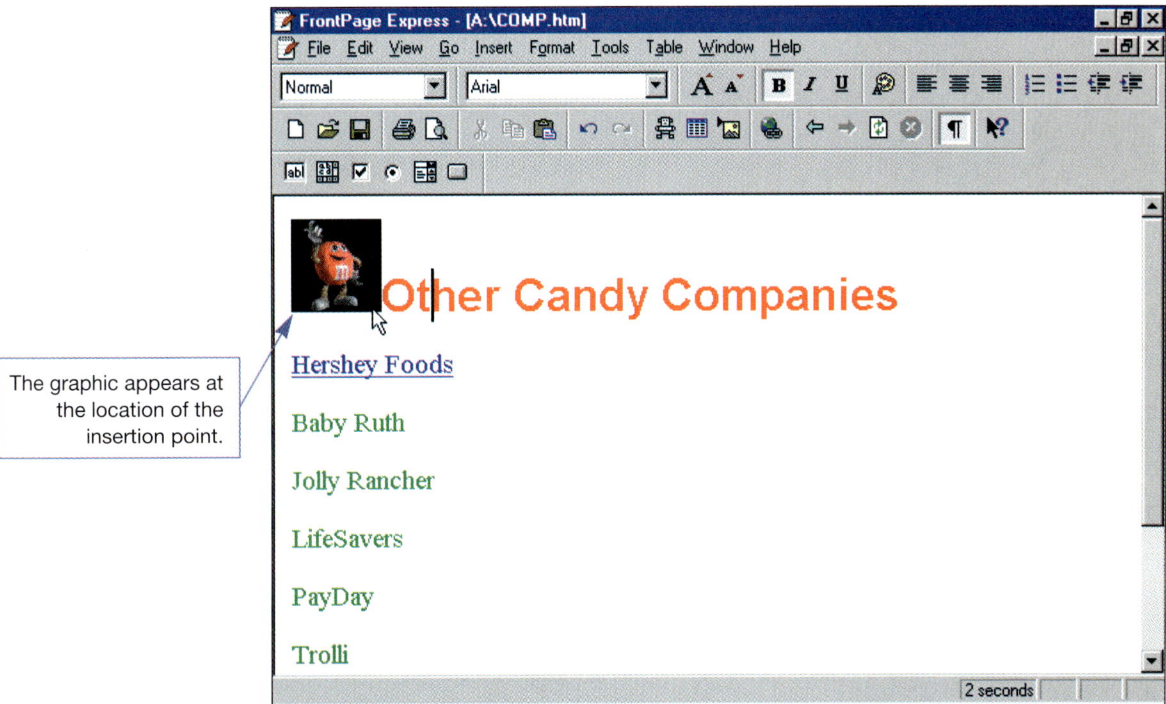

9. Right click on the graphic in your Web page and select Image Properties.
   The Image Properties dialog box opens (Image 9-16).

10. Insert the URL for *Learning Online* in the Location text box: http://www.mhhe.com/cit/net/learning (Image 9-16).

Image 9-16

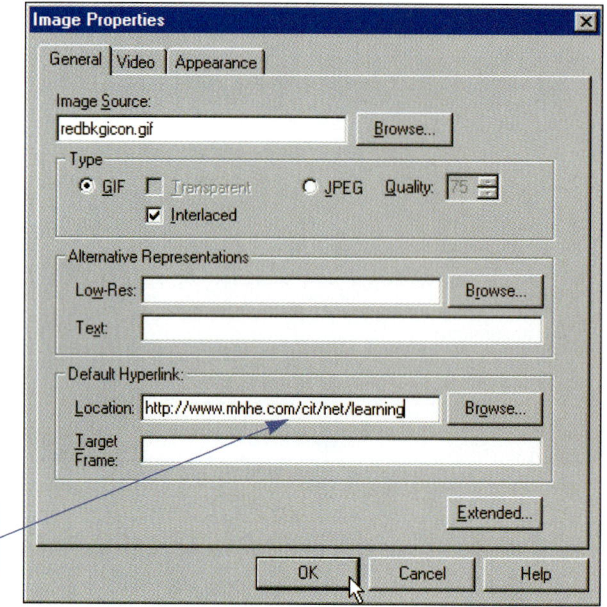

11. Click on OK.
12. Save your document and then use Internet Explorer to examine your Web page. Make sure your new graphic is a link.
13. Place the insertion point anywhere in the document; then click on the Horizontal Line command from the Insert menu.
    Notice that a horizontal line is added to the Web page.
14. Delete the horizontal line by clicking on the line; then press the Delete key.

EXERCISE 9-4

Now that you have used some of the content design fundamentals, you can adjust the AGEE.HTM document so that it is visually appealing. It is up to you to use your creative abilities to determine how this page should look. Be sure to save your updated document.

BACKGROUND COLORS AND IMAGES

Black text, even colored text, on a simple white or gray background can be a very effective design. However, there may be times that you want to use a different color, or even graphics, in the background. Changing the background color for a Web page with FrontPage Express is rather simple. Choose the Background command from the Format menu and then select the Background tab.

You have several options for setting colors, including setting colors for various types of text as well as the background color. To set any one of these colors, click on the color box and select a desired color. The color

> **Tips, Tricks, and Ideas 9-8**
>
> *Create Your Own Backgrounds*
>
> Many Web pages use the same background. Try creating your own background images—they will add a sense of personal style to your Web pages and make them unique.

that you select appears in the preview area. Always try to select colors that enhance the content and style of your Web page. Poor color selection can drive people away from your Web page.

If you are interested in adding more excitement and interest to your Web page, you can specify a background image. You can use any image as long as it is in a supported format (.jpg or .gif) and as long as you are not violating copyright protections. When a background image is used, it is placed in a tiled format. In other words, several images appear to fill your entire background. Consequently, some designers prefer to use images that look seamless when tiled. The Image site at *Learning Online* has links to excellent sources for seamless background images.

ACTIVITY

1. With your AGEE.HTM document available in FrontPage Express, select Background from the Format menu (Image 9-17).
2. Select the Background tab (Image 9-17).
3. Change the Background color to yellow.

Image 9-17

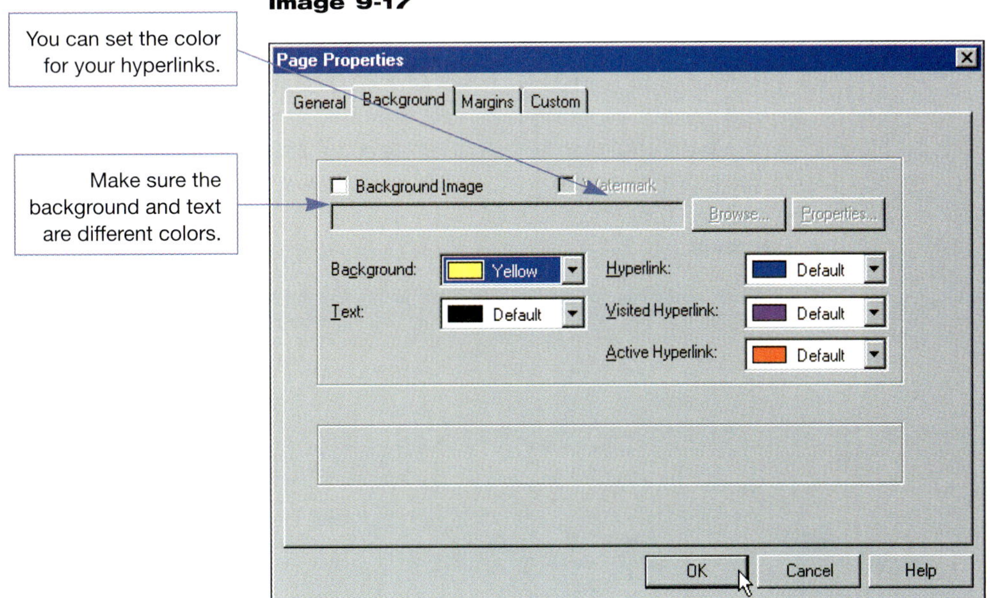

4. Click on OK.
   Notice the background change in FrontPage Express.
5. Activate Internet Explorer and then go to the *Learning Online* site.
   Notice the background image.
6. Point and right click anywhere on the background.
   Notice the pull-down menu (Image 9-18).

Image 9-18

Right click anywhere on the background.

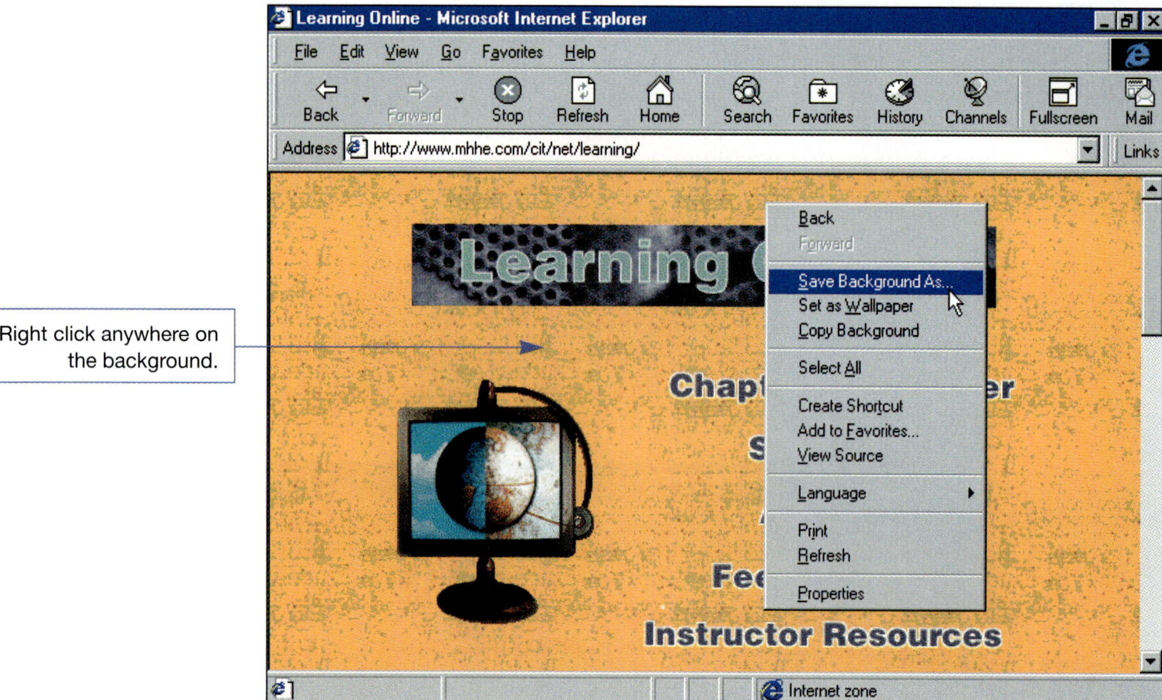

7. Select Save Background As and save this image to your disk.
8. Return to FrontPage Express and select Background from the Format menu; then choose the Background tab.
9. Click on the check box next to Background Image.
10. Select the background file you just downloaded (Image 9-19).

Image 9-19

Activate this option.

Include the file name for the background graphic.

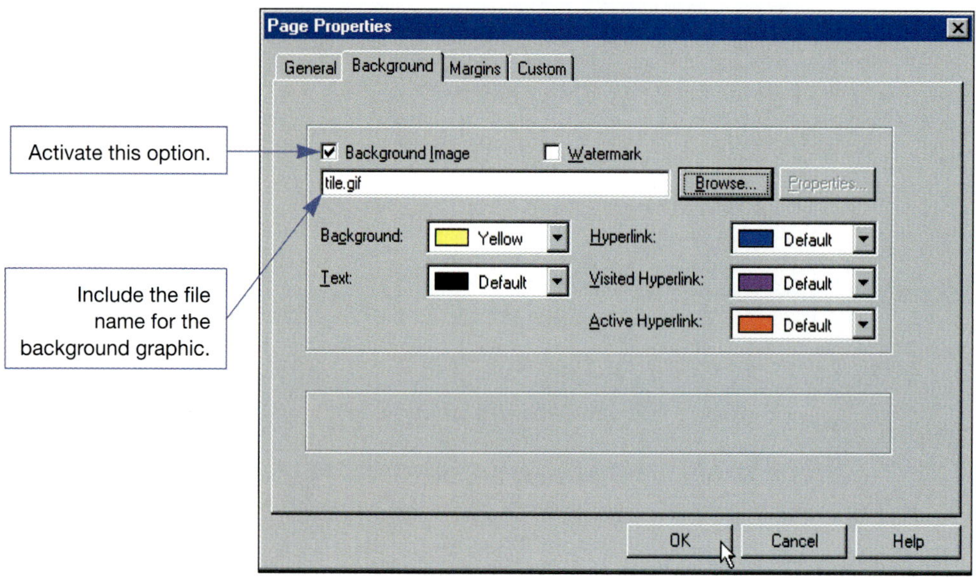

11. Click on OK.
    Notice the results.

EXERCISE 9-5

Go to the Background section of the Image site on *Learning Online.* Here you will find access to a wide range of backgrounds. Download a new background; then apply this new background to AGEE.HTM. Print a copy of your Web page.

PARAGRAPH STYLES

Up to this point you have been able to set attributes for specific text. However, what happens if you want to use the same attributes on several sets of distinct text? This approach is common for such things as section titles and subtitles. The solution is to use Paragraph Properties. A **paragraph property** is a predefined set of attributes that can be applied to text. One advantage of using a paragraph property, or style, is that you can quickly set a wide range of attribute settings with just a few clicks of the mouse.

To establish paragraph style settings, place the insertion point in a paragraph and then select the desired style from the Paragraph Properties style list box on the Format toolbar.

Tips, Tricks, and Ideas 9-9

Character versus Paragraph Settings

Although paragraph style settings are quick, they are considered secondary to character style settings. In other words, if you set a font for a specific portion of text, the text will retain that font attribute even if you change the paragraph settings.

ACTIVITY

1. Select New; then select Normal Page from the File menu.
   Notice that a new blank document appears.
2. Type the following entries (Image 9-20):
   Address
   Bulleted List
   Defined Term
   Definition
   Directory List
   Formatted
   Heading 1
   Heading 2
   Heading 3
   Heading 4
   Heading 5
   Heading 6
   Menu List
   Normal
   Numbered List
3. Click on Address in the composition area; then click on the Change Style list box on the Format toolbar and select Address. You can also select the Paragraph command from the Format menu and select Address. Both actions apply the Address style.
4. Repeat this process and apply the style that has the same name as the entry to each paragraph in your document (Image 9-20).

Image 9-20

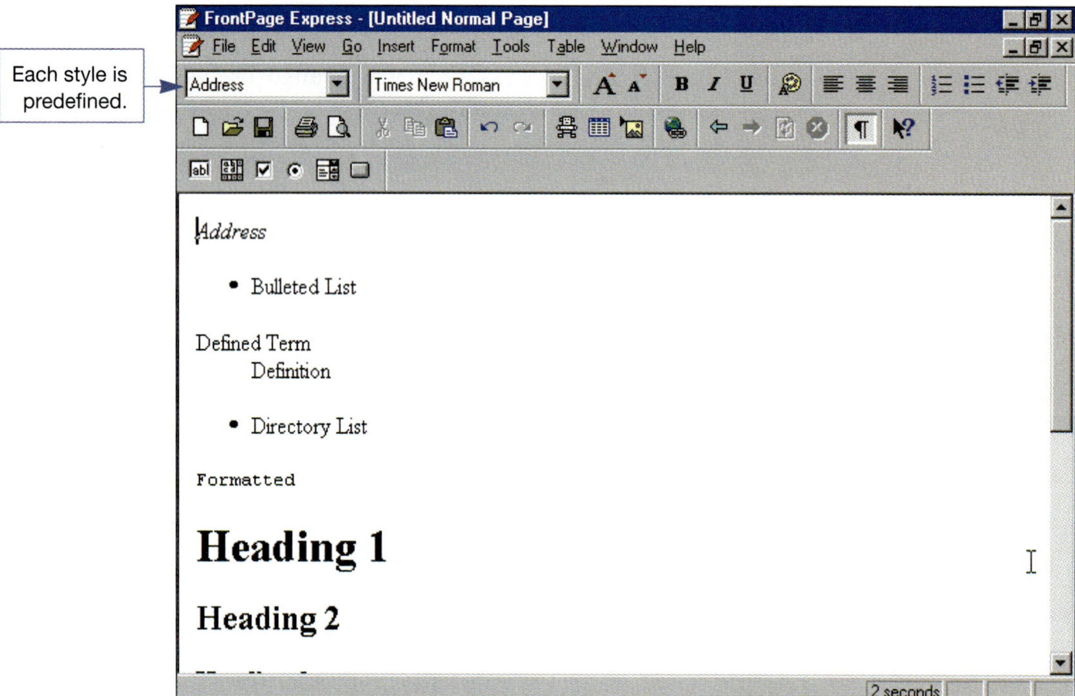

5. Print your document.
6. Exit FrontPage Express.

USING TEMPLATES AND WIZARD

Now that you have gone through some of the basics and learned how FrontPage Express works, you will appreciate the tools that make the creation of Web pages even easier. These tools are the page templates and wizards.

The **Personal Home Page Wizard** provides an easy-to-follow, step-by-step approach to generating a Web page. To use this wizard, select the New command from the File menu and then select Personal Home Page Wizard. A series of windows will guide you through the process of generating a simple Web page.

Page templates are useful because they provide a complete Web page; all you need to do is go in and change the text. In other words, with a template you take a predesigned Web page and modify it to fit your unique needs. Two of the most useful templates include the Confirmation Form template and the Survey Form template.

Another method for creating a new Web page based on a template is to open a page from the Web, modify that page, and then save the new HTML document to a new location. If you use this method, it is very important that you not use another person's Web design without written permission. Stealing someone else's work is just that—stealing.

ACTIVITY

1. In FrontPage Express select the New command from the File menu and then choose Personal Home Page Wizard.
   The Personal Home Page Wizard dialog box opens (Image 9-21).

Image 9-21

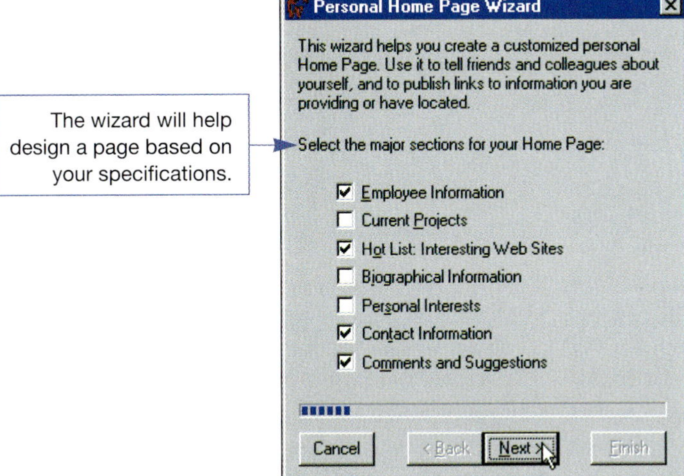

2. Select the major sections you would like to include in your Web page.
3. Click on Next>.
4. Follow the instructions for each step in the wizard and then click on Finish.
   Your Web page appears in a Front Page Express window (Image 9-22).

Image 9-22

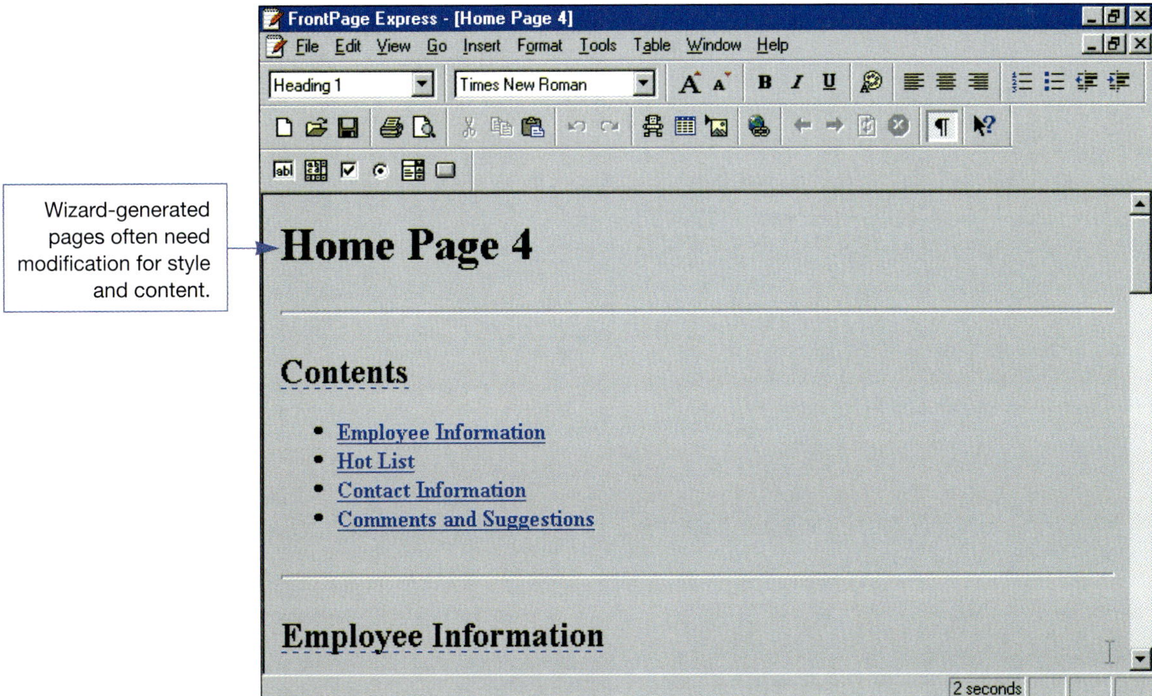

5. Take a few minutes to edit this new Web page and then save the document on your disk.

EXERCISE 9-6

It is time for you to create your own personal Web page. The design, style, and content are entirely up to you. You may start from scratch, use a template, or even use a wizard. Whichever method you choose, make your personal Web page reflect your interests and your style. When you complete your Web site, print copies of your Web pages to share with others.

KEY POINTS

- Microsoft's FrontPage Express is an HTML authoring tool that is used to create Web documents.
- Using FrontPage Express to generate HTML documents is much like using a word processor.
- To create and edit an HTML document, you must have a location on the Web where you can place your document. That is, you must have a URL.
- FrontPage Express is very similar to a word processor in that they both use a WYSIWYG orientation.
- Before you begin any Web page, you should take time to plan what information to include on your Web page and how you want your Web page to look.
- One of the most critical elements of planning is to identify the number of Web pages you want to include.
- After text is entered, several tools are available for setting the appearance of text. The four primary text attribute tools are Font, Size, Style, and Color.
- To set a text attribute, highlight the text you want to change. Then either choose the setting you want from the Format toolbar or use the Format menu.
- As with text attribute tools, FrontPage Express provides several text alignment tools. The three primary alignment options are left, center, and right.
- There are always two issues when saving any type of file: location and name.
- Most Web pages include links to other Web pages. These links can be to Web pages you create or to any page found on the Web.
- Graphics add life to an otherwise dull and drab Web page.
- FrontPage Express enables you to insert almost any graphics image you desire in a Web page. The image can be a drawing, picture, clip art, or virtually any graphic.
- You have several options for setting colors, including setting colors for various types of text as well as the background color. You can also specify a background image.
- When a background image is used, it is placed in a tiled format.
- A paragraph style is a predefined set of attributes that can be applied to text. One advantage of using a paragraph style is that you can quickly set a wide range of attribute settings with just a few clicks of the mouse.

KEY TERMS AND COMMANDS

Color
Font
Format toolbar
FrontPage Express
horizontal line
Insert Image
page composition area
page templates
paragraph property
Personal Home Page Wizard
right clicking
sans serif
serif
Size
Style
text alignment

STUDY QUESTIONS

1. Describe the process for setting text attributes.
2. In addition to setting text alignment, there are other features for making text appear more attractive on a page. What are these features and how do they work?
3. What type of graphics are available in Internet Explorer and what are the issues concerning the use of graphics?
4. What is FrontPage Express and why is it important?
5. Describe three tools on the Format toolbar.
6. What elements should be included in the planning of a Web page?
7. Why is the size of a graphics file important when you are developing a Web site?
8. What issues are important when you are saving an HTML document?
9. What is a Personal Home Page Wizard?
10. Describe the process for using templates and wizards to help develop a Web page.

PRACTICE TEST

1. Fonts, or typefaces, that have the small extensions on each character are called:
   a. Serif
   b. Fontless
   c. Sans serif
   d. Serifless
2. What type of font appears more like block letters?
   a. Serif
   b. Fontless
   c. Sans serif
   d. Serifless
3. The acronym HTML refers to
   a. Hypertext Transfer Markup Language.
   b. Hyper Text Markup Language.
   c. Hyperlink Transfer Makeup Language.
   d. Hyperlink Textransfer Markup Language.
4. FrontPage Express is very similar to a word processor in that they both use a WYSIWYG orientation.
   a. True b. False
5. A predefined set of attributes that can be applied to text is called:
   a. Paragraph style
   b. Paragraph property
   c. Text type
   d. Paragraph type
6. The four primary text attribute tools are
   a. Font, Size, Style, and Typeface.
   b. Font, Size, Typeface, and Color.
   c. Font, Typeface, Style, and Color.
   d. Font, Size, Style, and Color.
7. The Numbered List and Bulleted List tools can also be used to align text within a paragraph.
   a. True b. False
8. A complete Web page where all you need to do is go in and change the text is a:
   a. Page image c. Insert image
   b. Page template d. Web template
9. When a background image is used in a document, it is placed in a tiled format.
   a. True b. False
10. A graphics image may be a link.
    a. True b. False

FILL-INS

1. Font, sometimes called ____________________ , refers to the overall appearance of text.
2. The two major types of font types available in FrontPage Express are ____________________ and ____________________ .
3. The three primary text alignment options are ____________________ , ____________________ , and ____________________ .
4. There are always two issues when saving any type of file. These are ____________________ and ____________________ .
5. A good Web design always considers the ____________________ and ____________________ of graphics.
6. Most Web pages use graphics in one of two dominant graphics image formats. These are ____________________ and ____________________ .
7. When a background image is used, it is placed in a ____________________ format.
8. A ____________________ is a predefined set of attributes that can be applied to text.
9. ____________________ provide a complete Web page where all you need to do is go in and change the text.
10. The ____________________ option starts a process that will take you step-by-step through the procedure for creating a new Web page.

PROJECTS

1. Create a Web page that serves your own Internet needs. For example, create a page that contains links to several search engines. Do you have hobbies, sports interests, music or art pastimes? Create links to sites that deal with your interests. Try to incorporate a little animation, but don't overdo it. Look at the bookmarks you have used in the past. Develop categories of Web sites that include your bookmarks. Can you attach sound, video, or graphics to specific links? Develop this Web page from scratch.
2. Use a template to create a Web page. Again, develop a page that you can use for school, hobbies, recreation, music, art, sports, skiing, snowboarding, fly fishing, camping, or any other of your interests.
3. Use a wizard to create a Web page. This time create a Web page for a friend to use to follow his or her interests on the Web.

INTERNET AT WORK

Edith has become addicted to the Web. She wants her own Web page, and she wants you to design and develop it. Further, she wants it completed in just a few days. She just barged into your cubicle and described what she wants included on her page. She would like a background (not tiled) of some type of candy. If you cannot locate this for her, you better have a good explanation. She would also like you to create links that will help her with her hobbies. She likes to raise and care for tarantulas. She also likes to watch, feed, and house wild birds. In addition to her hobbies, she likes to listen to country and western music. She wants to be able to link to several country and western sites and play this music when linking to these sites. And finally, she would like you to create a few links that will enable her to examine a variety of candy recipes, especially chocolate candy.

You need to impress Edith because she has caught you playing games on the Internet. You know what it takes to impress Edith. You will have to include sound, animation, and other multimedia effects. Be careful, though. Don't include these elements just because you can. You should use these elements to impress Edith, but don't overdo it.

Index

M

N

O

P

Q